SPEED AND MICROPOLITICS

This book provides a th   he micropolitics of
speed; a rich, nua   ting world. What
does it feel   kinds of affects,
percept   nswers to these
question   speed; they also
mean und   xenophobia and anti-
immigratic   cation and solidarity, social
isolation and   ...ia to coordinate social movements.
    While dra   of contemporary theorists, Simon Glezos
recognizes that   .ot a purely recent phenomenon. He therefore turns
to thinkers such   , Spinoza, Bergson, and Merleau-Ponty, to ask how they
sought to underst.   and respond to, the rapid changes and unsettling temporalities of
their eras, and how their insights can be applied to our own.
    Advancing theoretical understanding and offering a useful way to analytically
conceptualize the nature of time, *Speed and Micropolitics* will be of interest to students and
scholars studying affect theory, theories of the body, new materialism, phenomenology,
as well as the history of political thought.

Simon Glezos is an assistant professor in the department of political science at the
University of Victoria, in Victoria, BC, Canada. He has a Ph.D. in political theory and
international relations from The Johns Hopkins University in Baltimore, MD, USA.
He is the author of *The Politics of Speed: Capitalism, the State, and War in an Accelerating
World*, also from Routledge press, and has published articles in *CTheory*, *Contemporary
Political Theory*, *The Journal of International Political Theory*, *International Politics*, *Postmodern
Culture*, *The European Journal of Political Theory*, and *Philosophy in Review*.

"Simon Glezos is one of our foremost thinkers on the relationship between speed and politics. In this book, he argues that social acceleration can be both destructive and energizing for democracy. Examining embodied experiences of speed in canonical thought and contemporary neoliberalism, Glezos masterfully illuminates affective practices that can best address the perils of acceleration in our time."

Elisabeth Anker, *The George Washington University*

"Even locked in our houses with nowhere to go we are beset by the need for speed. Bandwidth for telecommuting, wait estimates for grocery and toilet paper deliveries, guarantees of vaccines in unprecedented time, all promises or disappointments of a faster future. In this moment of anxious temporality Simon Glezos offers us a phenomenology of speed at the scale of the body rather than the supply chain or the fiber wire. Against the technical questions of fast and slow, Glezos redirects us to our experience of embodied, radically unsettled perceptive interchanges—feelings of speed. For Glezos this is the pressing philosophical provocation of our contemporary moment. *Speed and Micropolitics* is a gorgeous adventure following speed's trail through the thinking of Spinoza, Henri Bergson, Wendy Brown and Maurice Merleau-Ponty among many others. In each supple reading we find openings for meaningful reflection and even the possibility of ethical encounters amidst the hemorrhaging resentment of our accelerating times."

Jarius Grove, *Associate Professor of International Relations, The University of Hawai'i at Manoa*

SPEED AND MICROPOLITICS

Bodies, Minds, and Perceptions in an Accelerating World

Simon Glezos

Routledge
Taylor & Francis Group

NEW YORK AND LONDON

First published 2021
by Routledge
52 Vanderbilt Avenue, New York, NY 10017

and by Routledge
2 Park Square, Milton Park, Abingdon, Oxon, OX14 4RN

Routledge is an imprint of the Taylor & Francis Group, an informa business

© 2021 Taylor & Francis

Library of Congress Cataloging-in-Publication Data
Names: Glezos, Simon, 1981– author.
Title: Speed and micropolitics : bodies, minds, and perceptions in an
    accelerating world / Simon Glezos.
Description: New York, NY : Routledge, 2021. | Includes
    bibliographical references and index.
Identifiers: LCCN 2020026238 (print) | LCCN 2020026239 (ebook) |
    ISBN 9780367280635 (hbk) | ISBN 9780367280659 (pbk) |
    ISBN 9780367280642 (ebk) | ISBN 9781000195569 (adobe pdf) |
    ISBN 9781000195590 (mobi) | ISBN 9781000195620 (epub)
Subjects: LCSH: Time—Sociological aspects. | Speed—Social aspects. |
    Technology—Social aspects. | Political science—Philosophy.
Classification: LCC HM656 .G58 2021 (print) | LCC HM656 (ebook) |
    DDC 303.48/3—dc23
LC record available at https://lccn.loc.gov/2020026238
LC ebook record available at https://lccn.loc.gov/2020026239

ISBN: 978-0-367-28063-5 (hbk)
ISBN: 978-0-367-28065-9 (pbk)
ISBN: 978-0-367-28064-2 (ebk)

Typeset in Bembo
by Apex CoVantage, LLC

For Sarah, who was there right at the beginning,
and Waverly, who was there right at the end.

CONTENTS

ACKNOWLEDGEMENTS

This book was written over a number of years, and the research and ideas developed in it go back to my time in graduate school. As such, there are a very large number of people who contributed to its completion, and who have my deepest appreciation. First and foremost, I want to acknowledge my colleagues in the department of political science at the University of Victoria. They have provided me with support, kindness, and an academic home, and for that Colin Bennett, Michelle Bonner, Marlea Clark, Claire Cutler, Rita Dhamoon, Avigail Eisenberg, Wilfred Greaves, Matt James, Jamie Lawson, Mara Marin, Oliver Schmidtke, Heidi Kiiwetinepinesiik Stark, Reeta Tremblay, Jim Tully, Amy Verdun, Rob Walker, Scott Watson, Michael Webb, Guoguang Wu, Andrew Wender, and Feng Xu have my sincere thanks.

In addition to my departmental colleagues, many others have provided help in developing this manuscript, whether through comments at conferences, discussions over drinks, or simple encouragement. As such, I wish to acknowledge the contributions of Libby Anker, Jeremy Arnold, Marta Bashovski, Emily Beausoleil, Adam Culver, Francois Debrix, Daniel Deudney, Emily Eaton, Simon Enoch, Kathy Ferguson, Mark Franke, Jake Greear, Liron Lavi, Alexandre Lefebvre, Liam Mitchell, Matthew J. Moore, Benjamin Mueller, Morton Schoolman, Michael Shapiro, Brent J. Steele, Mina Suk, Heike Schotten, Rob Watkins, Dylan Weller, David Webster, and Melanie White.

Several individuals provided incalculable aid by reading portions of the manuscript, and providing me with thoughtful commentary, including Stefanie Fishel, Smita Rahman, Daniel Levine, Nina Hagel, and James Rowe, and I am thankful for the contributions they've made. Arthur Kroker and the late Marilouise Kroker were both supportive in the development of this manuscript. I am especially grateful for having had the opportunity to work with, and know, Marilouise, who was a brilliant thinker, and an immensely kind person. Warren Magnusson has been a teacher and mentor for years and provided feedback and commentary at multiple points in the life of this manuscript. William Connolly and Jane Bennett, although technically no longer my advisors, continue to provide support and for that I thank them. As always, Jairus Grove has been an invaluable friend and colleague throughout all of my work. Finalizing this book was helped immeasurably by the contributions of my research assistants David Miller and Gizem Sozen. Emily Shoichet and Pete Raskovsky provided both material and emotional support throughout the writing of this book, and for that I thank them. Michael Erickson continues to let me ramble about whatever I'm thinking whenever I need to, which is a crucial contribution to getting a book written. (I would also like to thank the good people of Habit Coffee and Discovery Coffee in Victoria, BC, for letting me use their establishments as makeshift offices. You were very tolerant, and I appreciate it.) Finally, I would like to thank my family for their continued support, both Sarah Mundy and Waverly Glezos Mundy, to whom this volume is dedicated, as well as Peggy, Jim, Matthew, Dawn, James, Ben, Caleb, Silas, and Tommy Glezos.

Chapter 1 was originally published in a slightly different version in *The Journal of International Political Theory*, and portions of Chapter 2 were published in *Postmodern Culture*. Both are reprinted here with permission.

INTRODUCTION

Beyond Fast and Slow

On Socrates, and the Fear of Speed and Politics, Respectively

> Socrates: A rhetorician, then, isn't concerned to educate the people assembled in lawcourts and so on about right and wrong; all he wants to do is persuade them. I mean, I shouldn't think it's possible for him to get so many people to understand such important matters *in such a short time*.
>
> *(Plato 1994: 17)*[1]

It is a brief reference, almost an aside, in a dialogue mostly devoted to questions of morality. In *Gorgias*, Socrates engages in a dialogue with three rhetoricians, criticizing the art of rhetoric, and debating the nature of morality. However, in the middle of this discussion, Socrates makes the statement earlier as a way of distinguishing rhetoric (and sophistry) from philosophy, arguing that the latter is about expertise and truth, while the former is about flattery. Though only briefly mentioned, this passage is crucial for Socrates' argument, since it explains why rhetoric can't ultimately be about truth. This is because the conditions of these kinds of discussions (public debate in the *agora*) are such as to make real understanding impossible. Bruno Latour, in his discussion of the *Gorgias*, notes that these conditions are threefold: number, priority, and urgency. Such discussions happen in the context of large groups of people, about important issues, and, crucially, frequently must happen quickly (either because they are responding to fast-moving events, or because the people involved do not have the time to devote to the kind of in-depth discussion and study that would be necessary to produce genuine expertise). According to Socrates, these conditions make 'real' understanding impossible. However, as Latour points out, such an approach means that Socrates has, out of hand, dismissed the very possibility of demo-cratic politics. As Latour says

> Yes, there are too many of them, the questions are too important *[megala pragmata]*, there is too little time *[oligô chrono]*. Are these not, however, the normal conditions of the Body Politic? Is it not to deal with these peculiar situations of number, urgency, and priority that the subtle skills of politics were invented?
>
> *(Latour 1999: 221)*

Socrates' vision of truth as purely the domain of the expert – the philosopher – working slowly and assiduously outside of the agora, ultimately means a rejec-tion of the practice of democratic politics.

Of course, Socrates (or rather Plato's) anti-democratic politics have been extensively discussed. Most of this commentary focuses on Plato's elitism, his rejection of the demos for its failure to possess the understanding of the true and the good necessary to be able to govern themselves. However, the reason I bring this dialogue up is to note the less frequently remarked upon condition that makes Socrates opposed to democratic politics: the condition of urgency. Rhetoric fails not just because it tries to get 'so many people' to understand, but because it attempts to do so in 'such a short time'. The danger of politics is exactly that it must, at least sometimes, be done *quickly*. And this problem of urgency is, arguably, a greater problem for Socrates than number or priority. While the conditions of number and priority can be resolved through the abo-lition of democracy and the imposition of a philosopher king, this does not nec-essarily solve the problem of urgency. While certainly there are many thinkers that argue that a centralization of political authority is the correct response to the problem of urgency,[2] this does not free us from the problem of urgency, but, at best, provides a new set of tools for responding to it. What this means is that it is potentially the condition of urgency that shifts Socrates' position from anti-*democratic* politics, to simply anti-politics. Socrates hatred of politics *qua* politics is, I would argue, at root a hatred of *speed*. To commit to the practice of politics is ultimately to accept that there will be times in which one cannot avail oneself of leisurely reflection and analysis before making decisions and taking action.

As a result, by the end of the *Gorgias* Socrates has thoroughly rejected the politics and debates of the *agora*, and shifted his argument to the court of the afterlife, describing how the moral man will be judged righteous in the world to come. But as Latour puts it 'Politics is not about "freshly dead" people, but about the living; not about ghoulish stories of the afterworld, but about gory stories of this world' (1999: 246). Socrates escapes the world of becoming to the world of being exactly because he cannot ultimately cope with the conditions of politics he experiences within it. And it is, ultimately, the *speed* of the world of becoming that Socrates seeks to transcend; its uncertainty, its changeability and accelerations.[3] R. B. J. Walker describes Plato as a man who 'seek[s] to flee from politics into the world of forms' and refuses to 'take seriously the world of fleeting impressions, of flux, becoming, and illusions' (1993: 109).

Crucially, as Latour points out, the problem is not just that Socrates seeks to 'flee from politics', but that in fleeing he seeks to also destroy the practices that make politics possible.

> To see a political project through, with the crowd, for the crowd, in spite of the crowd, is so stunningly difficult that Socrates flees from it. But instead of conceding defeat and acknowledging the specificity of politics, he destroys the means of practicing it, in a sort of scorched earth-policy the blackened wreckage of which is still visible today.
>
> *(1999: 239)*

Having identified the problems of number, priority, and urgency which constrain the process of democratic decision making, Socrates attacks the practices of rhetoric (as well as several other allied arts) by which the Athenian community had learned to grapple with these constraints because they do not meet the standards of his rigorous, slow-moving, didactic philosophical knowledge. Says Latour of this kind of necessarily *speedy* democratic, political deliberation:

> Of course 'it does not involve expertise,' of course 'it lacks rational understanding'; the whole dealing with the whole under the incredibly tough constraints of the agora must decide in the dark and will be led by people as blind as themselves, without the benefit of proof, of hindsight, of foresight, of repetitive experiment, of progressive scaling up. In politics there is never a second chance – only one, this occasion, this *Kairos*. There is never any knowledge of cause and consequence. Socrates has a good laugh at the ignorant politicians, but *there is no other way* to do politics, and the invention of an afterworld to solve the whole question is exactly what the Sophists laugh at, and rightly so! Politics imposes this simple and harsh condition of felicity: *hic est Rhodus, hic est saltus.*
>
> *(1999: 242)*

In short, what we get is a surprisingly common worldview. Truth and understanding can only be developed slowly. Politics necessarily happens quickly. Therefore, Politics cannot be about truth and understanding. In turn, the tactics and practices which are developed to make a speedy politics possible must be devalued and degraded. Socrates' fear and anxiety of speed translates into his hatred of politics (especially democratic politics) and vice versa.

Beyond Fast and Slow

I discussed this connection between dromophobia, or a fear of speed, and a hatred of politics in my previous book, *The Politics of Speed: Capitalism, the State, and Warfare in an Accelerating World.* In this book, I wish to carry forward that analysis, understanding the ways in which our fears, anxieties, and resentments around speed hamper our ability to engage productively with both the theory and practice of politics. The reason I begin with Socrates is because in the *Gorgias* this dromophobic/anti-political worldview is connected to three other themes which will be central to the way in which this book approaches questions of speed and politics.

1. *Political anxieties around speed are not a recent, or even modern, phenomenon. Neither are political or theoretical attempts to grapple with, and respond to, the problem of speed.*

To talk about speed, especially its political or social dimensions, is frequently to face a set of assumptions about what you're discussing. It conjures up any number of high-tech, high-velocity images of an accelerating society, from fiberoptic cables, to supersonic jets, to always on social media networks connected to always present smartphones. From this perspective, speed is viewed as a contemporary phenomenon, and dealing with the theory and politics of speed means dealing with the up-to-date world of cutting-edge technology. At most, it might be conceded, that to talk about speed is to talk about the nature and conditions of industrial modernity in which 'All fixed, fast-frozen relations, with their train of ancient and venerable prejudices and opinions, are swept away, all new formed ones become antiquated before they can ossify. All that is solid melts into air' (Marx 2000: 249). Such assumptions are fair enough, so far as they go. It is demonstrably the case that contemporary society (both in North America and Europe, where much of the analysis of this book is focused, but also globally) is undergoing a period of what Hartmut Rosa terms 'social acceleration', and therefore, if we are going to understand and engage with the political present, we must understand the nature of this social acceleration.

Rosa, in his extended sociological investigations into speed, defines social acceleration through three categories – 'technological acceleration', 'social change and transformation', and 'the heightened tempo of everyday life' (2003: 6–9). The first category refers to 'the speeding up of intentional, *goal-directed* processes of transport, communication and production' (6).[4] The second refers to the rate at which we see changes in social, political, and economic patterns (7). This can mean anything from changes in business models or political movements to small matters of fads and fashion. Crary provides a particularly pessimistic account of this phenomenon, saying

> the very different actuality of our time is the calculated maintenance of an ongoing state of transition. There never will be a 'catching up' on either a social or individual basis in relation to continually changing

technological requirements. For the vast majority of people, our perceptual and cognitive relationship to communication and information technology will continue to be estranged and disempowered because of the
velocity at which new products emerge and at which arbitrary reconfigu-
rations of entire systems take place. This intensified rhythm precludes the
possibility of becoming familiar with any given arrangement.

(37)

Rosa's third category of social acceleration, 'the heightened tempo of everyday
life' refers to the experience had by many that in contemporary life there is the
ability (and pressure) to perform an increasing number of tasks and activities in
a decreasing period of time (2003: 8–10). As Hassan describes it:

the tempo of the pulsating dynamics of a globalizing world economy
affects more of us at the same time, than ever before, and more inti-
mately than ever before. Acceleration is almost palpable . . . the dynamic
of velocity, acceleration, urgency, momentum or whichever noun we
choose to employ, suffuses culture and society to an extraordinary extent.
Acceleration stems not simply from new industrial processes, but also
rises up from the ways in which we interact and communicate across all
walks of life.

(2009: 19)

Work from several disciplines shows ample evidence of this sense of an accelerating tempo of contemporary life.[5]

As we will discuss, this general experience of social acceleration has diverse
effects. On the one hand, this increasing capacity to experience more things
and perform more tasks is sometimes experienced as part of the exhilarating
thrill of life in an accelerating world (Garhammer 2002). On the other hand, it
can have wide-ranging negative effects, from large scale phenomenon such as
the increasing speed of warfare, and the dangers of accelerating capital flows,[6]
to more day-to-day experiences of stress and hurriedness. However, regardless
of whether we view this social acceleration as a positive or negative phenomenon (or, as we will discuss, both), we can accurately describe speed as one of
the central aspects of late modernity and respond to this social acceleration as
one of the central political problems of our present day. As such, this book will
spend its share of time on contemporary, high-tech symbols of speed.

And yet, the danger of focusing too closely on social acceleration within late
modernity is that we might be led to believe that speed is primarily, or worse
only, a contemporary phenomenon. That the arrow of time travels from a 'slow'
past to a 'fast' future. As Mark C. Taylor puts it, history moves 'From old to
new, pre-modern to modern, pre-industrial to industrial, the direction is first
from slow to fast, and then from fast to faster' (14). Such an assumption elides

the way in which experiences of, and anxieties over, social acceleration have been present throughout human history. Rosa describes how in

> 1877 W.G. Greg already formulates it like this: "doubtless the outstanding mark of life in the second half of the nineteenth century is *speed* – the hurry that fills it, the speed with which we move, the great pressure under which we work – and it behooves us, first, to consider the question whether this great speed is something intrinsically good, and second, the question whether it is worth the prices we pay for it – a prices that we can only estimate and reliably determine with difficulty."
>
> *(2013: 40)*

And Hassan notes that

> [d]uring 1825 Goethe complained to his friend, the composer Zelter, that: Everything is now 'ultra'. . . . Young people are swept along in the whirlpool of time; wealth and speed are what the world admires and what everyone strives for. All kinds of communicative facility are what the civilized world is aiming at in outpacing itself.
>
> *(2010: 359)*

And although these two examples are still generally from within industrial modernity, we can see similar accounts as we go back further in history. We might, for example, think of Machiavelli's famous account of *fortuna* in *The Prince*, in which he discusses the character of his time as being defined by 'the great variability of things which have been seen and are seen every day, beyond every human conjuncture' (98), echoing Rosa's accelerating rate of 'social change and transformation'. And, of course, we can return to where we began, with the *Gorgias* and Socrates' fear of the condition of urgency within which political action must be taken. This shows us that the idea of speed as a political problem has a much older pedigree than we might at first assume.

The ability to trace out this deeper history of speed is related to the fact that, of Rosa's three markers of social acceleration, only one – technological acceleration – is properly speaking 'unilinear', moving from a 'slow' past to a 'fast' future. The other two categories speak to subjective responses to a perception of an accelerating contexts, which don't need to be tied to any particular 'threshold' of velocity. Though the transportation and communication technologies of Machiavelli's renaissance Italy would have moved substantially slower than their 21st century counterparts, that doesn't mean that actors and thinkers were necessarily less anxious or overwhelmed by a perceived accelerating pace of events and social change.[7] This separating out of the 'objective' and 'subjective' dimensions of social acceleration is why, in my previous book, I sought to make an ontological distinction – following the work of

Deleuze and Guattari – between 'velocity' and 'speed'. Velocity is an extensive metric, indicating 'the objective measurement of movement as displacement over time' (Glezos 2012: 19). Speed, on the other hand, is an intensive metric, which speaks to the experience of radical change and acceleration. Speed is 'the swerve of the car, the sudden burst of acceleration' (22). In this regard we can feel speed at any velocity (whether it be riding a bicycle down a steep hill or feeling a plane accelerate off the runway). This is why Deleuze and Guattari make the seemingly paradoxical statement that 'It is thus necessary to make a distinction between *speed* and *movement*: a movement may be very fast, but that does not give it speed; a speed may be very slow, or even immobile, yet it still has speed' (1987: 381).[8] This is why we cannot restrict speed to any one historical era (although we certainly can discuss certain periods as having a more broadly identified sense of social acceleration).

Insisting on the historicity of speed isn't just an academic point. The assumption that speed is a purely contemporary phenomenon carries with it two important dangers. First, it serves to foster a sort of nostalgia, in which the past is viewed as slow, idyllic, thoughtful, and thus capable of fostering the kinds of engaged political action that the present is lacking. Such a nostalgia runs the risk of producing a reactionary rejection of the present. While we might think of such a position as being a fundamentally conservative formation (and as we shall see in the first chapter, this kind of longing for an idealized past, and resentment of the speed of the present, can crystallize into violent and reactionary politics), we also see it on the left. We might think here of Sheldon Wolin's anxiety over the lack of leisure time for proper political reflection, and his lionization of ancient Athens for the space and time they provided for political deliberation (1997).[9] Such a vision lets us imagine that there was a time when politics was possible, but that we have crossed an event horizon at some point (whether that point be the 1970s or the 1870s depends on the analyst) putting us in a situation in which politics is now impossible, absent some sort of radical social deceleration, cutting us off from the possibility of a productive political response to speed (which we will discuss shortly).[10]

This directs us to the second danger of assuming speed is a purely contemporary phenomenon/problem. It ignores the way in which speed has perpetually been a problem for politics. As Carmen Leccardi puts it, 'Social Acceleration is certainly not a unique phenomenon of our times' (2007: 25). Merriman makes a similar point, when he states that 'there is a danger that focusing on the transformation of mobilities and the speeding up of communications overstates the novelty of such experiences of mobility, speed and acceleration' (2012: 11). Indeed, it is ironic that the ancient Athenian democracy that Wolin lionizes for its leisurely pace is exactly the community that Socrates' decries for its speedy and insufficient mode of political deliberation. This disjuncture between our nostalgic depictions of the slow past, and their own political anxieties and resentments around speed can partly be blamed on the limitations of a unilinear vision of social acceleration (in which we note the accelerating pace of events to which politics must respond but fail to acknowledge the acceleration of the tools available to us to engage in political deliberation) but partly due to a failure to grapple with how deeply rooted this dromophobia (and attendant fear/hatred of politics) is in Western philosophy and political theory.

Dealing with speed as not only a contemporary phenomenon, but one present throughout history, means looking at the way in which the history of political thought can be read as a series of responses to the problem of speed. Thus, alongside Plato's anxieties around speed as expressed in *Gorgias*, we might look at Augustine's *City of God* as a response to the accelerating changes in late antiquity, attempting to fix and secure theological concepts in the face of a rapidly crumbling social order.[11] Or we might read Hobbes' *Leviathan* as an attempt to fix the boundary lines of the state in response to the violent upheavals of post-reformation Europe (and post-civil war England).[12] Conversely, we might look at how other thinkers sought to develop a theory that responded to the phenomenon of speed without lapsing into the kind of anxieties and resentments we see expressed in *Gorgias*.[13] As such, one of the central themes of this book is to turn to writers throughout the history of western thought, to see what kind of tools and insights they provide for dealing with speed. We look at Spinoza, responding to the radical social change of the early enlightenment from the centre of the increasingly global Dutch trading empire. We see Nietzsche and Bergson responding to the technological acceleration of the industrial revolution, and Merleau-Ponty analyzing the changing media landscape of the mid-20th century. These more historical thinkers are put into conversation with contemporary thinkers such as Paul Virilio, Gilles Deleuze, N. Katherine Hayles, Wendy Brown, Hasana Sharpe, and Jane Bennett, amongst many others.

The point here is that speed is not a new phenomenon, and that taking a more historical perspective on the question can help us in developing productive responses to an accelerating world. What this also means is that the question of speed is not always about whatever has the fastest velocity. Thus, alongside accounts of fighter jets and fiberoptic cables, this text will also discuss slow-moving freighters, stone age weaponry, telegraph wires, railroads, the trip through the desert in the American southwest, and flows of transnational capitalism, amongst other, ambiguously 'speedy' phenomena.

Such a historical perspective (and the rejection of a nostalgic, unilinear narrative of speed and politics) connects us to the next major theme of this text.

2. *Developing a set of practices that can aid us in living in an accelerating world frequently requires an attentiveness to the micropolitics of bodies, minds, and perceptions.*

One of the surprising reoccurring topics in the *Gorgias* is that of cookery. In his critique of rhetoric and sophistry, we saw how Socrates rejects the possibility that they can be forms of truth or expertise. When pressed to define what type of thing he takes them to be, Socrates says they are a type of flattery and likens them to cookery. Socrates makes the analogy with cookery according to two qualities. First, like cookery, rhetoric concerns itself only with producing pleasure in the subject, and second, that it involves no real understanding of the truth but is only a 'knack' based on memory and habit. As he says of cookery (and also of rhetoric):

> There is absolutely no expertise involved in the way it pursues pleasure; it hasn't considered either the nature of pleasure or the reason why it occurs. It's a completely irrational process – it hasn't itemized things at all, so to speak. All it can do is remember a routine which has become ingrained by habituation and past experience, and that's also what it relies on to provide us with a pleasant experience.
>
> *(Plato 1994: 95)*

This rejection of rhetoric (and cookery) because they are based on habit and pleasure, and not on 'true understanding', ultimately means doing away with the tools that a community might use to deal with fast-moving sphere of politics.

What is important here is the way in which the rejection of forms of practice which lack 'real understanding' is also frequently a rejection of modes of thought and practice which are rooted in the body. In rejecting flattery – whether cookery or rhetoric – Socrates explicitly rejects forms of practice and understanding rooted in the affects (pleasure), and in habit (embodied forms of knowledge). Indeed, Plato's account of knowledge and morality ultimately ends up not just with a flight from the world of becoming, but very explicitly with a flight from the body, as he explains his vision of judgement in the afterlife wherein 'the soul has been stripped of the body' (131, 524d). Here we see the way in which Socrates' rejection of politics is tied to his rejection of speed, and both are tied to his rejection of the body. Socrates is, in the language of Nietzsche (to which we will return in the fourth chapter), a 'despiser of the body' (1976: 146). His rejection of the body also means the rejection of a variety of mechanisms that the Athenian body politic uses to interrogate political and ethical questions, articulate beliefs, and manage conflicts. As Latour says of the political tools which Socrates jettisons:

> About what do[es Socrates] talk so irreverently? Cookery first, and then the skills of the greatest playwrights, the greatest sculptors, the greatest musicians, the greatest architects, the greatest orators, the greatest statesmen, the greatest tragedians. All of these people are dumped because they don't know what they know in the didactic fashion that Professor Socrates wants to impose on the people of Athens.
>
> *(Latour 1999: 244)*

What Latour is here describing is a society that manages the conditions of politics – number, priority, urgency – by relying on a variety of arts, occurring at a variety of tempos. Whether it be tragedies in which political and moral issues are dramatized (Butler 2000) (Honig 2013), sung poems which communicated moral and political norms (Havelock 1963), public orations in which political questions are debated (Aristotle 1991), public works of art and architecture which create a public space to manage and organize these political debates (Arendt 1998) (Cuboniks 2018: 77), or even arts of cookery which underpin communal experiences of eating (Panagia 2009: Ch. 5). Crucially even as many of these sites rely on conscious thought and reflection, they also fold in affects, habits, memories, and corporeal qualities which prepare and shape political sensibilities for the complex and speedy encounters of the *agora*. As we will discuss in Chapters 2 and 3, it is exactly the affect imbued character of thought that allows it to respond effectively to a quickly unfolding pace of events. And in both our discussions of Spinoza and Bergson, we will see accounts which, *contra* Socrates, seek to valorize the role of habit as a way of building both individuals and societies which can respond effectively to a 'speedy' pace of life and politics.

Socrates' rejection of the tools of politics is thus ultimately tied to his rejection of the body, and both are crucially tied to his fear of speed. One of the central goals of this book will be to tease out the relations between speed, politics, and the body, noting that theoretical work on the body is frequently helpful, and indeed necessary, in navigating the seeming impasses that the problem of speed introduces into the practice of politics. This focus on questions of bodily practice links us to the last theme that this book will explore.

3. *Developing a political theory, and practice, which can effectively grapple with the problem of social acceleration, requires a rejection of either a simplistic pro- or anti-speed orientation.*

In the *Gorgias* we see the way in which anxiety over speed can lead to a wholesale rejection of the political, authorizing, first, authoritarian leadership, and ultimately a kind of nihilistic rejection of the body and the world. We see similar articulations in our brief discussions of Augustine and Hobbes earlier. As such, any analysis of the relation of speed and politics must start with a refusal to succumb to a wholesale rejection of speed (a point to which we will return in the first chapter). However, to identify the reactionary and nihilistic dangers of an anti-speed political orientation is not to automatically succumb to an unthinkingly pro-speed account. Any number of contemporary thinkers provide extensive accounts of the dangers, exclusions, and violence produced through a contemporary condition of social acceleration.[14] Political positions which seek an uncritical embrace of speed (such as those discussed in Chapter 1) frequently abdicate our political responsibility to create a political space which are democratically inclusive, economically egalitarian, and robustly pluralistic (Noys 2014).

What this means is that an analysis which seeks to effectively theorize the relationship between speed and politics needs to think about how it can avoid lapsing into either a too resolute anti- or pro-speed orientation. In this regard, this analysis deviates from much contemporary work on the topic of speed. As Sarah Sharma points out, generally speaking,

> the contemporary theorist of speed is concerned about how a culture of speed is antithetical to democracy. They share a similar cautionary tale: Speed is the commanding byproduct of real-time communication technologies, military technologies, and scientific research on human bodies. Democratic deliberation gives over to instant communication.
>
> *(6)*[15]

Such an approach leaves us both open to resentful and reactionary political affects, and ill-equipped to respond to a world of accelerative technologies. As Wajcman describes:

> An implicit antipathy to science and technology forecloses appreciation of the scope that digital technologies might afford for control over time, enabling people to have not only more time but time of their choice. This stance is out of step with the widespread recognition that technoscience is a feverishly contested political field. Indeed, the plea for a slow down brings to mind the ecological feminists whom Donna Haraway chided over a quarter of a century ago for wanting to return to nature rather than becoming impure, hybrid cyborgs. A leading critic of technoscience, Haraway insisted on the liberatory potential of science and technology: 'The issue is no longer whether to accept or oppose technoscience, but rather how to engage strategically with technoscience, while, at the same time, being its chief critic.'
>
> *(26)*[16]

What is more, our discussion in the previous section of the kinds of tools which can help deal with the political problem of urgency makes clear the variety of tempos at which such political practices take place. Sometimes it is a matter of embracing techniques and technologies which can accelerate our response times. Sometimes it is a matter of working vigorously to introduce institutional and political mechanisms which can slow down the pace of events. Sometimes it is a matter of creating slow spaces which can allow us to cultivate particular affects and habits through which we can respond effectively to an accelerating and uncertain world. Most importantly, it always involves pushing for circumstances in which questions of technological acceleration are increasingly subject to democratic control rather than the vicissitudes of the market, or control of the militaristic wings of the state. Again, Wajcman is thoughtful on the question of accelerating technology:

> I want to argue that a more well-rounded understanding of the relationships between temporality and technology must inform an emancipatory politics of time. This involves the democratization of technoscience, deciding what sort of technologies we want and how we are going to use them. Resisting technological innovation and calling for deceleration or a digital detox is an inadequate intellectual and political response. Indeed, wistfully looking back to idealized slower time and mourning its passing has long been the preserve of conservative political theory.
>
> *(26–27)*

Again, this does not mean an uncritical embrace of accelerative technologies. It means, rather, an approach which refuses to presume a fundamental or necessarily 'human' pace which requires a unilateral deccelerationist stance. Indeed, if at times this text seems to be more of a 'pro-speed' manifesto, this is only because, as Sharma points out, it is fighting against a more broadly 'anti-speed' tendency in the literature. But this should not be mistaken for an uncritical or unthinking accelerationism. Indeed, at several points throughout the text, I will point to either specific contexts in which we might wish to reject or challenge accelerative technologies, as well as provide general theoretical rubrics which might help us to judge the value and desirability of certain types of technological change.

This rejection of an 'either/or' response to the question of speed and politics is another case in which our historical approach to speed is enlightening. Recognizing the reoccurring engagement with the political problem of speed throughout human history helps to show the insufficiency of either a pro- or anti-speed approach. It shows the way in which anti-speed accounts' nostalgia for the slowness of the past was rarely experienced by the actual participants of those periods themselves. And for those who wish a vision of social acceleration as tied to a vision of human progress, we see how repeated human societies articulate questions of speed in terms of danger and violence.

Ultimately what this means is that, in interrogating the question of speed and politics, we must go *beyond fast and slow*. We must refuse to see it as a matter of either embracing speed or negating it but rather developing a nuanced and complex account of the ways in which social acceleration shapes bodies, minds, communities, and futures, and develop theories and tools which can tell us when we might want to accelerate and when we want to slow down, when we want to embrace speed and when we want to reject it.

Outline

With these three themes in mind, this book then seeks to develop a micropolitics of speed, helping to understand the way in which speed shapes bodies, minds, and politics. In doing so it endeavours to develop a nuanced theory which takes seriously the ways in which speed can be a violent and dangerous force in the world, without presuming that there is a natural or essential pace at which human bodies or politics naturally exist. Starting from a historical perspective helps to de-essentialize such accounts of speed, and allows us to develop approaches to speed which let us grapple with particular sites and situations and develop particular responses.

The book is split into two parts: 'Speed and Affect' and 'Speed and Perception'. In the first section, I interrogate what kinds of affects an accelerating world gives rise to, what some of the political implications of these affects can be, and what kinds of productive ethical and political tools and tactics we might want to develop in response. Chapter 1 uses the works of Wendy Brown and Friedrich Nietzsche to interrogate the way in which social acceleration can give rise to what I term a '*ressentiment* against speed' crystallizing into reactionary and xenophobic political movements. This affective account of speed is carried over into Chapter 2 which uses Spinoza's theory of the body and affect to interrogate the effects of different encounters between speed and the body. Chapter 3 then draws out these affective and corporeal dimensions of Spinoza's theory of politics, discussing what kinds of tactics and politics are necessary to combat the reactionary effects of *ressentiment* against speed.

Part II, 'Speed and Perception', interrogates the way in which new information and communication technologies (ICTs) shape human perception and thought. It begins with Chapter 4, which constitutes a critique of some dominant accounts of the relationship between speed and perception (especially, though not only, as represented in the work of Paul Virilio). Central to this analysis is the idea that accelerating ICTs have a fundamentally disembodying and dislocating effect on human thought. In this chapter I argue that such an approach presumes that human perception is always already disembodied and shifts their anxieties around the body to concerns around speed. In the next three chapters, I then seek to interrogate how a theory of perception that is properly embodied would help us understand the impact of accelerating ICTs. In Chapter 5 the intensive dimension of acceleration is interrogated, as I look at the dramatic increases in the *amount* of information subjects are exposed to. In response to this, I look to Bergson, whose work argues that human perception is always at root about grappling with the exposure to too much information. In Chapters 6 and 7, I look at the extensive dimension of the acceleration of information, in the increasing *scope* over which information is projected, and specifically the claim that this has a dislocating and alienating effect on human perception and subjectivity. In response I turn to the work of Maurice

Merleau-Ponty, who develops a phenomenological account of perception, in which human subjectivity and spatiality is always dynamic and fluid. I argue that Merleau-Ponty's account gives us a vision of the subject at speed which can better be described as *trans*located rather than dislocated.

Notes

1. Emphasis added.
2. I discuss this line of reasoning in Glezos (2012: Ch. 1). See also Scheuerman (2004).
3. For a discussion of speed as not just velocity, but uncertainty and changeability, see Glezos (2012: Ch. 1).
4. See Lübbe (2009), Hassan (2009), Urry (2009), Gleick (2000), amongst many others.
5. See Crary (2013), Eriksen (2001), Sharma (2014), and Wajcman (2016).
6. For a discussion of these two phenomena, see chapters 2 and 4 respectively in Glezos (2012).
7. Indeed, one might make the point that contemporary actors potentially have access to resources and technologies that allow them to get a handle on the changing character of the times in a way that actors in the past did not. For a discussion of this in a political context, see Glezos (2012: 15–18).
8. For a much more in-depth discussion of the ontology of speed and velocity, see Glezos (2012: 18–26).
9. For a more extensive reading of Wolin, see Glezos (2012: 34–41).
10. For example, in the aforementioned *Social Acceleration*, Rosa says that 'My guiding heuristic hypothesis here is that *the acceleration that is a constitutive part of modernity crosses a critical threshold in "late modernity" beyond which the demand for societal synchronization and social integration can no longer be met*' (20). Hassan makes a similar claim in (2009: 34)
11. See Connolly (1993).
12. See Campbell (1998: Ch. 3), Connolly (1991: Ch. 3), and Walker (1993).
13. By way of example, look at my reading of Machiavelli in Glezos (2016).
14. See Rosa (2013), Virilio (1983), Wajcman (2016), Wolin (1997), and Scheuerman (2004).
15. For my general account of the relationship between speed and democracy, see chapter one of Glezos (2012).
16. See, also, Cuboniks (2018: 17)

Works Cited

Arendt, H. (1998) *The Human Condition*, Chicago, IL: University of Chicago Press.

Aristotle (1991) *The Art of Rhetoric*, Trans. H. C. Lawson-Tancred, London, UK: Penguin Book.

Butler, J. (2000) *Antigone's Claim: Kinship between Life and Death*, New York, NY: Columbia University Press.

Campbell, D. (1998) *Writing Security: United States Foreign Policy and the Politics of Identity*, Minneapolis, MN: University of Minnesota Press.

Connolly, W. (1991) *Identity/Difference: Democratic Negotiations of Political Paradox*, Minneapolis: University of Minnesota Press.

Connolly, W. (1993) *The Augustinian Imperative: A Reflection on the Politics of Morality*, Newbury Park, CA: Sage Publications.

Crary, J. (2013) *24/7: Late Capitalism and the Ends of Sleep*, London: Verso.

Cuboniks, L. (2018) *The Xenofeminist Manifesto: A Politics for Alienation*, London, UK: Verso.

Deleuze, G. and Guattari, F. (1987) *A Thousand Plateaus*, Trans. B. Massumi, Minneapolis: University of Minnesota Press.

Eriksen, T. H. (2001) *Tyranny of the Moment: Fast and Slow Time in the Information Age*, London, UK: Pluto Press.

Garhammer, M. (2002) 'Pace of Life and Enjoyment of Life', *Journal of Happiness Studies*, 3(3): 217–56.

Gleick, J. (2000) *Faster: The Acceleration of Just About Everything*, New York, NY: Vintage.

Glezos, S. (2012) *The Politics of Speed: Capitalism, The State, and War in an Accelerating World*, Abingdon, UK: Routledge.

Glezos, S. (2016) 'Virtuous Networks: Machiavelli, Speed, and Global Social Movements', *International Politics*, 53(4): 534–54.

Hassan, R. (2009) *Empires of Speed: Time and the Acceleration of Politics and Society*, Boston, MA: Brill.

Hassan, R. (2010) 'Social Acceleration and the Network Effect: A Defence of Social "Science Fiction" and Network Determinism', *The British Journal of Sociology*, 61(2).

Havelock, E. A. (1963) *Preface to Plato*, Cambridge, MA: Belknap Press.

Honig, B. (2013) *Antigone, Interrupted*, Cambridge, UK: Cambridge University Press.

Koselleck, R. (2009) 'Is There an Acceleration of History?', *High-Speed Society: Social Acceleration, Power, and Modernity*, eds. H. Rosa and W. E. Scheuerman. University Park, PE: The Pennsylvania State University Press.

Latour, B. (1999) *Pandora's Hope: Essays on the Reality of Science Studies*, Cambridge, MA: Harvard University Press.

Leccardi, C. (2007) 'New Temporal Perspectives in the "High-Speed Society"', *24/7: Time and Temporality in the Network Society*, eds. R. Hassan and R. E. Purser, Stanford, CA: Stanford Business Books.

Lübbe, H. (2009) 'The Contraction of the Present', *High-Speed Society: Social Acceleration, Power, and Modernity*, eds. H. Rosa and W. E. Scheuerman, University Park, PE: The Pennsylvania State University Press.

Machiavelli, N. (1998) *The Prince*, Trans. H. Mansfield, Chicago, IL: The University of Chicago Press.

Merriman, P. (2012) *Mobility, Space and Culture*, Abingdon, UK: Routledge.

Marx, K. (2000) *Selected Writings*, Oxford: Oxford University Press.

Nietzsche, F. (1976) 'Thus Spoke Zarathustra', *The Portable Nietzsche*, Trans. W. Kaufmann, New York: Penguin Books.

Noys, B. (2014) *Malign Velocities: Accelerationism and Capitalism*, Alresford, UK: Zero Books.

Panagia, D. (2009) *The Political Life of Sensation*, Durham, NC: Duke University Press.

Plato (1994) *Gorgias*, Trans. R. Waterfield, Oxford, UK: Oxford World Classics.

Rosa, H. (2003) 'Social Acceleration: Ethical and Political Consequences of a Desynchronized High-Speed Society', *Constellations*, 10: 3–33.

Rosa, H. (2013) *Social Acceleration*, Trans. J. Trejo-Mathys, New York: Columbia University Press.

Scheuerman, W. (2004) *Liberal Democracy and the Social Acceleration of Time*, Baltimore, MD: Johns Hopkins University Press.

Sharma, S. (2014) *In the Meantime: Temporality and Cultural Politics*, Durham, NC: Duke University Press.

Taylor, M. C. (2014) *Speed Limits: Where Time Went and Why We Have So Little Left*, New Haven, CT: Yale.

Urry, J. (2009) 'Speeding Up and Slowing Down', *High-Speed Society: Social Acceleration, Power, and Modernity*, eds. H. Rosa and W. E. Scheuerman, University Park, PE: The Pennsylvania State University Press.

Virilio, P. (1983) *Pure War*, Trans. M. Polizzotti, New York: Semiotext(e).

Wajcman, J. (2016) *Pressed for Time: The Acceleration of Life in Digital Capitalism*, Chicago: University of Chicago Press.

Walker, R. B. J. (1993) *Inside/Outside: International Relations as Political Theory*, Cambridge, UK: Cambridge University Press.

Wolin, S. (1997) 'What Time Is It?', *Theory and Event*, 1(1): 1–10.

PART I
Speed and Affect

1

BROWN'S PARADOX

Speed, *Ressentiment,* and Global Politics

Since the turn of the millennium, political theory has become increasingly concerned with the question of speed, as thinkers have attempted to grapple with the political, social, and economic implications of what Hartmut Rosa calls the 'social acceleration of time'. As we discussed in the introduction, the question of speed is hardly absent from the history of political thought.[1] However, in the last two decades there has been a dramatic uptick in theoretical work on the subject.[2] In her book, *Politics Out of History,* Wendy Brown nicely lays out the conditions which have given rise to this increasing attention to the question of speed, saying

> From every area of contemporary discourse, we know that the pace of contemporary social, cultural, economic, and political change is unprecedented. Technological obsolescence occurs at the inception of production, deracination in human lives is ubiquitous and normal . . . today's corporate giant is the material of tomorrow's dissolved or merged identity. If all that was solid melted into air in the last century, today's economic, social, and technological transformations occur so rapidly that they often do not even achieve solidity before metamorphosing into something else.
>
> *(138–139)*

And, as Brown goes on to point out, it is not just the existence of this accelerating pace of change that has sparked the interest of theorists. Rather it is the profound *ambivalence* of the phenomenon that gives us pause. As she says

> [m]oving at such speed without any sense of control or predictability, we greet both past and future with bewilderment and anxiety. As a

consequence, we . . . feel a greater political impotence than humans may have felt before, even as we occupy a global order more saturated by human power than ever before.

(138–139)

In this passage, Brown successful sums up the paradox of our accelerated lives. On the one hand we find ourselves possessed of powers the likes of which the world has simply never seen. We have access to technologies that even a decade or two ago would have seemed like science fiction. Smartphones achieve the goal of ubiquitous computing, satellites ringing the planet provide us with instantaneous access to the sum total of human knowledge regardless of location, and the biosciences examine, splice, and augment the human body. It is as if the velocity inaugurated with the industrial revolution has accelerated history beyond itself, landing us in the middle of our own future.[3]

And yet, despite these incredible new tools, we also feel a 'greater political impotence than ever before'. This acceleration which seems to have overtaken the future also seems to have overtaken us, dragging us along in its slipstream. Events happen too fast for us to effectively intervene in them. We are subject to a constant wave of contingency which denies us the possibility of stability or security. And what is more, this seems to hold across the globe. While it is true that the poor and disenfranchised have always been (and still are) more subject to change and uncertainty, now even those with the most effective access to futuristic technologies seem to have not much greater purchase on events (which is not to say that their experience of it is at all the same). This is true in seemingly every facet of our lives: personal, political, economic, and cultural. Indeed, it is the political that is perhaps most important sphere to observe, since it is the state that was supposed to serve as a bulwark against the winds of change and earthquakes of uncertainty. And yet even that fortress seems to be succumbing to the acceleration of the world.

What is the answer to this contradiction, this dual sense of our own power and our own impotence; this feeling of both living in the future and being behind the times? In this chapter, I will seek to investigate Brown's paradox – both responses to it, and the way in which it might be constitutive of our accelerating world. I will begin by looking at two alternate political responses to Brown's paradox: the first, the neoliberal embrace and valorization of the uncertainty of an accelerating world; the second, the reactionary attempt to aggressively (re)secure the foundations of politics and society (Note that these are not the only two possible responses, but they are central to our current political moment). The discussion of this latter approach will lead us to the central question of this first section of the book, the relationship between speed and affect. Understanding the rise of reactionary political movements in the contemporary era means understanding the ways in which an accelerating world can give rise to affects of uncertainty, insecurity, and defensiveness, which can ultimately produce what I have termed elsewhere a *ressentiment* against speed (Glezos 2011, 2012), a reactive and vengeful affective disposition against a world that refuses to provide the stability and security that many desire. The second half of the chapter will focus on *ressentiment* against speed, arguing that it is central to understanding contemporary responses to social acceleration and Brown's paradox, insofar as it inhibits our ability to productively respond to the challenges of an accelerating world, while at the same time frequently authorizing policies of violence, marginalization, and exploitation against those constituencies which are already most subject to the contingencies of acceleration. This understanding of *ressentiment* against speed will be used to point the way to a politics which, while not *resolving* the contradictions inherent in Brown's paradox, might teach us to live with it – and within it – in a productive and ethical manner.

Dealing With Brown's paradox

Neoliberalism

The easiest way of dealing with any paradox is to simply decide that there is, in fact, nothing paradoxical about it, and thus nothing to overcome. In regard to Brown's paradox, this can be achieved by reinterpreting an unsettling acceleration as an enriching progress. In this account – which finds its strongest advocates amongst an ascendant neoliberalism (although it resonates through other political positions)[4] – the acceleration of transportation, communication, and production technologies are making our world more developed, more efficient, more egalitarian, as well as more humane and democratic. The world is changing at an astonishing clip, these prophets say, but overall, for the better.

From this point of view, the sense of political impotence Brown identifies is nothing other than the uncomfortable letting go of a belief in the ability of politics to effectively intervene in matters which are better left up to the molecular processes of market economies, scientific innovation, and individual entrepreneurship. Our desire for 'stability' is nothing other than the vestiges of an obsolete ideology, one which might have been more 'stable' but also less advanced. According to this account, the state's attempts to provide us with 'security' were really doing more to hold us back, than prop us up.

Take neoliberal prophet Tom Friedman.[5] Friedman, is one of the great advocates of globalization, a process which he refers to as the 'flattening of the world'. He acknowledges that this flattening of the world introduces a new level of uncertainty and instability into the life of the average person. However, he argues, the rewards that globalization brings so outweigh any dangers, that we must embrace it. In this context, any attempt by politics to put limitations on globalization – to slow down the pace of development – is fundamentally hazardous to the future. In this context, citizens must learn to overcome their desires for stability, and states must overcome their desires to control and organize.

> The job of government and business is not to guarantee anyone a lifetime job – those days are over. That social contract has been ripped up with the flattening of the world. What government can and must guarantee people is the chance to make themselves more employable.
>
> *(2006: 367)*

From this perspective, the way to reconcile Brown's paradox is for people to simply accept the new uncertainty of their lives and learn to live within this newly flat world.

> In the flat world, the individual worker is going to become more and more responsible for managing his or her own career, risks, and economic security, and the role of government and business is to help workers build all the muscles they need to do just that.
>
> *(369)*

A government should not be there to provide 'protection'. By doing so it simply constrains the efficiency of the market and inhibits people's entrepreneurial natures. At most, the government should be preparing people to live in this newly accelerating world, helping them to adapt to this world of uncertainty and to use futuristic gadgets to navigate the flows and swells of this flat world.[6] Indeed, this is what government is supposed to do, say neoliberals; empower the individual, not fictitious, stultifying aggregations like 'society' (think here of Thatcher's 'There's no such thing as society'). Such an approach will ultimately empower us all.

> We all have to be owners as well as wage earners. That is where public policy has to be focused – to make sure that people have wealth-producing assets as they enter the twenty-first century, the way homeownership accomplished that in the twentieth century.
>
> *(370)*

The paradox thus resolves itself, as the security we lose with the flattening of the world, we gain in the establishment of an ownership society. The ownership of ourselves (as workers, as human capital) is compared to homeownership in the passage earlier. Thus, ownership of ourselves provides the grounding and security that our homes once did (now, of course, long washed away by the tides of rising home costs and mortgage foreclosures). The new image of *homo economicus* in a flat world: *homo gastropoda*, the snail-person, carrying her house around on her back, at home wherever she finds herself because of her ownership in herself.

For others, this accelerating world is less a world of opportunity, than an intensification of the processes of exploitation already endemic in capitalist modernity. Zygmunt Bauman has, since the turn of the millennium, done an exceptional job of tracing out the violence inherent in an accelerating world. He excavates the danger underlying Friedman's ownership society, saying

> the responsibility for resolving the quandaries generated by vexingly volatile and constantly changing circumstances is shifted on to the shoulders of individuals – who are now expected to be 'free choosers' and to bear in full the consequences of their choices. The risks involved in every choice may be produced by forces which transcend the comprehension and capacity to act of the individual, but it is the individual's lot and duty to pay their price, because there are no authoritatively endorsed recipes which would allow errors to be avoided if they were properly learned and dutifully followed, or which could be blamed in the case of failures.
>
> *(1998: 3–4)*

While Bauman is here discussing the experience of individuals, we could apply the same analysis to individual countries, as entire economies become subject to the fickle interests of the market, currency speculation, debt crises, and pressure from groups such as the IMF, the WTO and the various 'G's. These abrupt shifts, though conceived of by the neoliberal crowd as simple 'adjustments' or 'market pressures', bring untold levels of human suffering. In this context, the neoliberal emphasis on progress becomes more of an eschatological faith, than a grounded economic 'law'.

> 'Progress', once the most extreme manifestation of radical optimism and a promise of universally shared and lasting happiness, has moved all the way to the opposite, dystopian and fatalistic pole of anticipation: it now stands for the threat of a relentless and inescapable change that instead of maturing peace and respite portends nothing but continuous crisis and strain and forbids a moment of rest. Progress has turned into a sort of endless and uninterrupted game of musical chairs in which a moment of inattention results in irreversible defeat and irrevocable exclusion. Instead of great expectations and sweet dreams, 'Progress' evokes an insomnia full of nightmares of 'being left behind' – of missing the train, or falling out of the window of a fast accelerating vehicle.
>
> *(10–11)*[7]

Thus even if you don't find yourself one of the 'losers' of the neoliberal economy – if you manage to leverage your 'wealth-producing assets' and take ownership over your own 'human capital' – success is never secure. So-called 'progress' inculcates a sense of anxiety and instability as to how long the 'good times' will last (which makes one wonder exactly how 'good' those times really are).[8]

Reactionary Movements

The failure of Neoliberalism's claimed 'progress' to authoritatively manifest means that, for many people, it also fails to explain away the anxiety and immiseration of an accelerating world, and thus this 'solution' to Brown's paradox is rejected. In response, we frequently see the opposite tactic emerge, a solution which tries to aggressively reassert the capacity for human intervention in the world via the political sphere. Here political power is used to attempt to suppress the sources of insecurity which unsettles the lives and livelihoods of individuals and communities.

The trouble with this strategy, of course, is that the sources of this insecurity – globalizing capitalism, colonialism and neoimperialism, the military-industrial complex – are both diffuse (and hence difficult to identify and target) and powerful (and hence difficult to effectively challenge). In these contexts, there is a tendency for this attempt to reassert control to be expressed through reactionary political movements which target vulnerable constituencies that are taken as symbols of this new instability.

I should note that, unlike neoliberalism, which refers to a relatively unified political ideology, here I am attempting to draw together and name a more diverse set of phenomena. When I invoke the idea of 'reactionary' politics, I am pointing to a variety of political tactics, movements and organizations, in multiple countries (in both the global north and south) which seek to suppress the social acceleration of time in the contexts of increasing globalization. Such reactionary politics can manifest as anti-immigration sentiments and policies, fundamentalist religions, ethnic or nationalist movements, or the suppression of democratic institutions (amongst others).[9]

By way of example, one increasingly common reactionary tactic intended to suppress the acceleration of global flows is the dramatic rise in the building of fences and walls by states, a phenomenon Brown engages with in her book *Walled States, Waning Sovereignty*. Brown argues that the proliferation of wall building tactics is the result of states' attempts to prop up their 'waning sovereignty' against a world of accelerating global flows (81). Though occurring in a multitude of different states and societies (including, amongst others, the US, Israel, South Africa, Zimbabwe, Saudi Arabia, Pakistan, Uzbekistan, Botswana, Egypt, Brunei, China, Morocco, and Brazil [8–19]), in reaction to a variety of different local contexts, Brown identifies a common thread in the practice, noting that '[t]he popular desire for walling harbors a wish for the power of protection, containment and integration promised by sovereignty' (26). Brown identifies the flurry of contemporary fence building as a response to the global acceleration and flux, lauded – and induced – by neoliberalism. As she puts it '[v]isible walls respond to the need for containment in too global a world, too unhorizoned a universe' (119). This production of walls constitutes only the most visible manifestations of the proliferation of reactionary movements and tactics attempting to suppress difference, uncertainty, and flux (the three being necessarily linked in an accelerating, globalizing world). A wide variety of thinkers have shown how, in diverse countries, anxiety over acceleration and uncertainty have given rise to new reactionary political movements.[10]

It is, of course, potentially dangerous to subsume all of these diverse movements and activities under the same rubric. Unquestionably, specific political activities will be rooted in specific historical contexts, respond to specific local grievances, and draw on specific local narratives (and what is more, of course, reactionary, conservative, anti-democratic, and fundamentalist political movements predate the current era of acceleration). At the same time, I believe that there is something useful about linking these diverse political activities, recognizing the way in which they are at least partially responding to a similar set of anxieties over acceleration. As Brown points out in defence of linking together acts of wall building in diverse political contexts, despite 'their distinctive political and economic contexts, varied histories, various states purposes and effects . . . [e]ach of the new walls can be seen to issue from certain pressures on nations and states exerted by the process of globalization' (2010: 27).[11] I would argue that the same can be said about the broader world of reactionary politics, and about the phenomenon of 'ressentiment against speed' which I discuss later.

To provide an example of the kind of reactionary political stances I'm discussing, and to foreground how they can be linked to questions of speed and acceleration, I wish to turn to a specific case study, the *MV Sun Sea*, a refugee ship which arrived on the shores of Canada, sparking a wave of anti-immigrant sentiments. I believe that a close investigation of this case shows how, in addition to a general xenophobia and racism, this response has to be understood as tied to a more general anxiety over acceleration. Furthermore, close investigation of this case study will be helpful in articulating the central concept of 'ressentiment against speed'. The choice of case study is not arbitrary, as the figure of the refugee frequently manifests as the abject representative of accelerating globalization.[12] As Brown puts it 'almost nothing rivals the image of immigrant hordes as an incitement to xenophobic nationalism and to demands for fierce state protectionism amid globalization' (2010: 68–9).

The MV Sun Sea

In August of 2010, the *MV Sun Sea*, a ship carrying 497 Tamil refugees from Sri Lanka – fleeing the violent reprisals which Tamil populations had been subject to in the wake of the civil war (UNHCR 2010) – was captured and boarded by the Canadian Navy off the coast of Vancouver Island. The refugees were immediately detained. Although the government promised to 'to deal "aggressively" with the refugee determination hearings' (Canadian Council for Refugees 2015: 8), and sought to keep them detained for an unusually long period of time, ultimately around two-thirds of the refugees' claims for asylum were accepted.

The initial response in Canada was, however, disturbing to say the least. Almost immediately upon news of the *Sun Sea* hitting the media, then Prime Minister Stephen Harper and the ruling Conservative party began to fan the flames of fear. Canadian daily *The Globe and Mail* reported that '[t]he Harper government said intelligence sources give it reason to believe the passengers include human traffickers and people linked to the Tamil Tigers terrorist group' (Chase, Youssef and Lindell 2010), despite having little to no knowledge of who was actually on the boat (suspicions are that the intelligence source to whom Harper was deferring was the Sri Lankan government itself). Public Safety Minister Vic Toews claimed that that the Sun Sea was a 'test case', saying '[t]his particular situation is being observed by others who may have similar intentions and I think it's very important that Canada deals with the situation in a clear and decisive way' (Ibid). All the while, Harper ominously intoned 'We are responsible for the security of our borders' (Lablanc 2010). All of this served to effectively frame the case of the Tamil refugees not in terms of human rights, or social justice, but as a question of security.

With the spectre of terrorists being smuggled into the country, and with hordes more apparently just over the horizon, a disturbing portion of Canadians embraced the government's fear-mongering. In an Angus Reid poll, 'Fifty per cent of poll respondents want[ed] to deport the passengers and crew of the Tamil ship back to Sri Lanka, *even if their refugee claims are legitimate*'.[13] More broadly, '46 per cent of Canadians believe immigration is having a negative effect on the country, a five-point increase from [one year previous]' (Taber 2010). On the elite side of things, a new right-wing think tank, *The Center for Immigration Policy Reform*, was launched, focusing on asserting 'moral contracts' with migrants. As Gilles Paquet, professor of governance at the University of Ottawa, and member of the centre's advisory board helpfully explains 'Canada is not a bingo hall. When you come to this country, I expect you to abide by a number of things' (Ibbitson 2010). (This, I suppose, reassures those of us deeply concerned about the impending 'bingo-hall-ization' of Canada.)

Now, we might wish to dismiss this as a momentary xenophobic panic, whipped up in a fairly obvious bit of voter manipulation. The Conservative party was, at the time, a minority government, having failed to win a majority in the previous two elections, and saw their poll numbers falling. We could therefore potentially write it off as a moment of cynical politicking by a right-wing party seeking to gin up controversy.

Unfortunately, there is a long history of this kind of panicked response to migrants and refugees in Canada, happening in almost unnervingly similar ways, in seemingly regular cycles. Just a little over ten years previous there was another public outcry over immigration, this time caused by the arrival of several boats of Chinese migrants, again off the coast of Vancouver Island.

Their arrival again prompted sizeable protests and numerous denunciations in the press.[14] In more recent years, Canada once again underwent another such round of xenophobic politics in response to proposals to resettle refugees from the Syrian civil war.

These reoccurring uproars have to be put in the context of Canada's overall immigration situation. Canada has one of the highest per-capita immigration rates in the world – a rate which is rising. According to projections from Statistics Canada, by 2031, the Canadian population will be between 25% and 28% foreign born. Additionally, according to the report, 'nearly one-half (46%) of Canadians aged 15 and over would be foreign-born, or would have at least one foreign-born parent' (Statistics Canada 2010). As a result, between 29% and 32% of the Canadian population would be visible minorities, the first and second largest groups amongst which would be those of Chinese and South Asian descent.

These profound demographic shifts challenge easy and seemingly stable images of what Canada, and Canadians, look like. In such contexts, attachments to supposedly cherished principles of 'multiculturalism' and 'diversity' run the risk of becoming weakened. Multiculturalism – and robust immigration and refugee policies – might be an acceptable practice when one can guarantee that it will happen in a cultural context which is predominantly white, Christian, European, and colonial. However, as white settler privilege in Canada becomes increasingly challenged, pluralism becomes more of a gamble.

In these broad demographic shifts we see, as discussed in the introduction, what Rosa (2003) identifies as one of the key elements of the social acceleration of time, the perception of an increase in the rate of 'social change and transformation' (7). This perception gives rise to a profound anxiety over an accelerating world. The perception of the loss of impermeable borders leaves people feeling adrift in a world of accelerating global flows. In such a context, there is a tendency to seek out authoritative narratives, ones which will hopefully re-affirm traditional borders and boundaries, securing both space and identity (As Brown describes it, a world of accelerating global flows 'threatens an imaginary of individual and national identity dependent upon perceivable horizons and the containment they offer' [2010: 26]). Thus, the Conservative government proposed a draconian overhaul of refugee and immigration policy (Baluja 2012). Such reactionary actions must be understood in the context of global acceleration, and the desire to resist Brown's paradox through authoritative reimpositions of political authority, even if only against the weakest and most vulnerable instantiations of this broad process.[15]

The story of the *MV Sun Sea* could be repeated *ad nauseum*, both within Canada and around the world. Anti-immigration movements, xenophobic panics and the scapegoating of migrants have become the norm.[16] There are, of course, countless specific reasons that these movements occur – particular histories of racism, nationalism, colonialism; economic, cultural, political, social, and personal assemblages which allow these movements to gain ground. But at least one of the factors driving these reactionary movements is an increasing anxiety over acceleration, and a sense of insecurity that comes with the seeming dissolution of borders which provided stability for narratives of identity, morality, community, etc. As Brown puts it, in the current political context 'xenophobia is . . . overdetermined by the economic and political insecurities generated by globalization' (2010: 69).

What is more, anti-immigration movements are not the only manifestation of this anxiety over speed. Everywhere in contemporary political culture, we see reactionary calls for 'security' and 'stability' in the face of acceleration. This frequently manifests itself as a move away from democratic deliberation and towards centralized authoritarian power. In a previous work (2011), I discussed this shift to centralized and arbitrary authority in the American context, discussing the passing of the PATRIOT ACT and the willingness to hand over enormous unquestioned power to the American president, both by congress and the American public. This was done, both explicitly and implicitly, because of the perceived threat of the acceleration of the pace of events, and the increasing pace of dangerous global flows. But such anti-democratic reforms are by no means the sole purview of America. We have seen a similar rightward turn in Canadian politics since (at least) the turn of the millennium.[17]

The Conservative party's undemocratic policies and behaviour while in government were well documented.[18] Prime Minister Stephen Harper was notorious for legislating through the Prime Minister's office, avoiding bringing key issues to a vote in parliament. The conservative party muzzled government scientists, preventing them from discussing their work with the media (Burgman 2012); attempted to control the flow of information to the press; and used an unelected senate to veto legislations passed by the elected house of commons. All of this led to the Harper government being held in contempt of parliament, something that has never happened in the history of Canadian politics (indeed, something which has never happened in any commonwealth country ever).

For all this, in 2011, the Conservatives were rewarded with a majority government for the first time since 1993. This of course had to do with the unique institutional and regional composition of Canadian politics. However, the Conservative party, like many reactionary movements, gained at least some success by preying on anxieties and insecurities over acceleration. *The Globe and Mail*, the major national Canadian daily, in their endorsement before the election, said '[o]nly Stephen Harper and the Conservative Party have shown the leadership, the bullheadedness (let's call it what it is) and the discipline this country needs'. What's curious is that the endorsement then goes on to criticize his anti-democratic behaviour saying:

> Mr. Harper could achieve a great deal more if he would relax his grip on Parliament, its independent officers and the flow of information, and

instead bring his disciplined approach to bear on the great challenges at hand. That is the great strike against the Conservatives: a disrespect for Parliament, the abuse of prorogation, the repeated attempts (including during this campaign) to stanch debate and free expression.

(The Globe and Mail *2011)*

That last paragraph would seem like a damning indictment. And yet clearly it did not stop *the Globe and Mail* from given Harper their endorsement. Indeed, given their appreciation for his 'bullheadedness', it's unclear what that could mean *other* than his willingness to ignore traditional constraints and democratic checks. The tone of the *Globe*'s endorsement is clear: democracy is good, but in a time of uncertainty, it is more important that we have 'leadership' and 'discipline'. Thus, where the neoliberal approach seeks to 'wish' Brown's Paradox out of existence, the reactionary approach seeks to force it out through sheer 'bullheadedness'.

Ressentiment Against Speed

In my previous book, *The Politics of Speed*, I argued that this willingness to hand over authority to centralized executives and reject democratic consultation is not due to the technical challenge of speed (any more than the panic over the *MV Sun Sea* had anything to do with the actual scope of immigration in Canada, the 500 Tamil refugees constituting a drop in the bucket of Canada's 250,000 annual new permanent residents) but rather its existential challenge (31). In times of acceleration, people fear democratic consultation, and crave authoritative renderings because of the way in which stable identities and narratives come under threat. This reactionary mindset is rooted in a phenomenon I called *ressentiment* against speed. *Ressentiment* against speed is a kind of crystallized cultural dynamic which craves a stability and a certainty which the world is incapable of providing.[19] This disappointment becomes activated as a drive for revenge against the world which is viewed as the source of instability; against scapegoats who are identified with this instability; and ultimately against ourselves, through calls for authoritarian governance to control us. Here I wish to make a more thorough study of this concept of *ressentiment* against speed, uncovering its specifically Nietzschean roots, which are not extensively discussed in the original text. This investigation is important because I think that a *ressentiment* against speed is, in fact, one of the central components of Brown's Paradox. To understand this, we must understand Nietzsche's philosophy of *ressentiment* in greater detail.

Ressentiment should not be confused with resentment. Resentment – a sense of anger over pain or injury we may have suffered – is a natural response, as is the attempt to challenge or overturn the sources of these pains or injuries.[20] Nietzsche does not council a kind of ascetic rejection of judgement, simply accepting everything as it comes (in which case, we would become, in his words, the ass which can only bray 'Yeah-yuh' [Nietzsche 1976: 424]), nor is he arguing for a Christian 'turning of the other cheek'. Being angry, resentful, unhappy, etc., are all perfectly acceptable to Nietzsche so long – and this is crucial – as they serve as a spur to action. So long as your resentment or anger become a vector for productive intervention in the world, then they have the potential to be good or noble.[21]

The trouble with *ressentiment* is that, counter to resentment, it does not act as a spur to productive action (although it does still frequently spur reactive behaviour, a distinction I will explain shortly). *Ressentiment* is resentment crystallized and spiritualized, and thus focused not on any particular actor but rather on the world as a whole. *Ressentiment* expresses itself as a generalized resentment against a world that allows pain and suffering to occur. It frequently manifests as a rejection of the world, and the imagining of a world of perfection in opposition to this 'imperfect' world. Nietzsche makes clear how this drive to idealization is linked to *ressentiment* and the spirit of revenge. 'To talk about "another" world than this is quite pointless . . . we *revenge* ourselves on life by means of the phantasmagoria of "another," a "better" life' (1968: 49). This link between idealization and revenge are displayed quite strongly, Nietzsche says, in many of the major works of metaphysics in the western canon.

> Psychology of Metaphysics – This world is apparent: consequently there is a true world; – this world is conditional; consequently there is an unconditioned world; – this world is full of contradiction: consequently there is a world free of contradiction; – this world is a world of becoming: consequently there is a world of being: – all false conclusions. . . . It is suffering that inspires these conclusions: fundamentally they are desires that such a world should exist; in the same way, to imagine another, more valuable world is an expression of hatred for a world that makes one suffer: the *ressentiment* of metaphysicians against actuality is here creative.
>
> *(1968a: 310–11)*

'It is suffering that inspires these conclusions' and *ressentiment* is 'expression of hatred for a world that makes one suffer'. This is the danger of *ressentiment* and how it differs from resentment. Resentment is a part of living in the world for Nietzsche, a world which produces suffering, and which therefore must be responded to. But *ressentiment* takes one out of the world. It orients one's actions to other worlds, worlds which don't exist.

In the context of a discussion of an accelerating world, *ressentiment* against speed manifests as an existential resentment over the refusal of the world to provide one with the stability – either in time or in space – that one craves. In response, we construct idealized spaces and times, located either in the nostalgia of the past, or in an eschatological future. Nietzsche discusses idealist philosophy and religious cosmologies, but we can just as easily see these drives expressed in political narratives of 'golden ages', 'the good old days', 'the end of history' or simply the security of 'strong borders'. These space-times become refuges, defences, and weapons against an uncertain world of flow and becoming. Just as to live in the world is to suffer, to live in time is to be subject to contingency, and to live in space is to see that space always invade, reshaped, and de/reterritorialized.[22] To wish otherwise is to close one's eyes and stop up one's ears, to refuse to intervene in the world as it is. This is exactly what *ressentiment* against speed produces.

Nietzsche's discussion of the philosopher's disdain for the 'world of becoming' shows how *ressentiment* is always already a *ressentiment* against speed.

> All that philosophers have handled for millennia has been conceptual mummies; nothing actual has escaped from their hands alive. They kill, they stuff, when they worship, these conceptual idolaters. . . . Death, change, age, as well as procreation and growth, are for them objections – refutations even. What is, does not *become*; what becomes, *is* not.
>
> *(1968: 45)*

This quote brings out another important element of Nietzsche's thinking. Looking at Nietzsche's critique of idealism, we might take him for a kind of vulgar realist, criticizing flights of philosophical fancy. This is to misunderstand Nietzsche's conception of the world of becoming. Nietzsche never takes what the 'world' *is* for granted and, with his focus on creativity, even were 'one' to know what the 'world' *is*, the world – and 'one' – would almost certainly change. But that is exactly the point. Nietzsche affirms that the world is a world of change, of becoming, of contingency (and therefore necessarily, at times, of suffering and disappointment). This is the world that we live in, and the world in which we must act.

Ressentiment and Political Action

This is the greatest danger of *ressentiment* from a Nietzschean perspective. Unlike that active power which a sense of resentment can potentially inculcate, *ressentiment* functions as a *reactive* power. Deleuze, in his analysis of Nietzsche, develops an important insight when he says that reactive powers are those which 'decompose, they *separate active force from what it can do*; they take away a part or almost all of its power' (2002: 57). By orienting us towards idealized space/times, and rejecting intervention in 'this world', *Ressentiment* separates us from our power. This is the crucial point which brings us back to Brown's Paradox, where we seem to have so much power at our fingertips, and yet are able to do so little with it.

Note, the fact that *ressentiment* separates us from what we can do does not mean that we stop doing things. Quite the opposite. When under the sway of *ressentiment* we are just as prone to take action in the world. This is because in *ressentiment* we have judged the world and found it wanting. We find this world of speed and becoming to be a world of evil and suffering. This is why *ressentiment* also manifests as a spirit of revenge. We feel that the world has punished us, and we wish to punish it back, and this frequently means punishing those who are viewed as agents or avatars of that evil.

Once again, this is different than the active behaviour that might be undertaken in response to resentment. There the idea is to stop those who injure us or overcome those things or people who block our way. It is never just the reactive desire for revenge but always the active desire to achieve some goal, to further our plans, to assert our values. The reactive movement of *ressentiment* manifests as revenge. It is thus premised upon a moral judgement and is itself a moralizing move (i.e. one acts primarily to punish an evil rather than achieve an end). It is this ability to moralize suffering, to assign blame, that is so useful to the agent of *ressentiment*. Nietzsche explains the difference between resentment and *ressentiment* quite well in the passage that follows.

> In my judgement, we find here the actual physiological causation of *ressentiment*, revenge and their ilk, in a yearning, then, to *anaesthetize pain through emotion*: – people generally look for the same thing, wrongly in my view, in the defensive return of a blow, a purely protective reaction, a 'reflex movement' in the case of any sudden injury or peril, such as that performed even by a headless frog to ward off corrosive acid. But the difference is fundamental: in the one case the attempt is made to prevent harm being done, in the other case, the attempt is made to *anaethetize* a tormenting, secret pain that is becoming unbearable with a more violent emotion of any sort, and at least rid the consciousness of it for a moment – for this, one needs an emotion, the wildest possible emotion and, in order to arouse it, the first available pretext. 'Someone or other must be to blame that I feel ill'.
>
> *(1997: 93)*

This desire to seek out somebody to blame is the pattern we see time and again in the reactionary politics of *ressentiment*. It is what we saw earlier in the case of the *MV Sun Sea*, and in other anti-immigration movements like it: the attempt to identify and blame particular actors as representative of what are broader movements and social forces, to take the individual migrant as a synecdoche of global acceleration as a whole. To return to Wendy Brown's analysis:

> If, as Nietzsche recognized, impotent rage inevitably yields a moralizing (re)action, how might we succeed in rereading contemporary political

life through this recognition? Might it help us understand, for example, the contemporary tendency to personify oppression in the figure of individuals and to reify it in particular acts and utterances, the tendency to render individuals and acts intensely culpable – indeed prosecutable – for history and for social relations?

(2001: 21–2)[23]

And what is more, we tend to personify that oppression in the weakest, most vulnerable constituencies, themselves caught up in the same history and social relations as their attackers. Having separated active force from what it can do, the politics of *ressentiment* naturally takes as its enemies those who are weakest, the most easily targeted and punished. (It is instructive that, for Nietzsche, one of the most important contemporaneous examples of the politics of *ressentiment* was the anti-Semite [1997: 48].)

But these moralizing expressions of revenge, and the feeling of power which accompany them, do not actually empower the bearer of *ressentiment*. This is because the standards *ressentiment* sets can never be achieved. A mindset overcome by *ressentiment* says that only a world free of suffering, of uncertainty, of insecurity, is of any value. One does not want less pain, but no pain. Not less insecurity, but no insecurity. No matter what is done, it will always fall short of this goalpost. Actual positive change which might improve their lot, or increase their power, is eschewed because it will never provide them with ideal world they crave. Better to engage in moralizing punishment which does nothing to solve their pain, but, as Nietzsche says, at least anaesthetizes them somewhat, gives them a feeling of moral superiority which will keep them going, at least for a while longer.[24]

What is more, this craving – for certainty, for stability, and most importantly, for moral superiority – makes these sufferers of *ressentiment* easy prey for those who wish to exploit them. Nietzsche discussed this in terms of 'the Priests', but in our days, it is more useful to speak of the politician of *ressentiment*, who doesn't just respond to the anxiety and fear of their public, but actively cultivates it. As Nietzsche describes it:

> He brings ointments and balms with him, of course; but first he has to wound so that he can be the doctor and whilst he soothes the pain caused by the wound, *he poisons the wound at the same time* – for that is what he is best trained to do, this magician and tamer of beasts of prey, whose mere presence necessarily makes everything healthy, sick, and everything sick, tame.

(1997: 93)

The politician of *ressentiment* provides ever more targets and scapegoats for moralizing punishment, knowing that it will never actually solve the problems of their constituency (my god, if it did, what then?). Indeed, it is not at all coincidental that reactionary politicians of *ressentiment* frequently institute neoliberal policies, making the conditions of insecurity and acceleration which give rise to the *ressentiment* against speed even more prevalent.[25]

The politician of *ressentiment* relies on their constituency's craving for certainty and stability, by presenting themselves as the source of the authority that will usher in this other world. The politician of *ressentiment* presents themselves to their constituency as 'their support, defence, prop, compulsion, disciplinarian, tyrant, God' (92). People feel themselves incapable of bringing into being the world of security they desire, and therefore become willing to submit to anyone who claims that ability. How else to explain the *Globe and Mail* endorsement which simultaneously decries the 'anti-democratic' behaviour of the Conservative party, while craving the 'discipline, leadership and bullheadedness' they possess? Here we see the final stage of *ressentiment*, and the final ascendancy of 'The Priests', of the politician of *ressentiment*:

> 'I suffer: someone or other must be guilty' – and every sick sheep thinks the same. But his shepherd the ascetic priest, says to him, 'Quite right, my sheep! Somebody must be to blame: but you yourself are this somebody, you yourself alone are to blame for it, *you yourself alone are to blame for yourself*'.
>
> *(94)*

When we authorize increasingly centralized and authoritarian governments, when we do not jealously guard our civil liberties and democratic rights, what are we saying, other than that we accept that *we* are the problem with politics, that we ourselves are to blame? Give us, then, a 'leader' who will provide us with the security we crave.[26]

Once again, *ressentiment* as that which separates an active force from what it can do, as that which separates people and communities from their power. And this is the irony of the *ressentiment* against speed. As people feel impotent in the face of acceleration, they become more willing to give up what power they do have to increasingly authoritarian structures or, when they do express their power, do so by attacking the weakest elements of the systems they oppose, usually in ways which actually shore up the systems they are supposed to be opposing.[27]

Living With/in Brown's Paradox

The result of this analysis is that both attempts to 'solve' Brown's paradox prove unsatisfying. The neoliberal approach of embracing the instability of this accelerating world requires us to ignore the violence and exploitation which goes along with it. Furthermore, it dismisses the very real desire for stability and security in our lives – and livelihoods – as somehow quaint, or even childish. We see how the frequent neoliberal complaint that 'government cannot provide for everything' borrows the tropes of oppressive parenting, making the dissatisfied citizen into nothing more than the stereotype of a peevish toddler rather than a stakeholder in a social contract with a legitimate grievance. Any response to Brown's paradox will require that we acknowledge the very real inequality and violence that are currently part of our accelerating world, and the impotence that most people feel in the face of it. It must also therefore have some sort of program for empowering people, for challenging these inequalities and violence, for providing people with genuine opportunities rather than the neoliberal offer of 'owning' one's own subjugation. Genuine efforts must be made both to constrain the violent flows of global capital, and to insulate individuals and communities from these flows, at the local, state, and global levels. One trajectory of future research on the question of speed therefore must be to look at effective policy responses to the violence and exploitations affiliated with social acceleration.[28]

And yet, at the same time as we try to empower people, we must be careful that our desire for stability and security, our desire to oppose the uncertainty of an accelerating world, doesn't manifest itself as a *ressentiment* against speed. Some measure of uncertainty and instability in the world is ineradicable. This is true for both historico-empirical reasons (we *are* undergoing a period of social acceleration, and we are unlikely to de-invent the wheel of technological speed any time soon) but also for essentially ontological reasons. As discussed earlier, we must recognize that we live in a world of becoming, and that this necessarily introduces a note of flux, uncertainty, and acceleration into our lives. Our teleological projections will always be disturbed by irruptions of radical futurity, and the borders we try to police will always be criss-crossed by deterritorialized lines of flight.

What is more, these contingencies are not necessarily bad things. First of all, they open us up to new experiences, new possibilities, and new worlds. Brown wasn't lying when she said that we now live in 'a global order more saturated by human power than ever before'. We must be careful how we think about, and use that power, but we cannot just ignore it or give it up lightly.[29] Indeed, in terms of achieving our first goal, a willingness to interact constructively with the powers and opportunities our accelerating world provides us with will be crucial (as will be discussed in later chapters). Second, genuinely slow worlds, worlds with firm borders and thoroughly policed lines of time, frequently require deep authoritarian power to maintain those borders and narratives. Indeed, it is exactly in the *ressentiment* of speed that the reactionary call for control is invoked; in the attempt to extinguish the novel, the unexpected, the different, the other. As William Connolly puts it:

> A slow, homogeneous world often supports undemocratic hierarchy because it irons out discrepancies of experience through which constituencies can

become reflective about self-serving assumptions they habitually use to appraise themselves in relation to others.

(2002: 144)[30]

Our response to Brown's paradox must, therefore, be careful not to turn stability and control into a fetish, to acknowledge the intractability – and also the benefits and pleasures – of a world of contingency, a world of becoming, a world of acceleration.

We must therefore begin to cultivate a third way, a response which does not so much try to resolve Brown's paradox, as re-inflect. Such an approach would seek to embrace the power and opportunities which an accelerating world provides, using them to resist the exploitation and violence inherent in the contemporary world. However, at the same time as it sought some amount of security for individuals, it would be willing to accept that a certain amount of contingency and instability in the world is ineradicable. It would ensure that this desire for stability did not manifest as a reactionary drive for the exclusion and erasure of difference, nor through a totalitarian drive for complete mastery over contingency. It would thus be a politics that attempted to express itself as an 'active force', which is to say a force which expresses itself, which builds a world to its specifications, but does so with an understanding, and even affirmation, of the limitations of life in 'this world'. Such a politics therefore would rigorously have to root out the sense of *ressentiment* against speed, and become comfortable with living, organizing, and acting, in an accelerating world of becoming. This does not mean letting go of our desire for stability, but it does mean loosening our attachment to it, recognizing the necessity (and indeed desirability) of some amount of difference, individuality, and flux in the world.

This loosening of attachment is not easy, and cannot simply be the result of policy prescription. It would mean working on the affective sensibilities of individuals and communities to make them more capable of coping with a certain amount of uncertainty and instability in the world. A second trajectory of future research on speed will therefore have to focus on how to utilize narrative and affective resources to inculcate a sense of comfort with uncertainty, and fight against the pull of *ressentiment*.[31] In the next two chapters we turn to just such a discussion of the affective dimensions of social acceleration, seeking to understand the roots of *ressentiment* and practices we might develop at both the individual and social levels to respond to them.

In an ideal world, this project of loosening people's attachments to stability would begin to integrate with the project of making them less subject to the violence of global acceleration, creating a virtuous cycle. As people become more secure, they potentially become less subject to *ressentiment*. At the same time, as they affectively fight off the *ressentiment* driven desire for stability, they potentially become more willing to engage in active political tactics which might actually provide for greater security and stability. Lessened *ressentiment* against speed might provide the conditions of possibility for greater solidarity and alliance building across borders and differences, a greater willingness to take advantage of some of the powers which global acceleration provides. Here we might look to increasing examples of global solidarity networks.[32]

Let us be clear, however; this possibility of a feedback loop associated with living within paradox should not be taken as a *resolution* of that paradox. We must remember that this paradox is fundamentally irresolvable, and thus that it will be the source of an ongoing political struggle over crucial questions ('How much stability is enough?'; 'How much velocity is desirable?'). This struggle will always run the risk of falling into either *ressentiment* against speed or indifference to the pain that it causes. This is as it should be. It reinforces our discussion from the introduction in which I argued that effective responses to social acceleration must go 'beyond fast and slow' as an uncritical embrace of either will leave us ill-equipped to grapple with the nature of Brown's paradox. As Chantal Mouffe describes, when it comes to paradox '[n]o final resolution or equilibrium between . . . two conflicting logics is ever possible, and there can be only temporary, pragmatic, unstable and precarious negotiations of the tension between them' (45). The best that we can do is try to ensure that we live that paradox deliberately.

Notes

1. A not at all exhaustive account would include Machiavelli on *fortuna* (1998), Locke on prerogative power (1988), Kant on cosmopolitanism (1983), and Marx on capitalist dynamism (2000), as well as 20th-century discussions such as Heidegger (1971), Derrida (1984), Deleuze and Guattari (1987), Baudrillard (1994), Simmel (1997), and Schmitt (2007).
2. A partial list would include Mackenzie (2002), Connolly (2002), Wolin (1997), Der Derian (2001), Rosa (2013), Scheuerman (2004), Agamben (2005), Tomlinson (2007), Glezos (2012), and Sharma (2014).
3. Note, we should be careful that we don't assume that access to such technologies are evenly distributed, either globally, or within any individual society. Dramatic asymmetries of wealth and power limit access to key technologies, processes and spaces. At the same time, we shouldn't ignore the way in which the social acceleration of time is very much a global phenomenon, changing the lives of people around the world (the wide dissemination of mobile phones throughout the developing world is just one small example). In this regard, the 'we' that this article speaks for should not be seen as a fully homogenous we but rather simply the collective experience of a diverse global population coping in different ways with an accelerating world. For a discussion of global variations in social acceleration, see chapter four in Glezos (2012), especially pages 131–134.
4. We see, for example, a Marxist version of it in Hardt and Negri (2000), or a cosmopolitan version in Held (2003). Accelerationism (Mackay and Avanessian 2014) also provides a somewhat more ambiguous version of this account. For a more detailed discussion of neoliberalism, see Brown (2015: 20).
5. It might be perceived as a bit cheap to turn to Friedman rather than more serious neoliberal thinkers such as Jagdish Bhagwati (2004). However, my goal is not so much to engage with Friedman as a political theorist, but as a spokesman for a

particular set of narratives and sensibilities; an archetype of neoliberal politics, and its way of responding to the paradoxes of an accelerating world. Friedman has been enormously influential in advancing a widely held narrative about life in an accelerating world. Engaging with his writings is a way of engaging with a neoliberal 'common sense'.

6. Furthermore, this perspective is not just relegated to Friedman's America, or indeed the first world. As is well documented, a combination of international economic organizations, multinational corporations, and international think-tanks have made such perspectives and policies equally common throughout the developing world. For a good introduction on this topic, see Klein (2008).

7. See, also, Wajcman (2016), Rosa (2013), Hassan (2007), Merriman (2012), Sharma (2014).

8. See, also, Virilio (1977), Sharma (2014), Crary (2013), Noys (2014), Wolin (1997). Hassan provides a useful account of the anxiety over social acceleration saying:

> The economy, globalization, job insecurity, levels of indebtedness, the institutionalization of the short-term perspective, the rapid turnover in product cycles, lower real wages, turbulent stock markets and so on, are objective social conditions that can be measured. These are social forces that give rise to an interconnected world that is far more complex and far less comprehensible that it was, say, a generation ago. This complexity, this opacity, this denial of the future and valorizing of the present, constitute a temporal context (speed-filled and future empty) within which the subjective experience of trauma and anxiety are given their locus and expression.
>
> *(2009: 111)*

9. Crucially, not every reactionary movement is motivated – still less motivated *solely* – by a reaction against speed, nor is every attempt to challenge social acceleration 'reactionary' as we will discuss in the final section. But, as discussed in this chapter, I feel there is evidence to support the idea that global social acceleration plays a role in a variety of reactionary movements, and thus that understanding the relationship between the two is valuable.

10. See, as a set of examples Steger (2005: 96), Harvey (2006: 61), Glezos (2012: Ch. 4). Furthermore – and somewhat ironically – we can see the way these local reactionary movements have organized as transnational activist networks, in what Clifford Bob refers to as the 'global right wing' (2012).

11. See, also, her broader methodological defence in (2010: 139).

12. See Nyers (2003).

13. Emphasis added.

14. For an excellent discussion of this incident, as well as prior incidents of the naval interception of maritime refugees in Canada, see Watson (2009: Ch. 3). For a broader discussion of the way that maritime refugees constitute particular challenges to, and opportunities for, state authority, see Budz (2009).

15. Budz provides an account of the way in which the punishment of these archetypally mobile actors serves to shore up the apparent stability of the state.

> The shifting justifications, as well as the necessary, if minimal, compromises made by government actors in the management of these maritime incidents work to produce the impression of an effective social ordering, in which people are correctly categorized and managed, where borders are impermeable, society is safe and the state is sovereign. Each new ship represents a potentially valuable opportunity to perform the ordering process and symbolize the strength of the state.
>
> *(21)*

16. Over the course of writing this book, we have seen violent xenophobic reactions in states around the world grappling with the refugee crisis resulting from the conflict

in Syria, and the establishment of concentration camps for asylum seekers on the southern US border, to name just two examples.

17. Nor is this centralization of authority to unitary executives unique to North America but instead has been a general global trend, even amongst liberal democratic states. See Glezos (2011) and Scheuerman (2004: 92–93, 108–109).

18. See Martin (2011).

19. As Leccardi puts it:

> When the accelerated sequence of social changes, chained to the speed of technological innovation, ties itself to the acceleration of the rhythms of life in a globalized space, the temporal dimension of the present will also contract . . . In this case a *loss* of the present as a space of choice and of reflexive action occurs. The present seems no longer to be a time open to experience (inasmuch as the mutilation of the temporal horizons of the past and future allows it) but rather precarious time, in the sense that Bourdieu . . . conferred on this term. That is to say, the present seems a time when not only forms of rational anticipation appear impracticable but when the idea of "hold" on the world vanishes.
>
> *(30)*

20. For an excellent discussion of the distinction between 'resentment' and '*ressentiment*', see Connolly (1995: 213–14)

21. Of course, what constitutes a 'productive intervention in the world' is itself contested, and will be based on judgements both pragmatic (i.e. ones related to questions of political efficacy, such as whether 'walls' actually fulfill their stated goal of decreasing immigration) as well as more broadly ethico-ontological (thus, as we will see later, in the discussion of whether particular actions or orientations constitute nihilistic rejections of the world). That such judgements will be contested and, at times, unclear, does not, I feel, diminish the usefulness of the language of *ressentiment* as a way of understanding contemporary responses to the question of social acceleration.

22. See my discussion of the radical futurity of speed in Chapter 1 of *The Politics of Speed,* and my discussion of the exteriority of speed in Chapter 2. Note, as we will discuss later, this is not to argue that we must uncritically accept any and all flows and becomings (just as we must not uncritically accept any and all forms of suffering). It is, rather to reject an orientation to the world that views flows as irruptions or deviations from a stable and secure world we would otherwise have. Rather we must understand that flows and becomings are foundations to life, and that we must reject orientations that are incapable of responding to them with anything other than *ressentiment*. As Peter Merriman puts it

> Movement, affect, sensation, rhythm, vibration, energy, force, and much more, then, might be taken to be fundamental to understand how life unfolds, and we might even go as far as to suggest that space-time is a Western fiction, a series of stories we tell ourselves, which in turn structure how we think about the world.
>
> *(2012: 2)*

23. And, as Brown says in *States of Injury*:

> the characteristics of late modern secular society, in which individuals are buffeted and controlled by global configurations of disciplinary and capitalist power of extraordinary proportions, and are at the same time nakedly individuated, stripped of reprieve from relentless exposure and accountability for themselves, together add up to an incitement to *ressentiment* that might have stunned even the finest philosopher of its occasions and logics. Starkly accountable yet dramatically impotent, the late modern liberal subject quite literally seethes with *ressentiment*.
>
> *(69)*

24. We can see this moralizing drive for punishment over results in countless aspects of contemporary politics from the 'War on Terror' to the 'War on Drugs' to mandatory sentencing laws, to the drive for abstinence only education, to the criminalization of poverty. For a discussion of this drive to revenge in the 'War on Terror', see Butler (2006). For a discussion of it in relation to criminal justice, see Connolly (1995). Brown's *Walled States, Waning Sovereignty* explicitly engages with the ways in which wall building not only fails but frequently makes the problem it seeks to solve worse (110, 112–113).

25. See the discussion of the evangelical capitalist resonance machine in Connolly (2008).

26. See Scheuerman (2004) and Glezos (2011).

27. And note that this is the drive towards *ressentiment* against speed does not only appear on the 'right' side of the political spectrum. Anxiety over acceleration exists across multiple ideologies. We therefore see it emerge in liberals and radical democrats. (See my discussion of Sheldon Wolin in [Glezos 2012: Ch. 1]) as well as amongst Marxists (see Brown [1999]).

28. Over and above work focusing on struggles for economically just worlds generally, we might look at specific policy prescriptions arguing for targeted forms of social deceleration, such as those discussed in Eriksen (2001: Ch. 8), Sharma (2014), Garhammer (2002), Wajcman (2016), and Connolly (2002).

29. Rosi Braidotti sums up this critical and thoughtful engagement with accelerative technologies quite well when she states:

> In this context, I want to side firmly with the technological forces but against the liberal individualistic appropriation of their potential. Let me instead emphasize the liberatory and transgressive potential of these technologies, against the predatory forces that attempt to index them yet again onto a centralized, white, male, heterosexual, Eurocentric, capital-owning, standardized vision of the subject.
>
> *(33)*

See also the discussion of sustainability in Chapter 2.

30. We should also be attentive to the point raised by Laboria Cuboniks in their *Xenofeminist Manifesto*,

> suggestions to pull the lever on the emergency brake of embedded velocities, the call to slow down and scale back, is a possibility available only to the few – a violent particularity of exclusivity – ultimately entailing catastrophe for the many.
>
> *(43)*

31. Early efforts at such a project can be seen in Connolly (2002), Mackenzie (2002), and Glezos (2012).

32. See Castells (2012), Glezos (2012: Ch. 5), Stillerman (2003).

Works Cited

Agamben, G. (2005) *State of Exception*, Trans. K. Attel, Chicago, IL: Chicago University Press.

Baluja, T. (2012) 'Tories Unveil Bill to Thwart Bogus Refugees', *The Globe and Mail*, February 16. Available at: www.theglobeandmail.com/news/politics/tories-unveil-bill-to-thwart-bogus-refugees/article2340521/ (Accessed February 16, 2012).

Baudrillard, J. (1994) *Simulacra and Simulation*, Trans. S. F. Glaser, Michigan: University of Michigan Press.

Bauman, Z. (1998) *Globalization: The Human Consequences*, New York: Columbia University Press.

Bhagwati, J. (2004) *In Defense of Globalization*, Oxford: Oxford University Press.

Bob, C. (2012) *The Global Right Wing and the Clash of World Politics*, Cambridge: Cambridge University Press.

Braidotti, R. (2006) *Transpositions*, London: Polity.

Brown, W. (1995) *States of Injury*, Princeton, NJ: Princeton University Press.

Brown, W. (1999) 'Resisting Left Melancholy', *Boundary 2*, 26(3): 19–27.

Brown, W. (2001) *Politics Out of History*, Princeton, NJ: Princeton University Press.

Brown, W. (2006) 'American Nightmare: Neoliberalism, Neoconservatism, and De-Democratization', *Political Theory*, 34(6): 690–714.

Brown, W. (2010) *Walled States, Waning Sovereignty*, New York: Zone Books.

Brown, W. (2015) *Undoing the Demos: Neoliberalism's Stealth Revolution*, Brooklyn, NY: Zone Books.

Budz, M. (2009) 'A Heterotopian Analysis of Maritime Refugee Incidents', *International Political Sociology*, 3(1): 18–35.

Burgman, T. (2012) 'Ottawa "Muzzling" Scientists, Panel Tells Global Research Community', *The Globe and Mail*, February 17. Available at: http://www.theglobeandmail.com/news/politics/ottawa-muzzling-scientists-panel-tells-global-research-community/article2342707/ (Accessed February 17, 2012).

Butler, J. (2006) *Precarious Life*, New York: Verso Press.

Canadian Council for Refugees (2015) *Sun Sea: Five Years Later*. Available at: https://ccrweb.ca/sites/ccrweb.ca/files/sun-sea-five-years-later.pdf (Accessed July 9, 2019).

Castells, M. (2012) *Networks of Outrage and Hope: Social Movements in the Internet Age*, Cambridge, UK: Polity.

Chase, S., Youssef, M. and Lindell, R. (2010) 'Tamil Migrant Ship Is a Test, Says Toews, and More Boats Are on the Way', *The Globe and Mail*, August 13. Available at: www.theglobeandmail.com/news/politics/tamil-boat-testing-canadas-response-toews/article1671766/ (Accessed August 13, 2010).

Connolly, W. (1995) *The Ethos of Pluralization*, Minneapolis: University of Minnesota Press.

Connolly, W. (2002) *Neuropolitics: Thinking, Culture, Speed*, Minneapolis: University of Minnesota.

Connolly, W. (2008) *Capitalism and Christianity: American Style*, Raleigh, NC: Duke.

Crary, J. (2013) *24/7: Late Capitalism and the Ends of Sleep*, London: Verso.

Cuboniks, L. (2018) *The Xenofeminist Manifesto: A Politics for Alienation*, London, UK: Verso.

Deleuze, G. (2002) *Nietzsche and Philosophy*, Trans. H. Tomlinson, New York: Columbia.

Deleuze, G. and Guattari, F. (1987) *A Thousand Plateaus*, Trans. B. Massumi, Minneapolis: University of Minnesota Press.

Der Derian, J. (2001) *Virtuous War*, New York: Westview Press.

Derrida, J. (1984) 'No Apocalypse, Not Now', *Diacritics*, 14(2): 20–31.

Eriksen, T. H. (2001) *Tyranny of the Moment: Fast and Slow Time in the Information Age*, London, UK: Pluto Press.

Friedman, T. (2006) *The World Is Flat*, New York: Farrar, Straus and Giroux.

Garhammer, M. (2002) 'Pace of Life and Enjoyment of Life', *Journal of Happiness Studies*, 3(3): 217–56.

Glezos, S. (2011) 'The Ticking Bomb: Speed, Liberalism and Ressentiment against the Future', *Contemporary Political Theory*, 10(2): 147–65.

Glezos, S. (2012) *The Politics of Speed: Capitalism, The State, and War in an Accelerating World*, Abingdon, UK: Routledge.

The Globe and Mail (2011) 'The Globe's Election Endorsement: Facing Up to Our Challenges', April 27. Available at: www.theglobeandmail.com/news/opinions/editorials/the-globes-election-endorsement-facing-up-to-our-challenges/article2001610/ (Accessed April 27, 2011).

Hardt, M. and Negri, A. (2000) *Empire*, Cambridge: Harvard University Press.

Harvey, D. (2006) *Spaces of Global Capital*, London: Verso.

Hassan, R. (2007) 'Network Time', *24/7: Time and Temporality in the Network Society*, eds. R. Hassan and R. E. Purser, Stanford, CA: Stanford Business Books.

Hassan, R. (2009) *Empires of Speed: Time and the Acceleration of Politics and Society*, Boston, MA: Brill.

Heidegger, M. (1971) *Poetry, Language, Thought*, New York: Harper Perennial.

Held, D. (2003) 'From Executive to Cosmopolitan Multilateralism', *Taming Globalization: Frontiers of Governance*, eds. D. Held and M. Koenig-Archibugi, Cambridge: Polity Press.

Ibbitson, J. (2010) 'Seeking Immigration Review, New Center Focuses on "Moral Contracts"', *The Globe and Mail*, September 28. Available at: www.theglobeandmail.com/news/politics/seeking-immigration-review-new-centre-focuses-on-moral-contracts/article1729389/ (Accessed September 29, 2010).

Kant, I. (1983) *Perpetual Peace and Other Essays*, Trans. T. Humphrey, Indianapolis: Hackett.

Klein, N. (2008) *The Shock Doctrine*, Toronto: Vintage Canada.

Lablanc, D. (2010) 'PM Takes Hardline on Tamil Migrants', *The Globe and Mail*, August 17. Available at: www.theglobeandmail.com/news/politics/ottawa-notebook/pm-takes-hard-line-on-tamil-migrants/article1676011/ www.theglobeandmail.com/news/politics/ottawa-notebook/pm-takes-hard-line-on-tamil-migrants/article1676011/(Accessed August 17, 2010).

Leccardi, C. (2007) 'New Temporal Perspectives in the "High-Speed Society"', *24/7: Time and Temporality in the Network Society*, eds. R. Hassan and R. E. Purser, Stanford, CA: Stanford Business Books.

Locke, J. (1988) *Two Treatises of Government*, Cambridge: Cambridge University Press.

Machiavelli, N. (1998) *The Prince*, Trans. H. C. Mansfield, Chicago: University of Chicago Press.

Mackay, R. and Avanessian, A. (eds.) (2014) *#Accelerate: The Accelerationist Reader*, Fallmouth, UK: Urbanomic.

Mackenzie, A. (2002) *Transductions: Bodies and Machines at Speed*, London: Continuum.

Martin, L. (2011) *Harperland: The Politics of Control*, Toronto: Penguin Canada.

Marx, K. (2000) *Selected Writings*, Oxford: Oxford University Press.

Merriman, P. (2012) *Mobility, Space and Culture*, Abingdon, UK: Routledge.

Mouffe, C. (2005) *The Democratic Paradox*, London: Verso.

Nietzsche, F. (1968) *Twilight of the Idols/The Anti-Christ*, Trans. R. J. Hollingsdale, New York: Penguin Books.

Nietzsche, F. (1968a) *The Will to Power*, Trans. W. Kaufmann and R. J. Hollingdale, New York: Vintage Books.

Nietzsche, F. (1976) "Thus Spoke Zarathustra", *The Portable Nietzsche*, Trans. W. Kaufmann, New York: Penguin Books.

Nietzsche, F. (1997) *On the Genealogy of Morality*, Trans. C. Diethe, Cambridge: Cambridge University Press.

Noys, B. (2014) *Malign Velocities: Accelerationism and Capitalism*, Alresford, UK: Zero Books.

Nyers, P. (2003) 'Abject Cosmopolitanism: The Politics of Protection in the Anti-Deportation Movement', *Third World Quarterly*, 24(6): 1069–93.

Rosa, H. (2003) 'Social Acceleration: Ethical and Political Consequences of a Desynchronized High-Speed Society', *Constellations*, 10: 3–33.

Rosa, H. (2013) *Social Acceleration*, Trans. J. Trejo-Mathys, New York: Columbia University Press.

Scheuerman, W. (2004) *Liberal Democracy and the Social Acceleration of Time*, Baltimore, MD: Johns Hopkins University Press.

Schmitt, C. (2007) *The Concept of the Political*, Trans. G. Schwab, Chicago, IL: University of Chicago Press.

Sharma, S. (2014) *In the Meantime: Temporality and Cultural Politics*, Durham, NC: Duke University Press.

Simmel, G. (1997) 'The Metropolis and Mental Life', *Simmel on Culture*, eds. D. Frisby and M. Featherstone, London: Sage Publications.

Statistics Canada (2010) 'Projections of the Diversity of Canada's Population'. Available at: www.statcan.gc.ca/daily-quotidien/100309/dq100309a-eng.htm (Accessed August 1, 2019).

Steger, M. (2005) *Globalism: Market Ideology Meets Terrorism*, Oxford: Rowman and Littlefield.

Stillerman, J. (2003) 'Transnational Activist Networks and the Emergence of Labor Internationalism in the NAFTA Countries', *Social Science History*, 27(4): 577–601.

Taber, J. (2010) 'Canadian View of Immigration Sours in Wake of Tamil Ship', *The Globe and Mail*, September 9. Available at: www.theglobeandmail.com/news/politics/ottawa-notebook/canadian-view-of-immigration-sours-in-wake-of-tamil-ship/article1701127/ (Accessed September 9, 2010).

Tomlinson, J. (2007) *The Culture of Speed: The Coming of Immediacy*, London: Sage Publications.

UNHCR Eligibility Guidelines for Assessing the International Protection Needs of Asylum-Seekers from Sri Lanka (2010) Available at: www.unhcr.org/refworld/pdfid/4c31a5b82.pdf (Accessed March 25, 2012).

Virilio, P. (1977) *Speed and Politics*, Trans. M. Polizzotti, New York: Semiotext(e).

Wajcman, J. (2016) *Pressed for Time: The Acceleration of Life in Digital Capitalism*, Chicago: University of Chicago Press.

Watson, S. (2009) *The Securitization of Humanitarian Migration: Digging Moats and Sinking Boats*, Abingdon, UK: Routledge.

Wolin, S. (1997) 'What Time Is It?', *Theory and Event*, 1(1): 1–10.

2

"NO ONE HAS YET LEARNED HOW FAST THE BODY CAN GO"

Spinoza, Speed, and the Body[1]

In the previous chapter we saw how the question of speed and politics is as much a question of affects as it is of policies and technologies. I argued that understanding contemporary reactionary politics means understanding this relationship between speed and affect. To further investigate this claim – and by way of beginning to develop one set of responses to the affective dispositions which can give rise to *ressentiment* and reactionary politics – in this chapter, I turn to three themes that have received increasing attention in contemporary political theory: theories of speed, theories of the body, and the work of Baruch Spinoza.

As discussed in the previous chapter, since the turn of the millennium we've seen a dramatic increase in work in political theory on the topic of speed. This theoretical investigation of speed has gone beyond discussions of macro sites (such as state governance and warfare) and has turned to the micro terrain of the body, applying the results of the extensive work that has been done in the realm of corporeal theory over the last few decades.[2] What is curious, however, is the relative absence of Spinoza from this discussion.[3] This is a missed opportunity, as the work of Spinoza is ideally suited to serve as a hinge point between theories of the body and theories of speed. Spinoza's *Ethics* explicitly conceives of the body in terms of 'relation[s] of motion-and-rest' (II, P13L3Pr) making speed and the body inherently related. My belief is that the philosophy of Spinoza can play an important role in helping us to better understand the relationship between our accelerating world and the human body and its affects, as well as to develop an ethical framework to help us navigate this relationship.

In pursuit of this goal, I begin this chapter by articulating three different types of 'encounters' (to use Spinoza's vocabulary) between the human body and an accelerating world. The first is exemplified by the experience of jet lag, the second by the technological apparatus of the flight suit, and the third, by the acheulean axe, one of the earliest human tools. Each of these encounters highlights a different possible outcome of the encounter between speed and the body, and helps to crystallize a set of assumptions and understandings about how speed and the body relate. Each is also linked to a different vision of life in an accelerating world: in the first, speed is destructive *to* the human body; in the second speed is a prosthetic *for* – and possibly parasitic *on* – the human body; and in the third speed is constitutive *of* the human body. Crucially my argument will be that none of them are sufficient to describe the relationship between speed and the body but rather that all three are necessary (although I will argue throughout that the first two have a prominence in our society that is potentially dangerous).

These three examples are not, of course, exhaustive of all possible encounters between speed and the body. Following Spinoza, I will argue that there is no way of knowing all the ways such encounters can take place. However, it is useful to focus on these three because they address influential accounts of speed, technology, and the body. Later, I show how the bundle of assumptions, implications, and ontologies involved in each of these encounters frequently cut across multiple philosophical traditions, and show up in widely divergent social contexts. Indeed, in these accounts, I very consciously draw from diverse sources (including literature, philosophy, history, and anthropology), and time periods (from the contemporary to the pre-historic). The goal is not to argue that these are novel or unique accounts but rather consistently reoccurring perspectives, as likely to be articulated in 'high philosophy' as in 'common sense'. What is more, these different accounts of the relationship between speed and the body can give rise to important political effects and affects, carrying forward our analysis from the previous chapter.

Having laid out these three visions of what speed does to bodies, I go on to show how Spinoza can provide a theory encompassing all three. I turn to Spinoza's monistic ontology, showing how differences are never metaphysically 'substantial', but the result of interacting patterns of 'motion-and-rest'. This is then linked up with his concept of *conatus*. The difference between the three encounters will be shown to be the way in which each affects the *conatus* of the human body. The result is a rubric which allows us to understand encounters between the body and speed less in terms of whether they are 'natural' and more in terms of their ethical effects. Spinoza, I argue, offers us today an important set of tools for understanding the status of the body in an accelerating world. This set of tools will, in turn, help us to develop a program of ethical and political response to *ressentiment*, and other reactionary affective dispositions discussed in the previous chapter (a problem we will carry forward into Chapter 3).

Part I: Three Encounters Between Speed and the Body

First Encounter: Jet Lag

William Gibson has always had a knack for identifying the ways in which life has changed in the digital age. (This is, after all, the author who coined the term 'cyberspace' while still writing on a typewriter). More, perhaps, than any other contemporary sci-fi writer, Gibson is able to cut through the superficial and identify genuine changes in the way people live. This is what makes the opening passage of his 2003 novel *Pattern Recognition* such a helpful place to being thinking through the relationship between speed and the body.

> Five hours' New York jet lag and Cayce Pollard wakes in Camden Town to the dire and ever-circling wolves of disrupted circadian rhythm. It is that flat and spectral non-hour, awash in limbic tides, brainstem stirring fitfully, flashing inappropriate reptilian demands for sex, food, sedation, all of the above . . .
>
> She knew, now, absolutely . . . that Damien's theory of jet lag is correct: that her mortal soul is leagues behind her, being reeled in on some ghostly umbilical down the vanished wake of the plane that brought her here, hundreds of thousands of feet above the Atlantic. Souls can't move that quickly, and are left behind, and must be awaited, upon arrival, like lost luggage.
>
> *(1)*

In this passage, Gibson points out that jet lag — as minor an irritation as it might be — speaks to a much greater rift in the world. To say that souls can't move as fast as bodies is to point out a fundamental disjuncture between the natural pace of the body, and the velocities at which technologies now allow us to travel. Jet lag is the result of the human body being exposed to something that evolution could not have prepared it for: a situation in which the body's internal clock does not sync up with external light cues. Prior to the invention of the airplane, such a situation would have been essentially unthinkable. Gibson presents us with the image of a reptilian brainstem desperately trying to make sense of — to gain purchase on — a world which follows none of the rules that the body's rhythms had adapted to.

Gibson's brief engagement with jet lag expresses the first of three stories describing the relation between speed and the body that I wish to present. It is not a new image, nor is it an uncommon one. In its simplest form, it says two things: 1) There is a natural speed of the body; an essential velocity, rhythm, or pace which is layered into its 'soul', enacted by its nervous system, encoded in its DNA, etc; and 2) as the world has accelerated, a disjuncture has formed between that natural pace of the body and the world in which it lives. This disjuncture produces a kind of friction where the body rubs up against the speed of the world, a friction which wears the body down, grinds it up, pulls it apart. In the scene earlier, Cayce Pollard lies in her bed, trying to immobilize her body for at least a little while, allowing its natural rhythms to reassert themselves, her 'soul' to catch up with her 'body'.

We should not view this story as unique to our modern, high-velocity world, for it tends to emerge regularly in times of social or technological acceleration. For example, a similar account of bodily anxiety over acceleration developed in the 19th century, driven by advances in the railroad and telegraphy.

> [T]here was, from at least the 1880s, a string of extravagantly alarmist prognoses of the effects of the pace of modern life on the human nervous system. In one of the earliest and most influential, *American Nervousness: Its Causes and Consequences* (1881) George M. Beard introduced the concept of 'neurasthenia' into psychotherapeutic discourse: 'Beard argued that the telegraph, railroads, and steam power have enabled businessmen to make "a hundred times" more transactions in a given period than had been possible in the eighteenth century; they intensified competition and tempo, causing an increase in the incidence of a host of problems including neurasthenia, nervous, dyspepsia, early tooth decay and even premature baldness'.
>
> (*Tomlinson 2007: 36*)[4]

Here we see a jet lag *avant la lettre*, an image of bodies decaying, falling apart from the pressures of high velocity society (compare this with the idyllic way that we frequently imagine journeys by rail today [Eriksen 2001: 54–5]). Indeed, in the early days of the railroad 'extreme skeptics argued that . . . speeds of 20 or 30 miles an hour could be "fatal . . . to human life"' (Fogel: 2). Though not always articulated in such extreme ways, wherever we hear of the unnatural or inhuman acceleration of the world, this story lurks in the background.[5]

Second Encounter: The G-suit

And yet, even as our anxiety about the pace of the world increases, technological acceleration continues relentlessly onward. Humans continue to travel at faster and faster velocities. And as humans are buffeted by the accelerating pace of technology, it is to technology that they turn in their attempts to shore up and protect their fragile bodies.

Though it turned out that train travel did not have quite the kick necessary to kill a human being, there are velocities which can overwhelm the human body's ability to function. Jet travel at supersonic speeds can be accompanied by g-forces which put so much pressure on the human body that blood pools in the lower extremities, causing pilots to black out. The most effective way to alleviate the effects of supersonic speeds is the G-suit. A G-suit is a flight suit that contains a set of bladders around the legs and abdomen (and in some cases lungs) of a pilot which inflate during high g-force acceleration, putting pressure on the body and thus maintaining blood pressure. A G-suit allows pilots to experience higher g-forces for longer stretches without passing out and losing control.

The flight suit thus provides a technological augmentation of the human body, allowing it to withstand the rigours of supersonic travel. It is an exoskeleton that protects the soft human interior from the disjuncture between internal and external velocities, between the 'natural' pace of the body and the artificial pace of technology. And the G-suit is only the most visible aspect of a wider web of technologies augmenting the human body during supersonic flight. Maintaining flight at supersonic speeds requires constant adjustments at a much faster pace than allowed for by human reflexes. Fighter jets are full of computers and sensors that produce micro-adjustments without human intervention. In this encounter then, rather than a simple opposition between the velocity of the body and the world (as in the previous encounter), we see how that same technological velocity can be grafted onto the body, with the G-suit serving as a kind of prosthetic accelerator.

Before we carry on, it is necessary to take a moment to discuss exactly what relationships between speed, technology, and the body, are being articulated in this story. To conceive of technology as 'prosthesis' in this context is to reject the claim that technological velocity can only destroy the body and its corporeal velocity. Nevertheless, it shares with the first story the idea that there is a disjuncture between natural and technological speeds. The body must be shielded and augmented, wrapped in a carapace of technology before it can be subjected to the violent pace of the future. The internal pace of the body and the external pace of the world are still opposed, though they can be harmonized through technical artifice. By maintaining the distinction between natural and technological velocities – between the pace of the 'inside' and the 'outside' – that which is essentially human is opposed to that which is essentially technological. Thus, implicitly, the more human one is, the less technological one is. And conversely, the faster you are, the less human you are.

This story is expressed in one of its most emphatic forms in the work of Jean-Jacques Rousseau. Rousseau begins his investigation into politics and philosophy in the same way as so many others; through an imaginary investigation of the 'state of nature'. However, where other philosophers found human life in this state of nature incomplete and inadequate, Rousseau finds the human being happy, robust, and, most importantly, complete. From this point, every increase in 'civilization' only brings the human further from perfection and self-sufficiency, and every technological advance distances us from our essence. Bernard Stiegler recounts the Rousseau-ian perspective, saying 'The man of nature, without prostheses, is robust, as robust as a man can be – and it is civilization that will weaken him' (1998: 115). In Rousseau's own words:

> Accustomed from childhood to inclement weather and the rigors of the seasons, acclimated to fatigue, and forced, naked and without arms to defend their lives and their prey against other ferocious beasts, or to escape them by taking flight, men develop a robust and nearly unalterable temperament. Children enter the world with the excellent constitution of their parents and strengthen it with the same exercises that produced it, thus acquiring all the vigor that the human race is capable of having.
>
> *(1987: 40)*

The second skin of technology that we wear, the exoskeleton, the G-suit, then serves to muffle and weaken us, to suppress the true vitality of the human body. Ironically, by accelerating the human body technologically, we actually rob it of its natural quickness. As Steigler puts it,

> Ax, slingshot, ladder, horse, these procedures and artifices are machines, already automated: they already carry the fate of all techniques, which is to be substituted for the natural, original force of the solitary man. They constitute an illusory power, always beyond the reach of the hand, unavailable and mediate, which must be prepared, transported, arranged, and in which one must enclose oneself.
>
> *(116)*

Thus, the opposition present in the first story – between the natural and the technological – is maintained. But here a crucial difference creeps in. It is not a matter of the inside of the body being killed or destroyed by the velocity of the outside. Rather, it is a matter of the inside being hollowed out. Look here again to Rousseau's account:

> Give a civilized man time to gather all his machines around him, and undoubtedly he will easily overcome a savage man. But if you want to see an even more unequal fight, pit them against each other naked and disarmed, and you will soon realize the advantage of constantly having all of one's forces at one's disposal, of always being ready for any event, and of always carrying one's entire self, as it were, with one.
>
> *(40–41)*

In this account, the natural human body has a unity and an interiority, as the pre-technological human carries 'one's entire self with . . . one'. By comparison, the 'entire self' of the 'civilized man' is always, as Steigler puts it, 'just out of reach'. In this worldview, 'Everything is inside: the origin is the inside.

The fall is exteriorization' (116). Thus, in this narrative, the threat of speed and technology to the human body is less to the 'body' and more to its properly 'human' character.

> Rousseau's narrative of the origin shows us through antithesis how every-thing of the order of what is usually considered specifically human is immediately and irremediably linked to an absence of property, to a process of 'supplementation', of prosthetization or exteriorization, in which nothing is any longer immediately at hand, where everything is found mediated and instrumentalized, technicized, unbalanced. This process would lead today to something inhuman, or superhuman, tearing the human away from everything that, hitherto, seemed to define him . . . a process by which the realization or the 'actualization' of the power of man seems to be as well the derealization of man, his disappearance in the movement of a becoming that is *no longer his own*.
>
> *(133)*

Pushed to its limit, this hollowing out of the body, this exteriorization of all activity and endeavour into technological prostheses, ends in the only way it can, with the full prosthetization of the human itself, as the human body becomes an extension of technologies rather than the other way around.[6]

These are some of the most extreme versions of this story, but we see this image in a host of different environments. Anywhere commentators are wor-rying about the way in which technology is 'dehumanizing' us, where we feel that the accelerating pace of life leaves us merely an 'automaton' a 'cog in the machine', we see an echo of this image.[7] In this image our bodies are not destroyed by speed. Rather they are hollowed out and incorporated into speed. We become servants of this new velocity and it is unclear, and unimportant, whether we wear the G-suit or whether it wears us.[8]

Third Encounter: The Acheulean Axe

While the first two stories describe a fundamental opposition between techno-logical speed and the human body, there is another account which sees speed not as a dividing line between the inside and outside of the body but rather as a point of connection between the two. We can see this by turning to a somewhat unexpected source, the acheulean axe. The acheulean axe is the old-est human tool ever found. Archaeological investigation shows evidence of its existence as far back as 1.5 million years ago, from the time of early hominids such as *Homo Erectus* all the way up to modern *Homo Sapiens*. In this way, the human and the axe are coeval in their emergence. Though of course any con-ception of the way in which these axes were used is highly speculative, there is the theory that they were used as both a hand tool and a thrown weapon. It is the latter use that is of most interest to us. Adrian Mackenzie, in his account of the acheulean axe, lays out the immense complexities involved in the seemingly simple act of throwing.

> A throw depends on timing. For the hand-axe, the window of control ranges between one and several tens of milliseconds depending on the length of its trajectory. That is, assuming that the hand-axe is thrown, it must be released at the right moment +/- 10 ms (milliseconds) from the hand during the throw if the device is to hit a small target five metres away. The problem here is that the neurones twitch. They can't modulate movement with any great accuracy. The timing jitter for spine-motor neurones is approximately 11 ms. On average they vary that much in their activation time. Neural feedback from arm to spinal cord and back at its fastest still requires approximately 110 ms. A problem of control develops because the window of control is less than the average variation in activation time, let alone the time of neural feedback.
>
> *(2002: 61)*

The result of this particular conjugation of physical and physiological facts is that '[t]echnical performance, if it is to have efficacy, must be much faster than certain raw facts of our own physiology seem to permit' (62).

The fundamental problem, says Mackenzie, is the existence of a race condition, which is to say the problem of syncing up several separate but parallel lines of activity and having them all reach their destination at the same time; in this case the firing of impulses in the nervous system, the release of the axe at a precise point in a throwing arc, and the trajectory and location of the target one wishes to hit. Given the varying speeds of those respective lines, all of them occurring in the right order and at the right time is a complex technical problem.

> The figures given then suggested that *if* the hand-axe . . . moved at speed, that is, if they were thrown or used to strike a blow, then a 'race condition' ensued. Assuming more or less stable timing constraints of human neurophysiology between now and then, a technical gesture involving the hand-axe could perhaps eventuate but not stabilize or be repeated. That is, its performance would not be repeatable, predictable, habituated or embodied. Because of the variation in firing times of neurones (11 ms) and the time of the feedback loop between peripheral muscles and the spinal cord (110 ms), the problem of controlling the trajectory of the throw or blow is . . . acute and difficult.
>
> *(81–82)*

What we have here then is a situation in which multiple tempos, both inside and outside the body, are what we might term 'out of phase' with one another.

This is a technical term in which the intervals of different waves fail to sync up. This inability to connect the 'raw facts of our own physiology' with the technical needs of the outside world leave us incapable of reliably producing important 'technical gestures' which could ensure our survival.

And yet, axes are thrown, with varying levels of accuracy and reliability. The gap between inside and outside is bridged through the simple act of practice. By practicing, one harmonizes internal processes with external ones, not so much speeding up internal response times, as training and distributing the process to sync it up harmoniously with external paces.

> The race condition involved in throwing or hitting is overcome because action is mapped out in a network of cortical zones associated with hand movements. Action is repeated both synchronically and diachronically: first, there are multiple circuits of control in parallel which together average out the activation times, thereby improving accuracy; second, the control paths are trained and adjusted by earlier repetitions; third, and most important, the sequence of neuronal firing is 'buffered' or stored up in advance and then released in one go. We do not guide a technical gesture in 'real time' so to speak, but only through an accumulation of previous gestures, and through their repeated performance all at once. . . . A gesture is the outcome of a living collective organizing itself around the mobility of a tool.
>
> *(82)*

Practice thus serves the function of a 'phase modulator', a process which syncs up disparate tempos, bringing them productively into phase.

Here the disjuncture between internal and external velocities isn't resolved just through the application or appearance of a technological prosthesis (the axe). Such an account would leave itself open to the charge of the creeping prostheticization of the body by technology. Rather here we see not an emptying out of the inside but instead the creation of a new relationship between outside and inside. Velocities which cannot be achieved by the human body in the thick of things, can be '"buffered" or stored up in advance and then released in one go'. Rather than the inside of the body being emptied out, the outside is invited in. As the body brings speed into itself it changes its internal rhythms, learns to make new ones, and learns new ways of using the old ones.

What is most important about this story is that it challenges the image of speed and technology represented by the extreme Rousseauian perspective in the last story. There, technology use by humans – the speeding up of human body – marked the decline of the human, the moment of its fall from completeness, self-sufficiency, and naturalness. Here, even in this early moment of axe-use, we are afforded a vision wherein speed and technology are coeval with the emergence of the human. Indeed, axe-use might very well have *contributed* to that emergence. Many paleo-anthropologists conjecture that the corticalization (expansion of the neocortex in the brain) which marks the emergence of what we think of as *Homo Sapien* was itself spurred by this expanded tool use. What this means is that the first human moment might indeed have been a moment of opening up the body to speed and interiorizing external velocities and structures. Technology and speed not as prostheticization/parasitization but as the syncing up of different rhythms, developing productive resonances between disparate tempos. In this context, the body itself becomes a phase modulator, a collection of modulations between different velocities. As Mackenzie says, '[i]f a stone speeds up, if its flight time is reduced, what a body can do has changed; its limits have altered' (85). While the axe might not always be ready to hand, the 'circuits of control' and 'sequence of neuronal firing' are.

From this perspective, rather than an opposition between a slow 'natural' internal velocity and a fast 'technological' external velocity – between a jet lagged body and an accelerating world – we would see speed, and the modulation of speeds, as being at the very heart of the body. The moment of 'humanization' was also the movement of 'velocitization' – of making stone axes (and neurons), accelerate. As Bernard Stiegler puts it,

> Mobility, rather than intelligence, is the "significant feature," [of the human] . . . What is specific to the human is the movement of putting itself outside the range of its own hand, locking in an animal process of "liberation": "The brain was not the cause of development of locomotor adaptation but their beneficiary."
>
> *(146)*

Thus, the Rousseauian ideal of the self-sufficient human body, with its own natural rules and rhythms, diminished, enslaved, and eventually nullified by technology, misses the central role that technology played in determining the body. And Gibson's image of a slow-moving soul in a fast-moving world also misses the way in which velocity can be a generative force for the human. The human body is hurled out into the world, develops new rhythms, new harmonies, runs new race conditions. Inside and outside learn to harmonize and modulate one another. Indeed, if pushed to its limit, (as we might later on), this story even begins to break down the duality of inside and outside, as target, rock, arm and neuron are brought into a singular assemblage, which cuts across boundary lines. The human was born in speed: speed outside and speed inside.

Taken in its simplest articulation – that there is an inherent interpenetration of the human and technological – we see this perspective emerge in several contemporary theoretical approaches, from Deleuze and Guattari's assemblage theory (1987), to Bernard Stiegler's technogenesis (1998), to Donna Haraway's Cyborg (1997).

The story of a mutually constitutive relation between the human and the technological reaches an extreme in the work of Ray Kurzweil and other technological teleologists. Here, this first moment of the modification and acceleration of the human body from within is conceived as the starting point of the long teleological arc of bodily enhancement. Kurzweil's techno-utopian analysis depicts a future in which a coming technological 'Singularity', will allow humans to 'transcend biology' (2005). For Kurzweil, this process of accelerating the human body to more effectively interact with the surrounding world is a natural, and inevitable, process. As he puts it (mimicking Mackenzie's account of the neurology of throwing an axe)

> [a]lthough impressive in many respects, the brain suffers from severe limitations . . . our thinking is extremely slow: the basic neural transactions are several million times slower than contemporary electronic circuits. That makes our physiological bandwidth for processing new information extremely limited compared to the exponential growth of the overall human knowledge base.
>
> *(8–9)*

According to Kurzweil, it is only a matter of time until this physiological lag is solved not through the medium of practice, but instead via the direct introduction of the technological into the biological. In the future:

> Billions of nanobots in the capillaries of the brain will . . . vastly extend human intelligence. Once non-biological intelligence gets a foothold in the human brain (this has already started with computerized neural implants), the machine intelligence in our brains will grow exponentially (as it has been doing all along), at least doubling in power each year.
>
> *(28)*

Thus, while Kurzweil too sees an increasing reliance on technology by the human body, he rejects Rousseau's pessimism in favour of a vision of this as an inherently empowering process: 'The Singularity will allow us to transcend [the] limitations of our biological bodies and brains. We will gain power over our fates' (9). For him, the increasing introduction of accelerative technology into the body is simply the continuation of the profoundly natural and human process which started hundreds of thousands of years ago with the throwing of an axe (9).[9]

Acceleration

We have here three different accounts of the relationship between the body and speed. The first conceived of the body as opposed to speed, the second conceived of speed as a prosthesis added to the body, and the third conceived of speed as something internal to the body. What is important as we proceed onwards is not to think of these stories as mutually exclusive, or as occurring linearly, each story supplanted by the one which comes after. Rather, each story describes a particular kind of encounter between speed and the body and is 'true' in its own way. Each story describes a different facet of what life is like in our accelerating world. Our experience of the accelerating pace of contemporary life is, at different times, destructive, enervating, and empowering. How are we to make sense of these diverse and seemingly contradictory experiences?

What is needed is a mode of analysis that is able to incorporate all three stories, that is able to think through these different types of encounters and, hopefully, providing us with a direction for how to seek out and develop productive interactions between speed and the body. It is here that the work of Spinoza is helpful.

Speed and the body are at the heart of Spinoza's philosophy. For Spinoza, bodies are defined not by substance but by particular patterns of motion-and-rest, of quickness and slowness. Moreover, he conceives of the ways in which different patterns of motion-and-rest can interact as different bodies come into contact with one another. He conceives of joyous encounters which can increase the power of the body, and sad encounters which diminish them. He conceives of ways in which patterns of motion-and-rest can be harmonized and ways that they can be opposed. Such a philosophy allows us to conceive of multiple types of bodily encounters with speed. Developing such a mode of analysis is crucial because, as we shall see in the next chapter, the encounter between speed and the body is one of the major factors which, in an accelerating world, gives rise to reactionary political orientations and movements. If we are to challenge these orientations, and learn how to live in an accelerating world with our ethical and political commitments intact, we must learn how to deal with the status of the body at speed. Spinoza's theory of the body (and the mind) is the starting point for such a challenge.

Part II: Speed, the Body, and Spinoza

Motion-and-Rest

We begin with Spinoza's idea that all bodies can be distinguished by relations of motion-and-rest: 'All bodies are either in motion or at rest . . . (P1A1) . . . Bodies are distinguished from one another in respect of motion and rest, quickness and slowness, and not in respect of substance' (*Ethics* II, P1L1).[10] This follows from Spinoza's argument in Book One that 'in Nature there exists only one substance, absolutely infinite' (P10S), of which all things take part to a greater or lesser extent. Differences between bodies result not from differences of substance but from differences in the vectors, velocities, and positions which organize that singular substance modally expressed as matter.

This horizontal ontology plays a crucial role in developing a more productive analysis of the relationship between speed and the body. Spinoza's monism disrupts many of the binary oppositions central to Western philosophical thought (thought and matter, natural and artificial, human and inhuman, etc.). Instead of these substantial differences, he introduces a continuum of difference based on patterns of motion-and-rest. It is true that Spinoza will speak of the 'essence' of a body, but this essence does not play the role of defining a form or substance. Rather, essence is always a singular thing, describing the particular relations of motion-and-rest which inhere to a particular body (III, P7Pr). As Hasana Sharp puts it, for Spinoza, '[s]trictly speaking, there is no human essence, there are only singular essences of similar beings that are called "human"' (2011: 86).[11] This is important for our understanding of the relationship between speed and the body. Contrary to the first two images of speed we presented, Spinoza's philosophy does not posit an essential distinction between stable, self-sufficient human bodies and the uncertain spaces of flow and flux that oppose these bodies or sap their energy. Instead, all bodies are marked by a certain motion (and a certain rest), a certain quickness (and a certain slowness). This is not to say certain relations of motion-and-rest cannot be opposed to one another, and won't destroy or sap the energy of one another. But we are left with a more complex and open image of the body.

Using this lens of 'motion-and-rest', Spinoza develops a complex analytical toolkit for understanding the composition of bodies and describing their relationships to one another.

> All the ways in which a body is affected by another body follow from the nature of the affected body together with the nature of the body affecting it, so that one and the same body may move in various ways in accordance with the various natures of the bodies causing its motion; and, on the other hand, different bodies may be caused to move in different ways by one and the same body.
>
> *(II, P13, L3, A1)*

Thus, in addition to explaining how we can differentiate between bodies, Spinoza's theory also shows how those bodies can interact. Here, again, the outcome of encounters between bodies is determined not by substance, but by how their different patterns of motion-and-rest relate. These relations can, for example, link up to form what Spinoza terms a 'composite' body.

> When a number of bodies of the same or different magnitude. . . are moving at the same or different rates of speed so as to preserve an unvarying relation of movement among themselves, these bodies are said to be united with one another and all together to form one body or individual

thing, which is distinguished from other things through this union of bodies.

(II, P13, L3, A2D)

For Spinoza, composite bodies are characterized by a distinctive movement-style, which is the particular choreography of the simple bodies it contains.

To fully understand this conception of composite bodies, two points are crucial. First this introduction of the idea of 'unvarying relations of movement' does not mean that composite bodies do not change (or worse, that they constitute some kind of internal 'essence'). Indeed, Spinoza immediately moves on to noting ways in which these composite bodies can change without losing their character as 'composite bodies'.

If the parts of an individual thing become greater or smaller, but so proportionately that they all preserve the same mutual relation of motion-and-rest as before, the individual thing will likewise retain its own nature as before without any change in its form.

(II P13L5)

If certain bodies composing an individual thing are made to change the existing direction of their motion, but in such a way that they can continue their motion and keep the same mutual relation as before, the individual thing will likewise preserve its own nature without any change of form.

(II P13L6)

Furthermore the individual thing so composed retains its own nature, whether as a whole it is moving or at rest, and in whatever motion it moves, provided that each constituent part retains its own motion and continues to communicate this motion to the other parts.

(II P13L7)

Says Spinoza 'We thus see how a composite individual can be affected in many ways and yet preserve its nature' (II P13L7S). This is crucial because it gives us a way to begin thinking of relations of speed without automatically thinking about oppositions between essential velocities. There can be interactions which speed up or slow down a body, which speed up or slow down its parts, which change the direction of its motion, without thereby decomposing that body.

Second, the distinction between composite bodies and simple bodies is not as straightforward as it may appear. This is because all composite bodies are themselves the simple bodies from which larger, other, composites are formed.[12] As Spinoza says, '[i]f several individual things concur in one act in such a way as to be all together the simultaneous cause of one effect, I consider them all, in that respect, as one individual' (II, D7). In this respect, for Spinoza, 'individual' bodies are always multiple. This is true for the human body itself which – thought it might be treated as an individual – is always already a layered and multiple thing. As Moira Gatens puts it:

> The human body is understood by Spinoza to be a relatively complex individual, made up of a number of other bodies. Its identity can never be viewed as a final or finished product . . . since it is a body that is in constant interchange with its environment. The human body is radically open to its surroundings and can be composed, recomposed and decomposed by other bodies. Its openness is a condition of both its life, that is, its continuance in nature as the same individual.
>
> *(1996: 110)*

All of this follows naturally from Spinoza's monism. Since all being is one, there are no ultimate ontological differences between bodies, and the universe can be conceived as a nested set of composite bodies (atoms make molecules, molecules make cells, etc.). There is thus an infinite chain stretching from the most infinitesimally singular body up to the most fully composite body, that totality of being which Spinoza terms *deus sive natura*, God or Nature (II, P13S).

> Now hitherto we have conceived an individual thing composed solely of bodies distinguished from one another only be motion-and-rest and speed of movement; that is, an individual thing composed of the simplest bodies. If we now conceive another individual thing composed of several individual things of different natures, we shall find that this can be affected in many other ways while still preserving its nature. For since each one of its parts is composed of several bodies, each single part can therefore . . . without any change in its nature, move with varying degrees of speed and consequently communicate its own motion to other parts with varying degrees of speed. Now if we go on to conceive a third kind of individual thing that composed of this second kind, we shall find that it can be affected in many other ways without any change in its form. If we thus continue to infinity, we shall readily conceive the whole of Nature as one individual whose parts – that is all the constituent bodies – vary in infinite ways without any change in the individual as a whole.
>
> *(II P13L7S)*

However, this unity of being is only present when we perceive the world *sub quadam specie aeternitatis* (II, P44C2), which is to say from the perspective of *deus sive natura*. When viewed from the perspective of individual bodies (a view which, being such bodies ourselves, we are almost always restricted to, barring the tactical, difficult, and always temporary application of philosophy), we see a world replete with opposition, conflict, and destruction. For in addition to bodies entering into relationships to form composite bodies, there are also interactions between bodies that lead to the decomposition of one of the bodies, which is to say the destruction or diminution of its relations of motion-and-rest. Indeed, this is actually presumed in the idea of composite bodies, since for composite bodies to exist, simple bodies must be absorbed into a larger aggregate, or previously existing composite bodies must be 'stripped for parts', as it were. (Note this is not the only way that composite bodies are formed. For example, the creation of the composite body that is 'society' requires the incorporation, but not the destruction, of various smaller composite bodies. Indeed, the creation of this larger composite body ideally empowers these smaller composite bodies.) Interactions between bodies, then, are frequently struggles between different relations of motion-and-rest to see which is able to gain the upper hand. As Deleuze puts it in his reading of Spinoza:

> The bodies that meet are either mutually indifferent, or one, through its relations, decomposes the relation in the other, and so destroys the other body. This is the case with a toxin or poison, which destroys a man by decomposing his blood. And this is the case with nutrition, but in a converse sense: a man forces the parts of the body by which he nourishes himself to enter into a new relation that conforms with his own, but which involves the destruction of the relation in which that body existed previously.
>
> *(Deleuze 1990: 211)*

The factor which drives these encounters is what Spinoza terms *Conatus*. *Conatus* means 'drive or impulse' in Latin (the full phase is *conatus essendi* 'the drive to exist'). For Spinoza, *conatus* is, more than anything else, the essence of the thing.

> Each thing, in so far as it is in itself, endeavors to persist in its own being.
>
> *(III, P6)*

> The conatus with which each thing endeavors to persist in its own being is nothing but the actual essence of the thing.
>
> *(III, P7)*

> Therefore, the power of any thing, or the conatus with which it acts or endeavors to act, alone or in conjunction with other things, that is . . . the power or conatus by which it endeavors to persist in its own being, is nothing but the given . . . essence of the thing.
>
> *(III P7Pr)*

Thus in any contest between two bodies, each will struggle to persist in its own way of being, and the 'winner' of any encounter can be determined by whose ability to persist – whose *conatus* – increases as a result of the encounter. The poison seeks to decompose the patterns of relation in the blood and the body seeks to decompose the patterns of relation in the food.

Bodies and Speed

This vision of different bodies attempting to maintain their particular patterns of motion-and-rest and subordinate those of others can help to explain all three of the encounters with which I began. In the case of jet lag we see how an encounter between the human body and a particular set of relations of motion-and-rest in the world (airplanes, time zones, light cues) overpowers the internal relations of the bodies of the composite called the human body, and – like a toxin – diminished that composite's power of action. In the case of the G-suit, we see an encounter which increases the body's power of action (it can now travel faster than the speed of sound), but does so in a way that potentially endangers that particular body's power of action (i.e. the human body becomes a component of a larger technological assemblage, and finds its capacity to enact its *conatus* to be heavily restricted or even disabled). And finally, in the case of the acheulean axe, we see an encounter that not only increases the body's power of action, but introduces changes that increase its power of action more broadly (reflex training, corticalization).

It is this last point that's the most challenging, for it introduces what appears to be a bit of a split in Spinoza's thinking. On the one hand he describes things as gripped by the desire to maintain their relations of motion-and-rest. And yet, any encounter with another will produce some change in ourselves. This tension is somewhat lessened by the fact, discussed earlier, that one's parts may change in any number of ways without signalling the destruction of the body, so long as its relations of motion-and-rest remain the same. Thus, in the case of food, individual organs are changed (nourished, rejuvenated, healed), but their overall relation remains the same.

The problem is somewhat greater, with the problem of corticalization. It would be something of a stretch to argue that a human before and after corticalization had 'retained the same pattern of motion-and-rest' (indeed, we'd probably say that it is only with corticalization that the human emerges). And yet from Spinoza's perspective, would it have been a proper expression of *conatus* for *homo erectus* to avoid this corticalization as a way of maintaining its essence? By this account, all evolution, all change of whatever type, biological or technological, would be against nature, since all change would go against our essential drive to 'persist in [our own] being' (an image which hews rather closely to the Rousseauian narrative).

This is the result of a fundamental misunderstanding of *conatus*. For though *conatus* is the drive by which '[e]ach thing, in so far as it is in itself, endeavors to persist in its own being' (III P6), it does not endeavour to persist solely as it is at any given moment (such a reading would be to presume an essentialist account that Spinoza explicitly rejects). Indeed, a being that only ever sought to exist as it was in a present moment would not last very long. The baby antelope that doesn't grow up to be an adult won't last long against predators. As Sharp puts it, 'Composite bodies must undergo constant change in order to remain themselves, and the more complex they are, the more changes they must undergo' (39). *Conatus* is thus not just the drive to persist, but the drive to persist as long as possible *and as much as possible*. Spinoza describes this conception of *conatus* as a body's drive to increase the number of ways in which it can affect, and be affected, by other bodies, which is to say to increase its power of action.

> That which so disposes the human body that it can be affected in more ways, or which renders it capable of affecting external bodies in more ways, is advantageous to man, and proportionately more advantageous as the body is thereby rendered more capable of being affected in more ways and of affecting other bodies in more ways. On the other hand, that which renders the body less capable in these respects is harmful.
>
> *(IV P38)*

Jane Bennett provides an excellent account of the creative characteristic of *conatus*:

> For Spinoza, both simple bodies (which are perhaps better termed *proto-bodies*) and the complex or mosaicized modes they form are conative. In the case of the former, conatus is expressed as a stubbornness or inertial tendency to persist; in the case of a complex body or mode conatus refers to the effort required to maintain the specific relation of 'movement and rest' that obtains between its parts, a relation that defines the mode as what it is. This maintenance is not a process of mere repetition of the same, for it entails continual invention: because each mode suffers the actions on it by other modes, actions that disrupt the relation of movement and rest characterizing each mode, every mode, if it is to persist, must seek new encounters to creatively compensate for the alterations or affections it suffers.
>
> *(2010: 22)*[13]

Thus, for example, prior to the acquisition of a G-suit, the body was severely limited in its ability to affect external bodies in ways which required high-g acceleration. In such contexts, the body literally could not 'persist in its being' and would pass out. The G-suit thus increases our *conatus* by introducing a wider array of encounters our body can have while still 'persisting in its being'. In doing so, however, it changes the nature of what that being is (the human body transforms from a thing which can't sustain high-g acceleration to a thing which can).

This acquisition of new powers to affect and be affected necessarily introduces changes in the relations of motion-and-rest within a composite body.
Indeed, Spinoza is willing to acknowledge that the changes a human body
undergoes while growing from a child into an adult are so great as to probably make it safe to say that it is a different thing in the end (IV, P38S). This
doesn't mean that it is against *conatus* for us to grow. For Spinoza, who rejects
substance and 'essential' differences, what's important isn't what a thing *is* but
what a thing can *do*. One could say that the 'nature' of the body is to self-alter
through encounters and to increase its ability to be affected. This is a direct
result of rejecting substance, and embracing speed and motion as the primary
ontological determinant. As Deleuze puts it:

> the kinetic proposition tells us that a body is defined by relations of
> motion and rest, of slowness and speed between particles. That is, it is
> not defined by a form or by functions. Global form, specific form, and
> organic functions depend on relations of speed and slowness. . . . The
> important thing is to understand life, each living individuality, not as
> a form, or as a development of form, but as a complex relation between
> differential velocities, between deceleration and acceleration of particles.
>
> *(1988: 123)*

This issue is further complicated by our early discussion of the fact that human
bodies (and, practically speaking, all bodies) are necessarily composite. This
means that not only are bodies inherently multiple, so too is *conatus*. It is not
enough to speak of the *conatus* of the body. We must also acknowledge a *conatus*
of the organ within the body, and the cell within the organ, and the mitochon-
dria within the cell. For the body – for any body – to survive, its *conatus* must
cooperate with the *conati* of multiple other bodies at multiple different scales,
and, most importantly, at multiple velocities. As Macherey describes it:

> The individual, or the subject, thus does not exist by himself in the irre-
> ducible simplicity of a unique and eternal being, but it is composed in
> the encounter of singular beings, who agree conjuncturally within him
> in terms of their existence, that is, who coexist there but without this
> agreement presupposing a privileged relationship, the unity of an internal
> order at the level of their essences, which subsists identically, as they were
> themselves before being thus assembled and without in so being in any
> way affected.
>
> *(2011: 176)*[14]

Here we see echoes of Mackenzie's discussion of the Acheulean axe, as the
human composes multiple different velocities, at many levels, incorporating the
conati of different bodies, to increase 'a' body's *conatus*.

The implications of this for our discussion of speed and the body is the suggestion that we might wish to let go of essentialist definitions of bodies and look instead to functional definitions. In the face of contemporary anxiety over the fate of 'the human', or fear of the dehumanizing effects of technology or 'unnatural' velocities, Spinoza leads us to consider not what a human body *is* but what it can *do*. Deleuze describes this as the shift to an 'ethological' perspective, a mode of analysis from zoology, which starts its investigation not on substance and essence, but on behaviour and practice.

> Such studies as this, which define bodies, animals, or humans by the affects they are capable of, founded what is today called *ethology*. The approach is no less valid for us, for human beings, than for animals because no one knows ahead of time the affects one is capable of; it is a long affair of experimentation, requiring a lasting prudence, a Spinozian wisdom that implies the construction of a plane of immanence or consistency. Spinoza's ethics has nothing to do with morality; he conceives it as an ethology, that is, as a composition of fast and slow speeds, of capacities for affecting and being affected on this plane of immanence.
>
> *(1988: 125)*

Such an approach would reject the extreme versions of the first two images of speed, which would seek to articulate an essentialist, transhistorical vision of human nature, as 'no one knows ahead of time the affects one is capable of'. Instead, it would push us to accept a more open, pluralistic vision of human life, refusing to allow our fears or frustrations with an accelerating world to calcify into a violent or reactionary politics (a topic which we will explore in the next chapter).

However, we must also note what Deleuze says here about prudence. To shift to this ethological approach, with its concern for increasing powers of action, doesn't mean an unthinking, uncritical acceptance of all technological acceleration, or all forms of change. Quite the opposite. A mode of analysis which asks, in the largest way possible, what a particular formation 'lets us do' – how it allows us to 'affect and be affected' – can just as easily lead to decisions to reject particular technologies, accelerations, or forms of change. On the one hand, the G-suit might allow the human body to travel at the speed of sound. But it might also require us to become an element in a military-industrialist complex, in which increasingly decisions are made on the basis of technical simulations which don't take human bodies into consideration. In this context, we might wish to reject many of the fruits of modern military technology. The acquisition of a car certainly increases our ability to affect and be affected, by radically increasing the velocities at which we can travel. But if the emissions it produces contribute to global warming, then it might very well decrease our ability to affect and be affected. Michael Mack argues that we must understand

Spinoza's conception of *conatus* 'in terms of sustainability on both an individual and a social scale'. By doing so 'Spinoza makes clear how humanity's will and power . . . self-destroys itself at the point where it loses track of human limitations' (2011: 102–3, 110). For one's *conatus* to be increased, the ability to affect and be affected must be sustainable.[15] I can become a faster runner by taking steroids, but if it ravages my health in other ways, in what way can I say I am actually able to exist at these higher speeds?

Such a perspective would take seriously the fears of the first two stories, recognizing that there can be bad encounters between speed and the body, encouraging us to evaluate whether or not a given technology or pattern of velocity is 'good' for 'us'.[16] At the same time, it would embrace the third story's open vision of humanity, rejecting those aspects of the Gibsonian or Rousseauian narrative which assumes they know what the human is in its essence. Spinoza rejects such an essence, or is, anyway, less interested in such an essence than in the possibilities of new formations. This is why scholars return time and again to Spinoza's injunction that 'nobody as yet has learned from experience what the body can and cannot do' (III P2S). Because it opens up a space of experimentation, of openness which is willing to explore the question of what the human body can do. This means that we might one day wake up and, like the child that has grown into the adult, realize that we are no longer something that we would describe as human. But then humans have surpassed any number of different limitations which people thought defined what it means to be human. Maybe we stopped being human a long time ago. Maybe we will be humans long after our bodies are unrecognizable. I am less interested in the essence of the human than in what we can do, how we can live, and, as we will see, what we can do for each other.[17]

Part II: Speed, the Mind, and Spinoza

Thoughts and Affect

Spinoza's analysis of the attribute of extension is not the only part of his philosophy that contains resources for investigating life in an accelerating world. Spinoza's account of the attribute of thought – and specifically his theory of affect and emotions – also helps to understand the relationship between speed and the body. It does so in two ways: 1) by helping us to tease out the affective dimensions of the three encounters discussed earlier, and the multiple speeds of the body; and 2) by helping us to understand the affective roots of the reactionary political responses to speed which we began to discuss in the previous chapter, and to which we will return in the next.

As with Spinoza's account of the attribute of extension, the starting point of his analysis of the attribute of mind is his monism. Spinoza's shift to a monistic ontology does more than limit possibilities of humanism.[18] The oneness of substance also serves to challenge one of the most pervasive assumptions of modern philosophy: mind-body dualism. Starting with Descartes, and travelling through a long lineage of western philosophy, mind-body dualism maintains that thought and matter are two different substances, creating the image of an idealized thought abstracted from, and unencumbered by, the mechanistic determinations of matter and the passions and emotions of the body. Spinoza's philosophy instead 'refuses every dualism between mind and body, where mind and body are imagined to play by different rules' (Sharp 2011: 2). Thus, Spinoza couples his ontological monism with a parallelism, in which thought and matter are simply two different modalities of what is one substance. As such for every change in thought, there is a concomitant change in the body, and vice versa (EII, P7).[19]

There are many implications of Spinoza's parallelism – binding, as it does, thought to matter – not least of which is the negation of any freedom of thought or will. As Hampshire puts it:

> The human mind cannot be, within Spinoza's metaphysics, a free agent, or an agent of any kind, in affirming or denying; for an individual mind simply consists of ideas of the modification of that finite order which is my body; and these ideas occur in an order which is determined within the order of Nature as a whole.
>
> *(87–88)*

This should not, according to Spinoza, surprise us since, as much as we might like to think of our minds as free and undetermined 'experience teaches us with abundant examples that nothing is less within men's power than to hold their tongues or control their appetites' (III P2S). We might, as many dualistic philosophers do, want to take these experiences as cases where 'somehow' the mind is overpowered by the body and rational thought is blocked by the unruly passions of matter ('somehow' because, Descartes' pineal gland aside, the way in which mind controls matter in the first place is usually pretty ambiguous[20]). Spinoza, however, rejects this idea, pointing out that assuming it is only in special cases where emotion over-rules thought – where the body becomes master of the mind – is to assume that we know thoroughly what is at the root of our conscious decisions. And yet we are perfectly aware of any number of times when it felt like we were making clear-headed, rational decisions, only to see later the ways in which they were really driven by unconscious impulses and unnoticed affects. As Spinoza says, 'we are in many respects at the mercy of external causes and are tossed about like the waves of the sea when driven by contrary winds, unsure of the outcome and of our fate' (III P59S). As much as we might wish to possess a perfectly rational and perfectly free mind,

> experience tell us no less clearly than reason that it is on this account only that men believe themselves to be free, that they are conscious of

the actions and ignorant of the causes by which they are determined; and it tells us too that mental decisions are nothing more than the appetites themselves, varying therefore according to the varying disposition of the body. For each man's actions are shaped by his emotion.

(III P2S)

Thus, if we acknowledge that thought is always matched and driven by emotion, that mind always walks hand in hand with the body, we are left with little reason other than humanism and vanity to posit mind and matter as different substances.

Now surely all these consideration go to show clearly that mental decision on the one hand, and the appetite and physical state of the body on the other hand, are simultaneous in nature; or rather, they are one and the same thing which, when considered under the attribute of Thought and explicated through Thought, we call decision, and when considered under the attribute of Extension and deduced from the laws of motion-and-rest, we call a physical state.

(III P2S)

Yet, despite his rejection of an autonomous, undetermined mind, we should not therefore take this solely as an argument for mechanism or, worse, as a depressing account of humans as nothing other than irrational creatures, ruled constantly by their passions. (There is little that Spinoza dislikes more than the cruel cynicism of satirists trying to outdo one another in their low-opinions of humanity [III, Preface].) Rather the goal of Spinoza's parallelism is to attune us to the ways in which conscious thought is driven – for better and for worse – by unconscious drives, layered corporeal memories, and affective patterns. Deleuze sums up the importance of Spinoza's parallelism quite nicely, saying that, as a doctrine:

it does not consist merely in denying any real causality between the mind and the body, it disallows any primacy of the one over the other. If Spinoza rejects any superiority of the mind over the body, this is not in order to establish a superiority of the body over the mind, which would be no more intelligible than the converse. The practical significance of parallelism is manifested in the reversal of the traditional principle on which Morality was founded as an enterprise of domination of the passions by consciousness. . . . According to the *Ethics* . . . what is an action in the mind is necessarily an action in the body as well, and what is a passion in the body is necessarily a passion in the mind. There is no primacy of one series over the other. What does Spinoza mean when he invites us to take the body as a model? It is a matter of showing that the body surpasses the knowledge we have of it, *and that thought likewise surpasses the consciousness we have of it.*

(1988: 18)

Spinoza realizes that there is no escaping the effects of the body, its passions, dispositions, and affects. There is no thought which is unconnected to the body and thus there is much in our thought and behaviour that derives its content from well beneath the surface of conscious awareness. 'Hence it follows that man is necessarily always subject to passive emotions, and that he follows the common order of Nature, and obeys it, and accommodates himself to it as far as the nature of things demands' (IV P4C).

Note that when we talk about thought being shaped by affect and emotion we are discussing substantially more than simply those experiences where we find ourselves caught up in the 'passion' of the moment. Rather this also refers to the way in which we can find our actions and behaviour subtly guided by emotional states and affective patterns. More importantly, this influence is not solely negative, inhibiting, or disruptive of the proper functioning of reason. Rather, emotions can also play a central role in the *proper* functioning of rationality. This is present in the work of Spinoza, for whom the joyful passions accompany and drive any increase in our understanding in the world (and in turn our understanding allows us to better, and more sustainably, produce joyful passions, in a productive feedback loop).

However, it is also a theme developed in contemporary neuroscience. Antonio Damasio, for example, is a neuroscientist who explicitly looks to the works of Spinoza as a guide to understanding the role that emotions play in cognition. Contrary to many dominant strains of thought in neuroscience, which start, either implicitly or explicitly, from the Cartesian assumption that emotions fundamentally inhibit rationality, for Damasio, emotions play a crucial role in cognition and rationality.[21] According to Damasio emotions constitute corporeal reactions to specific contexts. Thus, for example, when faced with a threatening object our body automatically produces a set of instinctive physical responses designed to ensure survival (secretion of adrenaline, shutting down various internal processes to save energy, etc). The same thing happens with a different set of bodily procedures when we are confronted with an object that we desire. Emotions then are layers of evolutionary produced procedures intended to quickly produce behaviour which encourages survival. Emotions then have, at their root, the highly 'rational' goal of survival.

> In general, drives and instincts operate either by generating a particular behavior directly or by inducing physiological states that lead individuals to behave in a particular way, mindlessly or not. Virtually all the behavior ensuing from drives and instinct contribute to survival either directly, by performing a life-saving action, or indirectly, by propitiating conditions

advantageous to survival or reducing the influences of potential harmful conditions.

(Damasio 1994: 115)

What you may have noticed is that these sets of corporeal responses which constitute 'emotions' happen almost entirely at a pre- or non-conscious level. When consciousness enters the picture, we find ourselves in the realm of what Damasio designates as 'feelings'.

> If an emotion is a collection of change in the body state connected to particular mental images that have activated a specific brain system, *the essence of feeling an emotion is the experience of such changes in juxtaposition to the mental images that initiated the cycle*. In other words, a feeling depends on the juxtaposition of an image of the body proper to an image of something else, such as the visual image of a face or the auditory image of a melody.
>
> *(145)*[22]

The crucial implication of this is that, contrary to our experience of how emotions and feelings work – namely that we have a conscious experience of some object, and then have an emotional reaction to it – what this model suggests is that feelings are the result of us first having an emotion, and then becoming consciously aware of it. Or, to paraphrase William James, we do not run from the bear because we are afraid. We are afraid because we run from the bear.

Emotions and affects then are not solely the 'irrational' passions. Quite the opposite really. They are evolutionarily developed patterns of behaviour intended to maximize our chances for survival and flourishing (it is, at this point, not a particularly large jump to reintroduce the concept of *conatus*). And they are not just activated in moments of life or death crisis. Rather, these instinctual emotional reactions are always taking place below the threshold of consciousness, evaluating encounters, and shaping conscious thought. Indeed, in most cases of decision making in real-world situations, the choice of options which conscious, 'rational' thought draws from, have already been winnowed down by preconscious 'emotional' processes.

> the emotional signal can operate entirely under the radar of consciousness. It can produce alterations in working memory, attention, and reasoning so that the decision-making process is biased toward selecting the action most likely to lead to the best possible outcome, given prior experience. The individual may not ever be cognizant of this covert operation. In these conditions we intuit a decision and enact it, speedily and efficiently, without any knowledge of the intermediate steps.
>
> *(Damasio 2003: 148–9)*

So great a role do preconscious emotional systems play in rational decision making that Damasio has shown a substantial decrease in the rational decision-making capabilities of people who have seen these emotional systems damaged or removed (1994: 53). Contrary to the dominant cartesian perspective on emotions and rationality, Damasio maintains that '*Reduction in emotion may constitute an equally important source of irrational behavior.* The counterintuitive connection between absent emotion and warped behaviour may tell us something about the biological machinery of reason' (53).

Speed and Affect

To return us to our dominant theme, what is important about these corporeal affective structures is the speed at which they function. By bypassing slower moving conscious thought, located in higher level cortical brain functions, emotional systems, functioning in speedier, lower order brain organs such as the amygdala and the prefrontal cortex are able to evaluate situations much quicker. 'Emotionally competent stimuli are detected very fast, ahead of selective attention' (2003: 60). In survival situations this ability to bypass slow-moving conscious thought and respond instinctually can be the difference between life and death.[23] We can think of these affect repertoires in terms of our discussion of the acheulean axe earlier. There we discussed the process of learning to throw as a kind of buffering mechanism, layering a set of behaviours into the body in such a way as to overcome the slowness of conscious thought. Affective responses provide a similar variety of general 'buffered' responses that can be activated by a variety of stimuli, allowing us to 'affect and be affected by' a wider range of events and contexts at different velocities. In a Spinozistic register, we can see this human body-brain-mind assemblage as a composite of different patterns of motion-and-rest, allowing for different paces of action in response to different situational requirements. Fast-moving, pre-conscious processes allow us to productively 'encounter' quickly emerging events in the world, while slower conscious thought allows for deeper, more leisurely analysis. Thus, contrary to our unitary conception of the self, and following along from our conception of composite bodies developed in the previous section, the self is a layered assemblage of different velocities. (One more reason to be leery of those narratives we saw in the first and second encounter, which seek to assert a 'natural' human speed, or oppose a violent technological speed to a slow-moving human thought.)

Identifying the crucial role that preconscious emotional structures and corporeal reactions play in rational cognition, is not, however, to necessarily assume that they will always be 'right' or beneficial. Neither Spinoza nor Damasio believe that all emotions are good, helpful, or productive. Nor is this to assume that there are not dangers to be being subject to fast-moving systems – corporeal or technological – which are not easily subjected to slow, deliberate reflection (as the first two encounters warned us). There are all sorts of ways in which emotional systems can inhibit our abilities to act both rationally and ethically. In the context of our discussion of speed and the body, there are at least two important ways in which emotions can be problematic for ethics and politics: stereotyping and the problem of potentially obsolete affective response patterns.

Preconscious corporeal emotional systems, because of the speeds at which they are designed to function, necessarily avoid in-depth analysis of phenomena. Such time-consuming activities are left up to the slower moving, higher level cognitive functions of consciousness. Instead, these lower-level functions primarily rely on stereotypes, rough and ready categories which lump together large numbers of phenomena under the same rubric, attached to the same evaluations and patterns of reactions. One of the factors playing a role in the development of stereotypes are somatic markers. A somatic marker is a corporeally layered memory, linking a particular stimuli or image with a particular outcome, which, when exposed to that stimuli again, prompts that same outcome.

> When the choice of option X, which leads to bad outcome Y, is followed by punishment and thus painful body states, the somatic-marker system acquires the hidden, dispositional representation of these experience-driven, noninherited, arbitrary connection. Re-exposure of the organism to option X, or thoughts about outcome Y, will now have the power to reenact the painful body state and thus serve as an automated reminder of bad consequences to come. This is of necessity an oversimplification, but it captures the basic process as I see it . . . somatic markers can operate covertly (they do not need to be perceived consciously) and they can play other helpful roles besides providing signals of 'Danger!' or 'Go For it!'
>
> *(1994: 180)*

Somatic Markers, and the stereotypes that they can encode can provide useful guidance for our behaviour, at speeds much faster than conscious thought allows. However, absent the discrimination of higher, slower brain functions, these stereotypes can be overly broad or incorporate unrelated phenomena into our evaluations. As Damasio points out:

> Under their influence and the agency of experience, the repertoire of things categorized as good or bad grows rapidly, and the ability to detect new good and bad things grows exponentially. If a given entity out in the world is a component of a scene in which one *other* component was a 'good' or 'bad' thing, that is, excited an innate disposition, the brain may classify the entity for which no value had been innately preset as it is too is valuable, whether or not it is. The brain extends special treatment to that entity simply because it is close to one that is important for sure. You

may call this reflected glory, if the new entity is close to a good thing, or guilt by association, if it is close to a bad one. The light that shines on a bona fide important item, good or bad, will shine also on its company.

(1994: 117)

The most obvious example to turn to here is to think about how this contributes to racist beliefs and behaviours. A negative encounter with a racialized other might result in a somatic marker which contributes to stereotyping all similarly racialized people negatively. More importantly, we do not even need the actual negative encounter in the first place. If we live in a culture where negative portrayals of particular groups or races are endemic, these will play a role in constructing particular affective patterns of response. Repeated exposures to portrayals of, for example, black men as criminals, or Arab people as terrorists, in TV and movies affectively mark these groups as sources of fear or danger. These beliefs and responses are then layered into body processes which move too fast for review and evaluation by the slow-moving processes of conscious thought, and therefore can influence the content of conscious thought. These fast-moving processes can then play a role in the implicit biases which sustain racist modes of interaction with racialized others.[24]

The fact that such somatic markers and stereotypes can be produced through cultural artefacts brings to the fore a crucial fact. Although thus far we have been talking in the language of neuroscience, affective responses are as much social as they are biological. Though the human body might possess certain innate capacity to encode encounters via somatic markers, the content of those encounters is provided by personal histories and social context. As Ross describes in his account of the role of somatic markers in the development of racism: 'Our brains are not hardwired to respond in fear to people who look differently than us. Rather, the brain is conditioned through experience to respond to certain stimuli with emotions considered appropriate to them' (2014: 81–2). What these experiences, and appropriate emotional responses, will be will depend very much on the dominant cultural context that we encounter (we will return to this problem in the next chapter).

In addition to the dangers of unreflective stereotypes activating emotional patterns of response that move too quickly for conscious thought, there are ways in which these patterns of response themselves might be problematic. Instincts and drives, developed over millions of years through evolution, might have been selected in response to a set of dominant encounters that might not be that prevalent in the modern world. Thus 'fight-or-flight' instincts, designed to maximize survival when confronted by a marauding bear, might be equally activated by our fear of an angry boss, but not particularly helpful. Damasio refers to the possibility of certain affective patterns becoming 'maladaptive' in new contexts, saying, 'Anger is mostly counterproductive in modern societies, and so is sadness. Phobias are major hindrance. And yet think of how many lives have been saved by fear or anger in the right circumstances' (2003: 39, 40). He goes on to note the way in which 'the value of each emotion differs so much in our current human environment' (40). What we have here is a disjuncture between tempos similar to what we saw in the phenomenon of jet lag in the first encounter. There the power of the body was inhibited by a disjuncture between the tempo of our internal clock and the tempo of an accelerating world. Here, there is a disjuncture between the pace of evolutionary, biological change, and the pace of social acceleration, leaving us with embodied emotional response processes that are potentially 'maladaptive' to our contemporary world. Still, as Damasio points out,

> '[w]e can be wise to the fact that our brain still carries the machinery to react in the way it did in a very different context ages ago. And we can learn to disregard such reactions and persuade others to do the same.
>
> *(40)*

We will return to this theme in Chapters 4 and 5.

Before we proceed it is important to take a brief moment to make clear what is being discussed here. By invoking questions of bodies, biology, evolutionary selection, and corporeal determinations of thought, it is very easy for us to lapse into biological or evolutionary determinism. While this account argues that both biology and evolution play a role in thought and behaviour, I am not saying that they are the sole, or even primary determinant. Any full explanation of thought and behaviour is going to have to take into consideration individual psychological and cultural level determinants (amongst others). Indeed, as we noted earlier, arguing that affective stereotyping can give rise to racist thought and behaviour is not the same as saying that we are biologically determined to be racist. Rather what was being argued was that humans have corporeal and affective structures which produce broad categorizations to encourage rapid survival responses to phenomena identified as dangerous. In that context, it was only as a result of a broader culture that provided imagery of particular racialized groups as dangerous (or indeed, the broad social construction of 'race' itself) that provided the content for that set of corporeal responses. More than this, such stereotyping would need to be reinforced by social, political, and economic forms of segregation which limit encounters across race and hence the formation of different somatic markers. These corporeal imbued stereotypes and assumptions then come to effect the behaviours of those who produce cultural artefacts (shaping decisions about casting films, for example, or framing stories on the news) and sustain modes of segregation (shaping decisions about hiring and housing, for example), creating a negative feedback loop which further entrenches racism in a society.

Analytically, what this means is we do not necessarily have to choose between biological and social constructivist accounts of emotions and thought.[25] Outcomes are always overdetermined by a set of interlocking assemblages – corporeal, psychological, cultural, ideological, economic, etc. But having a strong and robust understanding of the role that different subsystems play means having the best possible chance of intervening in these assemblages productively. In this case, understanding the corporeal as well as cultural and individual roots of racist thought and behaviour can play a crucial role in attempting to inculcate more anti-racist behaviour in both ourselves and others. It makes us aware that just tackling racism at the individual psychological or ideological levels will often not be enough to make substantial change.

Thus, the invocation of biology or evolution does not constitute a biological reductionism. Instead, it opens up new sites of action for conscious thought to encounter and engage with. As Deleuze puts it:

> One seeks to acquire a knowledge of the powers of the body in order to discover, *in a parallel fashion*, the powers of the mind that elude consciousness and thus to be able to *compare* the powers. In short, the model of the body, according to Spinoza, does not imply a devaluation of thought in relation to extension, but, much more important, a devaluation of consciousness in relation to thought: a discovery of the unconscious, of an *unconscious of thought* just as profound as the *unknown of the body*.
>
> *(1988: 18–19)*

Indeed, that is the fundamental benefit that Spinozistic monism provides us with in thinking about ethical and political practice. Contrary to a dualistic worldview, which runs the risk of focusing solely on improving reason, freeing it from the 'passions' that inhibit it, Spinoza acknowledges that there is a power to emotions *qua* emotions, and that they cannot simply be *thought* through. Emotions, affects, memories, somatic markers, have their own sets of rules and principles and, though they relate to conscious thought, they cannot be strictly controlled or understood through that thought. As Spinoza lays out in a series of principles:

> The force of any passive emotion can surpass the rest of man's activities or power so that the emotion stays firmly fixed in him.
>
> *(IV P5)*

> An emotion cannot be checked or destroyed except by a contrary emotion which is stronger than the emotion which is to be checked.
>
> *(IV P7)*

> No emotion can be checked by the true knowledge of good and evil in so far as it is true, but only in so far as it is considered an emotion.
>
> *(IV P14)*

What this means is that emotions have the power to affect our thoughts and actions but are not themselves always directly subject to rational thought. Emotions are primarily checked by emotions. Affects cannot be changed solely through an appeal to 'true knowledge' but rather 'only insofar as it is considered an emotion'. What this means is that any philosophy which seeks to reject the passions entirely will find itself a slave to them. Only by acknowledging the constitutive role they play in thought can we seek to live thoughtfully and ethically in the world. Indeed, Spinoza's conception of what a 'free' human looks like is not a human 'free' of their emotions but one who knows, as much as possible, the roots and causes of their behaviour. And such freedom can only come from understanding the passions and how they can be worked with – how they limit thought, yes but also how they enhance it. Thus, one of Spinoza's major projects in *The Ethics* is a deep investigation of the passions, understanding their sources, their relations to one another, how they are the result of bodily experiences, and how they are also the result of conscious thought.

> I think I have thus demonstrated why men are motivated by uncritical belief (opinio) more than by true reasoning, and why the true knowledge of good and evil stirs up conflict in the mind and often yields to every kind of passion. . . . My purpose in saying this is not to conclude that ignorance is preferable to knowledge, or that there is no difference between a fool and a wise man in the matter of controlling the emotions. I say this because it is necessary to know both the power of our nature and its lack of power, so that we can determine what reason can and cannot do in controlling the emotions.
>
> *(IV P17S)*

Once again, what is at play here is the question of the relation between different patterns of motion-and-rest, different paces, and tempos. The power, and problem, of emotions is that they function at tempos too quick to be directly intervened in by slow-moving conscious thought. There is a parallel to the problem of the acheulean axe. One can work out the physics of throwing an axe as much as you want (parabolic vectors, two body problems, etc). But so long as one relies on the slow-moving reflexes of conscious thought, the axe will never be thrown in time. The solution then is to work on the much faster layers of the human body-brain-mind network. Only then will we be able to produce productive encounters across multiple tempos (a topic to which we will turn in the next chapter).

These two discussions of Spinoza's philosophy (the first related to the attribute of extension, the second to the attribute of thought) provide us with a set of insights which, when folded together, provide us with a nuanced account of the relationship between speed and the body, an account which is able to encapsulate the three different images we discussed in the introduction. And it has already begun to give us some indications of the kinds of political affects which can emerge from this interaction between speed and the body. In the next chapter we will attempt to take these insights and use them to more robustly sketch out what politics in an accelerating world looks like, a picture which only comes into sharp focus when we introduce the crucial lens of the body into our analysis.

Notes

1. Copyright © Johns Hopkins University Press. This article was first published in *Postmodern Culture* 27.2 (2017). Reprinted with permission by Johns Hopkins University Press.
2. See Connolly (2002), Mackenzie (2002), Massumi (2002), Grosz (1994), and Bell (2010).
3. It should be noted that, while Connolly's *Neuropolitics* includes discussions of all three, his discussion of Spinoza is separate from his account of speed. The same is true of Deleuze who deals extensively with speed in *A Thousand Plateaus* but doesn't explicitly integrate this with his work elsewhere on Spinoza. For a discussion of Deleuze's account of speed, see Glezos (2012).
4. Compare this with Hassan's account of how speed can give rise to

   > a hyper anxiety, an epidemic that again has its roots in temporal changes associated with the compulsion towards increasing social acceleration. It is an anxiety that is fundamentally related to our failure to have a sufficient comprehension of what the future might have in store for us. Hyper anxiety, it is argued, is an actual clinical pathology that can have its origins in an unspecific apprehension about the future and what it may bring.
   >
   > *(2009: 97)*

5. This particular vision of speed and the body can rise to social and political efforts to slow down the pace of life in an accelerating world. In its more innocuous forms, these can manifest through movements based around 'slow-food' and 'slow-living' (although, see Sharma [2014: Chapter 4]). However, as discussed in the previous chapter, these efforts can give rise to reactionary political affects and movements. As Connolly argues, 'reactive drives to retard the pace of life' have a tendency to manifest 'in locating vulnerable constituencies to hold politically accountable for the fast pace of life' (2002: 142).
6. We will see another version of this account of the creeping prostheticization of the human body in the Chapter 4, when we engage with the work of Paul Virilio.
7. A review of just the titles of contemporary books on technology provides a wealth of examples of this sort of discourse, from Simon Head's *Mindless: Why Smarter Machines are Making Dumber Humans,* to Jaron Lanier's bestselling *You Are Not A Gadget.*
8. And as in the previous encounter, these humanist anxieties about an accelerating world can crystallize into conservative and reactionary political movements. We can, for example, look to Donna Haraway's discussion of how humanist anxieties over technology can enter into resonance with anxieties about race, difference, boundaries, 'purity', and 'normalcy' (1997: 61–2). More so, this critical stance on the negative influence of 'prostheticizing' technologies can carry with it a dangerously ableist politics, as it is premised on a normative vision of the 'whole' 'natural' body which ignores/erases the vast diversity of bodies and abilities. This is a topic to which we will return at various points in our discussions of speed and the body

9. The danger of such a worldview is that it can translate into an uncritical embrace of technological innovation, in which any 'enhancement' or 'acceleration' of the body is viewed as part of humanity's technological destiny. This techno–utopian worldview is by no means tied to our digital age. We can, for example, look to the *Futurist Manifesto*, with its embrace of the 'beauty of speed' and its goal 'to sing the man at the wheel' (Marinetti). What is more, if we note the Futurists' frequent fascist sympathies, we can make a connection here to the role that fantasies of technologically transcending the human body played in Nazi ideology (see Nussbaum [346–347]). We can see something similar in the work of Nick Land whose posthumanist accelerationism becomes connected to a belief in the 'dark enlightenment' and 'hyper-racism' (2014) (See, also, Noys [2014: x–xi]). The point here is not to suggest that the posthumanist outlook is somehow necessarily fascistic but rather to note how this view of the relation between speed and the body, when taken to its most extreme articulation, can have dangerous political implications (just like the other two encounters).

10. All Spinoza references are to *The Ethics*, unless otherwise stated.

11. See also Hampshire (2005: 115).

12. Indeed, the fact that all seemingly simple bodies are themselves composite bodies made up of simpler bodies leads Pierre Macherey to argue, 'The most simple bodies are thus abstractions, beings of reason, which allow us to construct a discourse on reality but do not exist in themselves in such a form that allows them to be isolated' (157).

13. Sharp makes a similar point, when she states that 'Nature, for Spinoza, names the necessity of ongoing mutation' (8).

14. For a further discussion of the multiplicity of the body in Spinoza, see Sharp (2011: 38). For a discussion of the multiple velocities of the body, see Connolly (2002: Ch.1).

15. See also Braidotti (2006: 148).

16. Crucially, this attentiveness to the question of sustainability – as well as the more global consequences of acceleration – is what stops this Spinozist approach from becoming what Noys terms the 'affirmationist and accelerationist model of increasing and developing powers whatever the costs', which 'debars critical assessment except in terms of higher or stronger powers versus lower or weaker powers' (2010: 38).

17. Michael Mack comes to a similar conclusion, saying 'Spinoza implicitly conceives of the human as an open-ended and not to be fully defined entity. From this perspective he is a post-humanist' (2012: 37). See, also, Skeaff (2013: 154) and Macherey (2011: 52–53, 75)

18. See here Montag (1999: xvii–xviii); and Sharp (2011: 1–8).

19. Hampshire conceives of this unification of mind and body as a kind of 'perspectival parallelism', in which we are aware of ourselves simultaneously as mind and body, and of the link between the two, even as we feel that the two are different things.

> We are aware of ourselves as mind/bodies, as having two entirely distinct aspects to our personality, and, when we reflect, we must recognize that this double aspect of ourselves is not unique to our species, as many philosophers have supposed. We look upon the world as consisting of things that exhibit in their behaviour thought or design, and at the same time as consisting of bodies moving in space according to laws of motion.
>
> *(xxi)*

20. For Spinoza's somewhat sarcastic account of Descartes' pineal gland, see (EII, Pr.35, S).

21. I am grateful here to the work of Bill Connolly, who has extensively discussed Damasio's insights, as well as the importance of contemporary neuroscience to discussions of political theory. See Connolly (2002). See, also, Mack (2011: 102).

22. There is at least some parallel here to the account that Spinoza gives of the relations between the mind and the idea of the mind which he develops in (EII, P21).
23. Indeed, even in non-survival situations emotions play a crucial role, as Damasio gives the example of a patient who had damage to his emotional systems, for whom even a simple decision such as when to schedule his next appointment took over half an hour of mulling over. In that situation, without the speedy work of pre-conscious emotional sub-systems to do an initial heuristic narrowing down of the options, he was forced to laboriously subject each choice to rational conscious calculation, effectively paralyzing his decision-making abilities.
24. See, for example, Plant and Peruche (2005).
25. For an extended discussion of this topic, see Protevi (2009: 24–5). William E. Connolly provides a similar argument in his account of the 'body-brain-culture network' in *Neuropolitics*.

Works Cited

Bell, S. (2010) *Fast Feminism*, New York: Autonomedia.

Bennett, J. (2010) *Vibrant Matter*, Durham, NC: Duke University Press.

Braidotti, R. (2006) *Transpositions*, London: Polity.

Connolly, W. (2002) *Neuropolitics: Thinking, Culture, Speed*, Minneapolis: University of Minnesota.

Cuboniks, L. (2018) *The Xenofeminist Manifesto: A Politics for Alienation*, London, UK: Verso.

Damasio, A. (1994) *Descartes' Error*, New York, NY: Grosset/Putnam.

Damasio, A. (2003) *Looking for Spinoza*, New York, NY: Harcourt.

Deleuze, G. (1988) *Spinoza: Practical Philosophy*, Trans. R. Hurley, San Francisco, CA: City Lights Books.

Deleuze, G. (1990) *Expressionism in Philosophy: Spinoza*, Trans. M. Joughin, Brooklyn, NY: Zone Books.

Deleuze, G. and Guattari, F. (1987) *A Thousand Plateaus*, Trans. B. Massumi, Minneapolis: University of Minnesota Press.

Eriksen, T. H. (2001) *Tyranny of the Moment: Fast and Slow Time in the Information Age*, London, UK: Pluto Press.

Fogel, R. W. (1964) *Railroads and American Economic Growth: Essays in Econometric History*, Baltimore, MD: The Johns Hopkins Press.

Gatens, M. (1996) *Imaginary Bodies*, London; New York: Routledge.

Gibson, W. (1984) *Neuromancer*, New York: Ace Science Fiction.

Gibson, W. (2003) *Pattern Recognition*, New York: Berkley.

Glezos, S. (2012) *The Politics of Speed: Capitalism, The State, and War in an Accelerating World*, Abingdon, UK: Routledge.

Grosz, E. (1994) *Volatile Bodies: Toward a Corporeal Feminism*, Bloomington, IN: Indiana University Press.

Hampshire, S. (2005) *Spinoza and Spinozism*, Oxford: Oxford University Press.

Haraway, D. (1997) *Modest_Witness@Second_millennium.FemaleMan_Meets_OncoMouse*, New York: Routledge.

Hassan, R. (2009) *Empires of Speed: Time and the Acceleration of Politics and Society*, Boston, MA: Brill.

Head, S. (2014) *Mindless: Why Smarter Machines Are Making Dumber Human*, New York: Basic Books.

Kurzweil, R. (2005) *The Singularity Is Near: When Humans Transcend Biology*, New York: Penguin Books.

Land, N. (2014) 'Hyper-Racism', *Outside In: Involements with Reality*. Available at: www.xenosystems.net/hyper-racism/ (Accessed July 9, 2019).

Lanier, J. (2011) *You Are Not a Gadget*, New York: Vintage Press.

Macherey, P. (2011) *Hegel or Spinoza*, Trans. S. M. Ruddick, Minneapolis: University of Minnesota.

Mack, M. (2011) 'Towards an Inclusive Universalism: Spinoza's Ethics of Sustainability', *Spinoza Now*, ed. D. Vardoulakis, Minneapolis: University of Minnesota Press.

Mack, M. (2012) *How Literature Changes the Way We Think*, London: Continuum.

Mackenzie, A. (2002) *Transductions: Bodies and Machines at Speed*, London: Continuum.

Marinetti, F. T. (1909) *The Futurist Manifesto*. Available at: http://cscs.umich.edu/.

Massumi, B. (2002) *Parables for the Virtual*, Durham: Duke University Press.

Montag, W. (1999) *Bodies, Masses, Power: Spinoza and His Contemporaries*, London: Verso.

Noys, B. (2010) *The Persistence of the Negative: A Critique of Contemporary Continental Theory*, Edinburgh: Edinburgh University Press.

Noys, B. (2014) *Malign Velocities: Accelerationism and Capitalism*, Alresford, UK: Zero Books.

Nussbaum, M. (2001) *Upheavals of Thought*, Cambridge: Cambridge University Press.

Plant, E. A. and Peruche, B. M. (2005) 'The Consequences of Race for Police Officers' Responses to Criminal Suspects', *Psychological Science*, 16(3): 180–3.

Protevi, J. (2009) *Political Affects: Connecting the Social and the Somatic*, Minneapolis, MN: University of Minnesota Press.

Ross, A. A. G. (2014) *Mixed Emotions: Beyond Fear and Hatred in International Conflict*, Chicago: University of Chicago Press.

Rousseau, J. J. (1987) 'Discourse on the Origin of Inequality', *The Basic Political Writings*, Trans. D. A. Cress, Indianapolis: Hackett.

Sharma, S. (2014) *In the Meantime: Temporality and Cultural Politics*, Durham, NC: Duke University Press.

Sharp, H. (2011) *Spinoza and the Politics of Renaturalization*, Chicago: University of Chicago Press.

Skeaff, C. (2013) '"Citizen Jurisprudence" and the People's Power in Spinoza', *Contemporary Political Theory*, 12(3): 146–65.

Spinoza, B. (1982) *The Ethics and Selected Letters*, Trans. S. Shirley. Indianopolis: Hackett.

Stiegler, B. (1998) *Technics and Time, 1*, Trans. R. Beardsworth and G. Collins, Stanford, CA: Stanford University Press.

Tomlinson, J. (2007) *The Culture of Speed: The Coming of Immediacy*, London: Sage Publications.

3

DOING WELL AND BEING GLAD

Spinoza and the Roots of Reactionary Politics

In this chapter, I wish to carry forward the account of *ressentiment* against speed which I began in the first chapter; to unpack its affective and corporeal roots, and thus to gain a better understanding of what sorts of practices and institutions might be useful in fighting these reactionary mindsets and movements. The account of Spinoza's work we developed in the previous chapter will be invaluable for doing so, both in terms of the analysis he develops of the corporeal and affective components of human thought, as well as the metaphysics and ethics he lays out as potential correctives to some of our more dangerous instincts and drives.

There are numerous ways in which encounters between the body and speed can give rise to *ressentiment* and produce reactionary mindsets and politics, and therefore any account given here will necessarily be abridged. Therefore, I wish to focus on two specific points of intersection, both of which were discussed in Chapter 1. The first is premised upon how affective responses to a sense of contingency and uncertainty in an accelerating world can give rise to a drive to establish authoritative, teleological accounts of time. Second is the development of reactionary mindsets in response to a perceived threat against interiority by a dangerous 'outside' (manifested most obviously in anti-immigration movements but also present in aggressive reactions to a rising sense of cultural diversity, and plurality amongst modes of life). Though these are merely two examples amongst many, their choice is not completely arbitrary, as they provide us with the opportunity to look at affective responses to both the temporal and spatial dimensions of speed: radical futurity and exteriority.

Part I: Speed, the Body, and Reactionary Politics

Teleology and Contingency

Turning to Spinoza as a way of helping to understand and combat the rise of *ressentiment* against speed might appear to be a curious decision as, at first blush, it seems as if Spinoza's metaphysics are themselves an instance of *ressentiment* against speed. This is because explicit in Spinoza's monistic ontology is a complete rejection of contingency. Spinoza views all things as unfolding according to a strict conception of necessity. As he says, '[n]othing in nature is contingent, but all things are from the necessity of the divine nature determined to exist and to act in a definite way' (I P29). Everything that happens is fully determined according to the requirements of being. Our perception of contingency is merely the result of our inability to grasp the complete web of causality that determines any action, outcome, or decision. Indeed, in Spinoza's metaphysics, even God is not capable of contingency saying, 'God does not act from freedom of will' (I P32C1) but rather from the necessity of his nature.

Despite this rejection of ontological contingency, Spinoza's work is actually surprisingly useful in helping us understand how people react to contingency in an accelerating world. This is because of the way in which his epistemology works alongside his ontology. For Spinoza, humans are always constrained by our finiteness, and hence our understanding will always be premised upon inadequate knowledge. As such, the perception of contingency in life is ineradicable. It is true that, through rational thought we are able, in a certain way, to perceive things *sub specie aeternitatis*. But this only relates to understanding the formal logical rules which govern existence. It does not lead us to be able to actively grasp (or predict) all of the web of causal factors which lead any individual 'thing' to occur (II P16–17). (And all of this before Spinoza's doctrine of parallelism, with its determinations and limitations of thought, is brought into the mix.) From this perspective, our perception of infinite being will always be incomplete, and we will always see the world as full of contingency. It does not matter if metaphysically there is no freedom or indeterminacy in *deus cive natura*. Our lives as modal beings will always be replete with uncertainty, no matter how much we might learn about the universe.

However, Spinoza believes that humans have a tendency to be dissatisfied with the contingency that they perceive in the unfolding of the world. When faced with this apparent uncertainty, humans struggle valiantly to give meaning to contingency. He notes that, in an uncertain world, rather than attempt to uncover what facts and laws *are* discernible to human perception and reason, and accept the limitations of this process, too many people have the impulse to make the world rational through the positing of an overarching goal or end point to time, explaining away all apparently meaningless contingencies. This is a result of believing that things happen in the world out of an intentional desire (by God, the universe, history, etc.) to bring about some particular end point or goal. As Spinoza says, 'all the prejudices which I intend to mention here turn on this one point, the widespread belief amongst men that all things in Nature are like themselves in acting with an end in view' (I Appendix). What Spinoza is criticizing here then is nothing other than teleological thinking. As Macherey puts it, 'The fundamental aspect of the Spinozist argument is its radical refusal of all teleology' (52).[1] While it is true that Spinoza rejects contingency and believes the world unfolds according to principles of logical necessity, he does not believe that it unfolds with some particular end point in mind. He states unequivocally that 'Nature has no fixed goal and that all final causes are but figments or the human imagination' (I Appendix).

More importantly, we still must grapple with the problem of contingency (intellectually and, as our discussion in the first chapter showed, ethically) because when we introduce the middle term of human intellect, it creates a great difference in terms of how we study the world and our metaphysical outlook. The belief in the necessity of the world which Spinoza counsels encourages us to seek to understand some of the logical rules which govern it. At the same time, he counsels an understanding of our own finitude which lets us know we will never have absolute knowledge of all of those rules, or how they will play out. Such an approach fosters an experimental orientation to the world, which seeks to understand while leaving open the future to new understandings. This is an epistemological and ethical orientation which can serve us well in an accelerating world of proliferating contingencies. Dimitri Vardoulakis nicely describes the limitations of a thought *sub specie aeternitatis*, saying:

> 'For this much is quite certain, and proved to be true in our Ethics, that men are necessarily subject to passions.' This statement, from Spinoza's Political Treatise (1, §5), encapsulates the importance of the present for his philosophy. Even though Spinoza insists on a knowledge from the perspective of eternity or the infinite, communal living is nevertheless permeated with the affects each one feels while living. A desire is always in the present. Thus philosophy for Spinoza is inextricably linked to life, to the now of existence.
>
> *(xi)*

Conversely, a teleological perspective begins by foreclosing the future, assuming that it grasps the trajectory of time and already knows its meaning and goal. In this context contingencies are not taken as opportunities for reflection and experimentation but are instead either explained as part of an unfolding plan, or worse, become dangerous threats to that plan, which must be suppressed.

Furthermore, for Spinoza teleological thinking is doubly dangerous since, in addition to assuming that *deus cive natura* has a plan, humans also have a tendency to assume this plan has *us* as its focus. Following along from his critique of the human prejudice to assume that all things in nature work like us, he goes on to say 'Indeed, they hold it as certain that God himself directs everything to a fixed end; for they say that God has made everything for man's sake' (I Appendix). This belief that 'God has made everything for man's sake' is to completely misunderstand the nature of being for Spinoza. As discussed earlier, human beings are one modal expression, one composite body, amongst the infinite expressions and bodies which make up the totality of being. Existence is no more 'for' us, than it is for any other finite being. We are all part of the unfolding of *deus cive natura*. The attempt to put human beings at the centre of the universe is simply the result of prejudice and narcissism. What is more, it requires increasingly tortured logic to force all contingencies to fit this narrative.

> But in seeking to show that Nature does nothing in vain – that is, nothing that is not to man's advantage – they seem to have shown only this, that Nature and the gods are as crazy as mankind. Consider, I pray, what has been the upshot. Among so many of Nature's blessings they are bound to discover quite a number of disasters, such as storms, earthquakes, diseases and so forth, and they maintained that these occurred because the gods were angry at the wrongs done to them by men, or the faults committed in the course of their worship. And although daily experience cried out against this and showed by any number of examples that blessings and disasters befall the godly and ungodly alike without discrimination, they did not on that account abandon their ingrained prejudice. For they found it easier to regard this fact as one among other mysteries they could not understand and thus maintain their innate condition of ignorance rather than to demolish in its entirety the theory that they had constructed and devise a new one. Hence they made it axiomatic that the judgement of the gods is far beyond man's understanding.
>
> *(I Appendix)*

Once again, a teleological outlook leaves us incapable of engaging with contingency and newness on their own terms. It leads us to interpret all things through our own finite framework rather than attempt to stretch our understanding. From Spinoza's perspective, part of the goal of philosophy is to understand our own finite nature, to understand that we are not the measure of all things.

> For many are wont to argue on the following lines: if everything has followed from the necessity of God's most perfect nature, why does Nature display so many imperfections, such as rottenness to the point of putridity, nauseating ugliness, confusion, evil, sin, and so on? But, as I have just

pointed out, they are easily refuted. For the perfection of things should be measured solely from their own nature and power; nor are things more or less perfect to the extent that they please or offend human sense, serve or oppose human interests.

(I Appendix)

For Spinoza every theodicy is flawed because they all start from the assumption that human beings are the point of the world, and that God does everything for them.[2] Only in such a world does evil have to be explained or worked around. But if serving humans is not God's goal, indeed if God cannot even be described as having goals, then any sort of justification of his 'actions' is completely beside the point.

As we move into a more secular age, such desires for a teleologically established meaning do not go out of the world. New teleologies take their place, narratives of progress, cosmopolitanism, revolution, and liberation present in worldviews across the political spectrum. All of them seek to provide an account of the world, seek to explain how seemingly 'evil' events – non-sensical events, *contingent* events (for what is evil except contingent events which escape the rubric of our plans) – are actually part of a broader teleological unfolding.

In this context, Spinoza's metaphysics can provide a useful corrective to these drives towards teleological thinking. This is because Spinoza's metaphysics fights against teleological thinking not just epistemologically (in terms of how we humans understand and interpret the world) but also ontologically. As he says earlier, he wants to overturn the 'belief among men that all things in Nature are like themselves in acting with an end in view'. For Spinoza *deus cive natura* doesn't pursue ends. It is not incomplete in some way and seeking after its perfection. The assumption of nature as being incomplete and pursuing some end is simply an attribution of the human mind.

There seems to be no other reason why even natural phenomena (those not made by human hand) should commonly be called perfect or imperfect. For men are wont to form general ideas both of natural phenomena and of artifacts, and these ideas they regard as models, and they believe that Nature (which they consider does nothing without an end in view) looks to these ideas and holds them before herself as models. So when they see something occurring in Nature at variance with their preconceived ideal of the thing in question, they believe that Nature has then failed or blundered and has left that thing imperfect.

(IV Preface)

Hegel's great accusation against Spinoza is that he ignores the power of the negative. But this is exactly the point of Spinoza's metaphysics, to reject the negative, to note the way the concept of the negative (of the 'imperfect' or the 'incomplete') is an attribution – an imposition – of the human mind, onto the perfection and totality of being. A meditation on Spinoza's metaphysics calls us to contemplate the sheer perfection and necessity of being, to understand that what has happened is not either a fulfilment of a plan or a deviation from it. Rather it is simply *what happened*. It simply *is*.[3]

This understanding of the ateleological nature of being has important political implications because, as discussed in the first chapter, one of the potential sources of reactionary mindsets and politics is the frustration of our teleological projections, as we become resentful when the contingent swervings of an accelerating world challenge them (Glezos 2011). Indeed, the contingencies of an accelerating world do not just result in overthrowing particular projections but seem to challenge the very possibility of a stable teleological trajectory (Glezos 2012: Ch. 1). In these contexts, we always run the risk of becoming resentful of a time that seems uninterested in our desire for a sense of stability or continuity. And as this resentment crystallizes into *ressentiment* we might become willing to endorse reactionary political perspectives; to enact violent revenge on those perceived as the agents of this contingency (more on this later); and to authorize increasingly despotic forms of political organization, in the hopes that they will be able to secure the future against these contingencies, and reestablish the legitimacy and functionality of our chosen narratives (Glezos 2012: 162). As Wendy Brown puts it in *States of Injury*:

> In a culture already streaked with the pathos of *ressentiment* . . . there are several distinctive characteristics of late modern postindustrial societies that accelerate and expand the conditions of its production . . . 'increased global contingency' combines with the expanding pervasiveness and complexity of domination by capital and bureaucratic state and social networks to create an unparalleled individual powerlessness over the fate and direction of one's own life, intensifying the experience of impotence, dependence, and gratitude . . . constitutive of *ressentiment*.
>
> *(68)*[4]

Spinoza is well aware of the link between reactionary politics and the affects of anger, fear, and resentment. For Spinoza, the sad passions of anger, fear, and resentment necessarily mark a decrease in power of the body (indeed, that is what defines their status as the sad passion). As we resentfully become attached to our teleological projections of time, we become unwilling to productively engage with the contingent emergence of being on its own terms. With this affective disposition, we become more interested in revenge against those who we perceive as threatening us, and more willing to authorize tyrannical authority to enact that revenge and to reestablish the master narratives we cling to.[5] In doing so, we lose sight of what would actually expand our *conatus*. Driven by fear and anger, we become willing to give our power over to a tyrant to rule us, and in doing so, become less able to secure our own lives. As Deleuze points out, for Spinoza, every tyranny, every reactionary politics, has its roots in the sad passions.

> The tyrant needs sad spirits in order to succeed, just as sad spirits need a tyrant in order to be content and to multiply. In any case, what unites them is their hatred of life, their resentment against life. The *Ethics* draws the portrait of the *resentful man*, for whom all happiness is an offence, and who makes wretchedness or impotence his only passion.
>
> *(1988: 25)*

Spinoza's metaphysics attempts to get us to overcome this hatred of life, this resentment of the world with its tendency to deviate from the teleologies we hold so dear. He wishes to convince us that we are wrong to expect this kind of certainty from time. He explains to us that time does not work like us, it does not have a meaning or a plan that we can decipher. That when it does not meet our expectations, we are not being wronged or being punished. That is simply how the world works. The best that we can hope to do is to rationally discern some of its laws of actions (the laws of physics, of biology, of ontology) while also understanding that, due to our finite nature, some aspect of this unfolding of time will always escape our comprehension. There will always be a sense of contingency in our experience of time, but this is not a failure, a punishment, or 'god working in mysterious ways'. It is simply the being/becoming of the world. By doing so, he also hopes to diminish the occurrence of these sad passions in the world, the fear, anger and resentment that lead us to give up our power to tyrants, or to focus our power in unproductive acts of revenge on those who might or might not have had anything to do with it in the first place.

Note this acceptance of the 'perfection' of the world (which for Spinoza merely means its completeness, its immanence to itself) does not translate into a kind of ascetic rejection of judgement. Spinoza has no problems with humans using concepts of good and evil, better and worse, and certainly understands them striving to change the world in ways that they prefer (indeed, as we've seen his entire concept of *conatus* is premised upon such a striving). Spinoza has no problem with things being described as incomplete or evil *from the perspective of finite modalities of being*. But, in the same way, Nietzsche's injunction against *ressentiment* is never a blanket injunction against resentment, and his call for a fundamentally affirmative existential outlook is not bound to a rejection of negativity or critique.

Spinoza expects and even requires us to judge things by the standard of the human, but in doing so he always asks us to understand that this is what we are doing, and that this is not the only standard from which to judge. That our lives are not lived as part of a teleological unfolding of god's plan but simply happen always in the fullness of time. For Spinoza there is no beginning or end to time[6] (this would limit god's infinity). Rather we are always in the middle. We join the world in the middle, and we will leave the world in the middle, and it is a middle without beginning and end, and thus a middle which changes the very nature of what a middle is. Meditation on this, attentiveness to this, learning to accept this, loosens our attachments to teleological projections, moderates our sense of *ressentiment* when our plans become frustrated or uncertain, and, therefore, seemingly paradoxically (but actually quite obviously) infuses us with an increased drive to action.[7] If *ressentiment* is that which separates us from our power and the world, Spinoza's metaphysics encourage us to affirm the world. And this makes us better able to act in an accelerating world.

And yet, following from Spinoza's account of the semi-autonomy of the affects, just knowing all of this does not therefore mean that we will be free of the desire for teleological projections, or the resentment, fear, and anger we feel when they are made frustrated. As we saw, the shift to a more secular age did not do away with conceptions of providence, fate, or destiny. This does not mean that we are fully a slave to them (indeed, Spinoza's overall argument is never that we are fully a slave to our bodies and their affects), but it does mean that they can't solely be rationally argued away. As Montag puts it

> the *Ethics* continues the arduous task of dismantling the apparatus of dualism, an apparatus that, according to Spinoza's own argument, can never be definitively abandoned given that the tendency to imagine another world, the double of this world which would give to it truth and purpose, is inescapable, arising as the necessary consequence of the variability of fortune.
>
> *(26)*

Thus, while rational argumentation is an important first step to altering behaviour, to acting ethically in the world, it is only a first step. For it to become an organizing principle of action, we must work out practices that work against – and with – the way in which it is corporeally and affectively layered into our actions and thoughts. We will turn to these practices in the second half of this chapter, but first, I would like to discuss this intersection between speed, the body, and reactionary politics from a different perspective.

Interiority and Exteriority

In terms of a *ressentiment* against speed, our anxiety about futurity – the existential resentment against a time which refuses to bow to our desire for simple stability and continuity – is twinned with a *ressentiment* against exteriority – a resentment against the eccentric flows which seem to puncture and fragment the unitary and stable boundaries of state, community, and identity (it is not even remotely coincidental that this sensibility mimics elements of our first two stories of the encounter between speed and the body in the previous chapter, with their anxieties about the purity and impenetrability of the body). I have investigated this phenomenon elsewhere,[8] and in the first chapter I discussed it in relation to the specific context of immigration politics in Canada. There, periodic panics over illegal immigration, refugees, and 'queue-jumpers' channel broader anxieties over the changing composition of the Canadian state, as well as fears over the perceived marginalization of a privileged white, European cultural milieu. Such anti-immigration sentiments (and nationalist/ civilizationalist panics) are, of course, not unique to Canada. These sentiments can provoke reactionary politics, and provide support for conservative and nationalist political parties and movements around the world. Although I have discussed these movements and instincts elsewhere, applying a Spinozistic lens provides additional insight, helping to flesh out the corporeal and affective dimensions which contribute to their rise.

Of course, nationalist and xenophobic movements have a much older provenance than just the contemporary accelerating world. But the specific discourses which are deployed in the context of many contemporary anti-immigration movements and sensibilities are related to the particular contexts of technological acceleration and neoliberal globalization. In such contexts, anti-immigrant and xenophobic sentiments are encouraged and expressed through the scapegoating of migrant labourers (as well as foreign labour pools) as the source of national economic decline (think here of Nietzsche's injunction that 'Someone or other must be to blame that I feel ill' [1997: 93]). As I put it elsewhere:

> This scapegoating can take form of a narrative about illegal Mexican migrants sneaking in to the United States to "steal" the jobs of Americans, or Chinese and Indian labourers who are "willing to work for less" in their home countries. Such scapegoating is aided by a failure to differentiate between foreign labour and foreign capital (or, for that matter, multinational or transnational capital). Therefore, migrant labour (whether legal or illegal) receives the same status and suspicion as does, say, the influx of Japanese capital in America in the mid-1990's. This is partly the result of the same liberal/neoliberal ideology of individualism which makes it impossible to view economic disenfranchisement as systematic. When transferred onto foreign workers alone, the movement of migrant labourers is seen as a result of a personal choice, and the willingness of foreign labour pools to work for less is seen as a ploy on behalf of foreign workers to steal jobs from the developed world. If one must conceive of these actions as the result of choices made by free individuals, rather than the coerced decisions of actors in different positions with regards to global capitalism, then one can a) devalue the moral status of these actors (turning migrants into 'illegals' or 'Queue-jumpers') and b)

see them as opponents competing for work, rather than fellow victims of a general system of economic exploitation.

(2012: 147)

It is this neoliberal discourse of individualism, and this perception of mobility as indicative of a 'free choice' on behalf of migrants (whether migrant labourers, refugees, or any number of other categories) within a fair and balanced marketplace that is crucial to our understanding of this *ressentiment* against speed, and the affective roots of reactionary politics. For it is this sense of the 'free choice' of the migrants that gives these mindsets their affective force. Here, once again, we can look to Spinoza's analysis of the force of emotions.

In his analysis of how things incite either love or hatred, he states that '[l]ove and hatred towards a thing that we think of as free must both be greater, other conditions being equal, than towards a thing subject to necessity' (III P49). We see how our moral judgements are weakened when considering agents who we feel are acting out of necessity. Such considerations are at the heart of our legal systems, as judges take into consideration mitigating circumstances when pronouncing sentences and we make distinctions between first degree murder, second degree murder, and manslaughter (all of which are nothing other than the degree of freedom with which we perceive that a killing took place). In the context of an already present anxiety over acceleration and global flows, the perceived freedom of migrants becomes a source of both sharpened moral judgement and heightened affective sensitivity. Indeed, it is the very mobility of the migrant which is interpreted as indicative of their freedom, and hence the marker of their morally suspect status. Affective responses of fear, anxiety or resentment are therefore premised upon the inability to perceive the mobility of migrants and refugees (whether 'economic' or otherwise) as the result of necessity. As I say elsewhere, the working class of developed countries frequently perceives itself as,

> essentially immobile, finding itself without much control, subject to the whim of global capitalism. In this regards then, it is assumed that since their immobility is tied to a lack of choice, mobility must represent a form of freedom or choice. Hence migrant labourers are attacked for impinging on a labour market that is already economically depressed. Such a perspective fails to conceive of a flow or movement that might be experienced not as . . . freedom and intentionality, but as . . . conditioned and forced. In short, they cannot conceive of a mobility that is just as constraining as their own immobility.
>
> *(2012: 147)*

This point is crucial because, in many contexts, when actors are able to perceive the various structural factors and contingent histories which constrain the supposedly 'free choices' made by migrants, they stop being threatening agents, economic competitors, or 'queue-jumpers' and instead become what they always were: fellow humans seeking to make the best possible choices in a complex, constraining and violent world.

In his article 'Abject Cosmopolitanism: The Politics of Protection in the Anti-Deportation Movement', Peter Nyers discusses the situation of non-status Algerian migrants primarily in Montreal facing deportation, and the *Comites D'Action des Sans-Status* (CASS), a group which acts in solidarity with them.

> The majority of the non-status Algerians arrived in Canada as refugees seeking asylum. All were fleeing the violence and conflict that has pitted armed Islamist groups and a corrupt military regime against one another since elections were suspended and a state of emergency was instated in 1992. The conflict in Algeria has taken a disastrous toll on the population: over 150 000 dead, 12 000 disappeared, a million displaced, and a civilian population harassed by regular kidnappings, summary executions and violent repression. Of the Algerians who managed to arrive in Canada, some were granted refugee status; many were not. While the individualistic bias of the Canadian refugee determination process separates 'genuine' and 'non-genuine' refugees, the Canadian government nonetheless deemed the situation in Algeria to be so dangerous that on 3 March 1997 a moratorium was instated prohibiting all deportations to that country. Many of the failed asylum seekers – now so-called 'non-status' persons – noted the irony of this situation: 'It's ironic that you can be refused as refugees but you can't be sent back to your own country because you'll be persecuted'.
>
> *(1082–1083)*

CASS wanted to avoid becoming spokespeople for the group, and hence duplicating a paternalistic structure in which CASS would 'speak for' the group that was already profoundly silenced. Instead CASS attempted to provide support in producing situations where the refugees could speak for themselves. One of the most powerful tactics was the staging of surprise 'delegation visits to immigration offices beginning in Summer 2002'. As Nyers points out, '[t]here is a number of advantages to these kinds of visits. An occupation by non-status people disrupts the normality of office affairs; they bring their own personal 'states of emergency' directly to the state apparatus' (1084). The refugees were able to leverage these disruptions into meetings with higher up officials in the Canadian immigration bureaucracy.

> These meetings usually include forcing officials to read the individual case files and hear the testimonies of the refugee claimants. This is the other key advantage of delegation visits: they allow for face-to-face

encounters with state officials invested with enormous powers of discretion. As one member of CASS complained, 'We are treated as file numbers, not as human beings'. Once the compelling individual stories behind these numbers are shared, it is not unusual for immigration staff to be moved to tears.

(1084)[9]

From a Spinozistic perspective, such an affective response is to be perfectly well expected (and twinned off against the previous affective response of anger and hatred at the perceived 'queue-jumpers' and 'economic refugees'). In this case, the anger that was directed at an actor perceived as being a free agent choosing to injure us is replaced by sympathy for an actor who we see as acting out of necessity when faced with complex and violent circumstances.

In principle these mitigating circumstances were already known by the government and immigration staff. As Nyers points out earlier, the Canadian government acknowledged the danger of the situation in Algeria by halting deportations. Paradoxically, this did not necessarily lead to migrants being granted refugee status. This tension speaks to Spinoza's point that affects can overpower true knowledge. As Sharp explains, '[t]o be adequate to the minds of others, the idea has to become compatible with their dispositions; it needs to be upheld by other ideas present in their minds' (2011: 73). For actors to accept a novel/challenging idea, they

> need the premises in order to be able to grasp the conclusions. Importantly . . . the premises are more than facts. The premises are the affective conditions, the ability to perceive and be transformed by an alien set of ideas and the bodies to which they correspond.
>
> *(73)*[10]

These in person meetings served to communicate not just the necessary ideas but the necessary affects as well.

Returning to the topic of the Algerian refugees, it is worth mentioning that this identification of the 'necessity' which determines these actors is not intended to transform them solely into 'victims' or 'passive agents' subject to the cruel whims of fate. Quite the opposite. By seeking to cultivate spaces wherein these migrants can speak with their own voices and tell their own stories, what is provided are often heroic accounts of actors overcoming fantastic obstacles, making countless difficult decisions, and surviving against the odds. Such accounts affirm the agency of these actors, while also making it clear that their 'choices' were always constrained and difficult, bearing little resemblance to the free economic 'choice' the neoliberal account lays out. Whatever choices they made, their 'intention' was never to 'steal jobs' or 'queue-jump'.[11] Hearing these stories, exposing oneself to these narratives, forces us to ask what we would have done in similar circumstances. We (I include myself here) hopefully can become aware of how first-world privilege has left us with a conception of 'choice' that is radically at odds with what is faced by the vast majority of the world's population.[12]

Interestingly enough we see how this account of the spatial characteristics of *ressentiment* against speed mirrors that of the temporal. In the previous discussion Spinoza counselled attentiveness to the necessity of being and the rejection of teleological projections as a way of avoiding resentfulness against a world that seems unwilling to provide us with stability and certainty. Here we see Spinoza counselling paying attention to the necessity which constrains human action as a way of avoiding resentfulness against actors who seem to interfere and intervene in spaces which we view as stable, certain, and ours alone.[13] Indeed, for Spinoza, attentiveness to this necessity inherent in being is a crucial component of his ethics. And here this ethics is not a juridical ethics in which actors are judged more or less guilty insofar as they are more or less free but rather a *conatus* driven ethics as a set of practices that cultivates greater power and freedom in terms of our own action. By focusing on the necessity constraining agents, we diminish the power of the sad passions – resentment, fear, and anger – and thus make ourselves freer and more open to the joyful passions which increase our power to act. As Spinoza puts it, 'In so far as the mind understands all things as governed by necessity, to that extent it has greater power over emotions, i.e. It is less passive in respect of them' (V P6).

Thus, as we come to understand the necessity which constrains the decisions of refugees and migrants, we first decrease the resentment which fuels reactionary political mindsets, and which is expressed in xenophobic rhetoric and actions. Furthermore, with an increased attention to necessity, new vectors of political action begin to open up as we become aware of the structural factors that contribute to refugee crises and large-scale economic migration. In such contexts we might reorient ourselves away from punitive immigration politics that target the most vulnerable manifestations of the phenomenon and instead focus on ameliorating the structural factors which give rise to these processes. We might seek to increase foreign aid budgets to encourage development, limit our involvement in violent conflicts that produce flows of refugees, seek peaceful solutions to conflicts, or reduce our support of oppressive regimes for tactical purposes.[14] What is more, we might even stop perceiving these flows of migrants as a violent imposition of the outside on the inside and instead see how we are always already bound up in the conditions and actions which put these flows into motion. Such an attentiveness to necessity would loosen our attachment to stable and static interiors and boundaries, making us aware that such boundaries are always already fictions we tell ourselves. For to return to an earlier Spinozistic point, we must always understand bodies which we perceive as stable and self-sufficient as actually being components of larger composite bodies. It would make us understand the webs of interconnection within which we are all bound up, and how we need to develop an ethics and a politics which focus on strengthening those interconnections, and engaging with them in an open and democratic way rather than attempting to violently expel and limit them (Sharp 2011: 53). In one of his lovelier passages, Spinoza lays out what is at the heart of his ethics, saying:

> It is of the first importance to men to establish close relationships and to bind themselves together with such ties as may more effectively unite them into one body, and, as an absolute rule, to act in such a way as serves to strengthen friendship.
>
> *(IV Appendix 12)*

A Spinozistic attentiveness to necessity thus serves as an important challenge to *ressentiment* against speed and, in overturning it, fulfils the key goal of reconnecting us with our power. By diminishing the sad passions of fear, anxiety, and resentment against contingency, futurity, and exteriority, we loosen the power of reactionary mindsets which limit the range of political options available to us (focusing on counterproductive politics of revenge and alienation), and instead offer us a whole new set of political possibilities, possibilities which can take advantage of the tools of an accelerating world. Such an approach is thus truly *ethical* in the Spinozistic sense, in that it increases our power, expresses our *conatus*, and yet does so in a way that is sustainable, which shows how increasing our own power requires attentiveness to the condition of others in a world of shared fate. As he says,

> Furthermore, as we have noted . . . the strong-minded man has this foremost in his mind, that everything follows from the necessity of the divine nature. . . . For this reason his prime endeavor is to conceive things as they are in themselves and to remove obstacles to true knowledge, such as hatred, anger, envy derision, pride, and similar emotions that we have noted. And so he endeavors, as far as he can, to do well and to be glad, as we have said.
>
> *(IV P73S)*

A politics and an ethics which seek 'to do well and to be glad'. We could do much worse for a guide in this accelerating world of ours.

And yet, as our discussion of affectivity earlier points out, just understanding this rationally is not enough to necessarily overpower the sad passions. Even as we might accept Spinoza's account of necessity, we will still find ourselves drawn towards teleological thinking, and individualist accounts of agents which focus on their free choices. Right thinking is not enough, on its own, to overpower affects. As I quoted earlier, 'No emotion can be checked by the true knowledge of good and evil in so far as it is true, but only in so far as it is considered an emotion' (IV P14). One last discussion therefore is necessary. In the next section we will turn to the question of how these understandings of the roots of *ressentiment* and reactionary politics can be fought through recourse to practices of the self which take the affective dimension of politics seriously.

Part II: Practicing Ethics in an Accelerating World

Thus far, we have seen that, in an accelerating world, the body becomes the site for a collection of encounters that can give rise to powerful affective forces which, if unchecked, can lead to reactionary political orientations, potentially manifesting as violent calls for revenge and anxiety-riddled demands for tyrannical authority.

Just in attempting to outline these affects, and the way that an accelerating world gives rise to them, we have already begun figuring out how to fight these tendencies. For as Spinoza points out, 'the more an emotion is known to us, the more it is within our control, and the mind is the less passive in respect of it' (V P3C). Thus, by bringing to the fore the affective drives which influence political behaviour, this analysis makes us aware of an entire space of political forces with which we must engage if we are to deal effectively with the politics of an accelerating world.

However, as we have said, an awareness of these affects does not necessarily mean overcoming them. This is why, despite Spinoza's statement earlier that the more we understand an emotion 'the more it is within our control', his theory of ethics is not purely a rationalist one. Or rather, though Spinoza is a rationalist insofar as he believes that rational thought is the main way we discern ethical guidelines, rational thought is not sufficient for ensuring ethical conduct. Emotions must be dealt with on their own terms. Understanding them merely gives us a starting point for figuring out how to diminish their power, excavate their roots, and challenge them with alternate affects. Any philosophy which accepts emotions as a substantial part of thought must develop some conception of how to deal with them on their own terms. As Spinoza says,

> I have already demonstrated that we do not have absolute command over [emotions]. Now the Stoics thought that the emotions depend absolutely on our will, and that we can have absolute command over them. However, with experience crying out against them they were obliged against principles to admit that no little practice and zeal are required in order to check and control emotions.
>
> *(V Preface)*

Or as Pierre Macherey puts it:

> The freedom of the sage does not consist of suppressing the passions and the effects of servitude but of modifying his relationship to his passions

and to the images that accompany them or elicit them; in recognizing the necessity that they express themselves in their own way, he transforms them into joyous passions, into clear images, which are explained in the totality of their determination. Spinoza's politics consists specifically of this because knowledge, which depends first on modes according to which it is practiced, is also a matter of politics.

(2011: 70)

This concept of 'practice' which both passages allude to is crucial to our understanding of the intersection of speed, the body, and reactionary politics because it make us aware of the dual sense in which we must not only 'practice' ethics (in the sense of *doing* ethics) but also 'practice' ethics (in the sense of repetition, training).

That is why, for Spinoza, the next step after beginning to understand emotions, and grasping our ethical responsibilities to others, is to ruminate upon these understandings, to meditate upon them, to repeat them. It might seem unclear what this has to do with the body (or with speed) if all we are counselling is simply the repetition of conscious, rational thought. However, this is to misunderstand the way that the repetition of an idea works upon us, and the way that meditation does more than simply make us aware of a fact. Rather it layers this thought – and an attendant set of behaviours – into a complex body-brain-mind network. The goal is to routinize ethical thought and behaviour so that such an orientation is second-nature, and ready to hand. As Spinoza says in his discussion of ethical conduct in the context of an uncertain future, and powerful affective drives

> the best course we can adopt, as long as we do not have perfect knowledge of our emotions, is to conceive a right method of living, or fixed rules of life, and to commit them to memory and continually apply them to particular situations that are frequently encountered in life, so that our casual thinking is thoroughly permeated by them and they are always ready to hand.
>
> *(V P10S)*

The goal is thus not just to become aware of these ethical principles but to produce a situation in which our 'casual thinking is thoroughly permeated by them, and they are always ready to hand'. Such a ready-to-handedness is crucial in the context of an accelerating world, when we do not always have the time to engage in rational reflection, and where contingent irruption of radical futurity will lead us to encounters for which we do not necessarily have precedent to draw upon.

Note the spectre of our discussion of the acheulean axe, where we learned how a temporal disjuncture between the speed of one line (the hand-axe-target line) required a pace that surpassed that of the necessary complementary line (that of the brain-nervous system-reflex line). This disjuncture was bridged by practice, a repetition which built new structures into thought and action, allowing a new pace and precision of action. Here we see the ethico-affective version of this process, which we alluded to in our discussion of affective response patterns and somatic markers in the previous chapter. We know that in an accelerating world, contingent situations which we might not be prepared for will occur, potentially unsettling our sense of stability, identity, community, etc., and in doing so give rise to *ressentiment*-laden reactionary politics. Furthermore, in an accelerating world, we might not have time to engage in a rational ethical analysis, or we might be overcome by those sad passions of fear, anxiety, hatred, and resentment. If beforehand, in slower times, we have meditated upon ethical principles, and practiced and engaged with them in other circumstances, we will find ourselves better equipped to fight these sad passions and affirm the joyful passions of love and friendship. In this case, as in the art of learning to throw, ethical behaviour is '"buffered" or stored up in advance and then released in one go'. Spinoza speaks thoughtfully about how this meditation and repetition of ethical principles better prepares us for ethical action in the future.

> For example, among our practical rules, we laid down . . . that hatred should be conquered by love or nobility, and not repaid with reciprocal hatred. Now in order to have this precept of reason always ready to hand in time of need we should think about and frequently reflect on the wrongs that are commonly committed among mankind and the best way and method of warding them off by nobility of character. For thus we shall associate the image of a wrong with the presentation of this rule of conduct, and it will always be at hand for us . . . when we suffer a wrong. Again, if we always have in readiness consideration of our true advantage and also of the good that follows from mutual friendship and social relations, and also remember that supreme contentment of spirit follows from the right way of life . . . and that men, like everything else, act from the necessity of their nature, then the wrong, or the hatred that is wont to arise from it, will occupy just a small part of our imagination and will easily be overcome. Or if the anger that is wont to arise from grievous wrongs be not easily overcome, it will nevertheless be overcome, though not without vacillation, in a far shorter space of time than if we had not previously reflected on these things in the way I have described.
>
> *(V P10S)*

It is said that the point of legal constitutions is to develop ethical principles beforehand, so that, when we find ourselves in a rapidly developing course of events, we don't have to redo these analyses and leave ourselves subject to error and bias. We can simply rely on the principles that we have already decided that we value. But such principles only work if they are already effectively layered into our legal and institutional structures. And, as we have seen in countless 'states of emergency', states and actors find any number of ways to overcome these limitations. Institutions and laws only have force if they are backed up by affective dispositions which do not succumb to resentment, hatred, and fear, and which are not willing to throw laws aside for a tyranny that will quiet these anxieties. And such affective dispositions will only have force if they are layered into thought and behaviour, rooted in the body and the mind, like a reflex arc, throwing an axe at a target.[15] Bill Connolly describes this process in this way:

> To work on an established sensibility by tactical means, then, is to nudge the composition of some layers in relation to others. You work experimentally on the relays between thought-imbued *intensities* below the level of feeling and linguistic complexity, thought-imbued *feelings* below the level of linguistic sophistication, *images* that triggers responses at both levels, and linguistically sophisticated patterns of *narrative, argument, and judgement*. You do so to encourage the effects of actions upon one register to filter into the experience and imagination available on others, thereby working tactically upon a dense sensibility whose layered composition is partly receptive to direct argument and deliberation, partly receptive to tactics that extend beyond the reach of argument, and partly resistant to both.
>
> *(2002: 107)*

Note that we might here perceive a tension between the two elements which are at play, namely practices which build up the habitual ethical 'reflex' arcs, embedded in corporeal dispositions and habit, and the unexpected contingencies to which they have to respond. Indeed, in many ways it might seem that the challenge is in breaking through calcified habitual thought to manifest an openness to new moral demands. Such a perspective would thus juxtapose the futurity of ethical thought, to the enclosed pastness of habit. There is an important concern embedded in this perspective, as much of the analysis I have developed regarding the ethical challenges of an accelerating world has to do with the character of radical futurity which marks it. And yet, to view futurity as opposed to habit is fundamentally to miss the point of Spinoza's critique. For to set up this opposition is to fundamentally conceive of a form of human thought which is *free* from habit, from affect, from bodily practice. The entire point of Spinoza's philosophy is to eschew the fantasy of a fully undetermined human thought. Instead, he counsels us to understand the ways in which affect shapes thought, and to consider how to intervene productively in that affect. As Sharp puts it:

Spinoza does not dismiss every notion of self-government, or self-moderation, but rather denies that we control our affects with non-affects. We do not impose order upon our affects with a different kind of power (e.g., reason). Our power, as well as our lack of power, is to be understood in terms of affect.

(50)

From this perspective, the opposition is not between habit and thought, affects and reason, or, practice and freedom, but between good habits and bad habits, between practices which open us up to the unexpected and practices which close us off. For make no mistake, even though we are talking here about practice producing ethical 'reflex arcs', this is not to say that we are seeking to set up one-size-fits-all responses to ethical quandaries. Quite the opposite. The ethico-affective dispositions which Spinoza is trying to get us to cultivate are based around open affects of love and friendship. They require us to decentre our own expectations and sense of self-identity (his critique of teleological thinking). He counsels a practice which seeks to look at things from other people's perspectives (his emphasis on understanding the necessities which constrain action). Reacting to a novel ethical demand from another by seeking to put ourselves in their shoes, or thinking about how our own privilege or assumptions might blind us to the claim they are placing on us is just as much a learned habit as rejecting the unfamiliar out of hand. This is exactly Spinoza's point. We must train ourselves to do this critical work, to interrogate ourselves, to be open to new demands, or else we will find other habits, bad habits of self-centredness, self-interest, and *ressentiment* to rule our thought and action. To bank on the spontaneous spark of conscience, or the iron-will of reason, is not enough for Spinoza. We must actively cultivate a practice of ethical openness. (Note, we will return to this intersection of habit, futurity, and ethics, in our discussion of Bergson in Chapter 5.)

The Practice of Ethics in Global Politics

Let us consider this image of ethical practice in the context of concerns over the reactionary politics which an accelerating world might give rise to. Here, we might try, in smaller scales and at slower tempos, to practice these ethics, as a way of preparing us for larger and faster venues. For example, in a world of accelerating migrant flows, one might track down narratives of migrant experiences, narratives which provoke affects of sympathy and compassion rather than resentment and revenge. Having encouraged these affects, one might then wish to involve oneself in solidarity movements that seek to provide spaces where migrants are able to give voice to these experiences, and develop networks, cultural artefacts, and media presentations where these narratives can be disseminated more widely, and thus prompt new affective dispositions in a wider audience. One might promote such narratives more widely and, when faced with those promulgating accounts of migration and acceleration premised upon the affects of resentment based on neo-liberal assumptions of 'free choice', challenge them with accounts of the contingent necessities which many migrants face. In doing so, you might shift the affective composition of others, in ways that produce positive feedback loops for individuals and communities.

It is worth noting that the deployment of such affective dispositions is not certain to bring with them ethical behaviour, or not to have unintended consequences. Just as rational thought alone is not enough to ensure ethical behaviour, neither is the engagement with affective registers. Affects and emotions are volatile things, and by engaging with them, we can never be assured of the outcomes that we desire. Indeed, Spinoza, like most good rationalist philosophers, would prefer human beings be perfectly guided by rationality and thinks that, if they were, they would function perfectly according to the dictates of ethics. However, such rational humans are rare, and even the most rational are still finite human bodies subject to emotions. As such, emotions can and must play a key role in bolstering rational critical thought. As Sharp says:

> Adequate ideas in finite intellects may not be robust enough to stand up to the affects that contradict them. True ideas need reinforcement from institutions, joyful passions, and, above all, fellow thinking powers, or they will be easily overwhelmed such that 'often we see the better and follow the worse.
>
> *(78)*

What is more, we must be aware of the different types of affects available to us. Earlier we talked about how interactions with the life-stories of migrants can spark affective responses of pity and sympathy. For Spinoza, these belong to the sad passions, affects that accompany a decrease of our power. And yet, Spinoza is willing to acknowledge that, in certain contexts, sad passions can be useful in prompting ethical behaviour (IV P54S). In the absence of perfect rationality, passive emotions such as hope and fear, sympathy and pity, can play an important role in ethical practice. However, he is also aware that there is a danger in the tactical use of the sad passions. People are subject to compassion fatigue, where constant meditation on the horrors of the world simply exhausts them and leads them to inactivity. (Remember that one of the key elements of an ethical practice is its sustainability. And an ethics that requires of us constant sadness and pity is simply not a sustainable affective disposition to hold.) Also a focus on personal affects of sympathy and pity for individual stories and experiences always runs the risk of: 1) leading us to evaluate people's experiences as 'deserving' and 'undeserving' of our attention based on how much sympathy and pity they produce in us, a problem exacerbated by 2) the fact that, as Spinoza points out, we will always feel more strongly the more we 'imagine a thing like ourselves' (III P27) and hence might be inclined to save our pity and sympathy for those who seem to most closely resemble our own understandings. These factors are limiting in a world of eccentric flows where we will frequently be called upon to engage ethically with people whose lives, cultures, ideologies, experiences, etc., are radically different from our own. Such an orientation would potentially run the risk discussed earlier of making our ethical practice an unthinking habit incapable of responding to the new.

So, affects of sympathy and pity are powerful, and might be important catalysts for seeking to understand the life experiences of others, and treat them not as enemies, but as possible friends. But in and of themselves, they aren't sufficient for producing a sustainable ethico-affective disposition. For that we must turn to the joyful, active passions, the emotions which mark an increase in our power, an expression of our *conatus*, an opening up of our possibilities. Joy and happiness – *hilaritas* in Latin – play a crucial role in Spinoza's ethics (IV P45C2S). The entire point of Spinoza's philosophy is to develop an ethics that has its roots in the joyful expression of the individual (and collective) body. This focus on the joyful goes beyond the personal and aesthetic – which encourages the proliferation of joyful (but always sustainable) encounters which increase the body's power – and infuses his political and ethical commitments, by encouraging the proliferation of joyful encounters between individuals in a growing community or 'multitude' for the purpose of increasing everyone's power. Such encounters are underwritten by joyful affects of love and friendship. The drive to joy is then the ethical drive *par excellence*. As Deleuze says,

> A man who is to become reasonable, strong and free, begins by doing all in his power to experience joyful passions. He then strives to extricate himself from chance encounters and the concatenation of sad passions, to organize good encounters, combine his relation with relations that combine directly with it, unite with what agrees in nature with him, and form a reasonable association between men; all this in such a way as to be affected with joy.
>
> *(1990: 262)*

Our attempts to cultivate an affective disposition capable of meeting the ethical and political challenges of an accelerating world must therefore be based on more than simply a sense of pity and sympathy (although these affects have their place). It must be based on a joyful sense of what kinds of new encounters can be gained from such a world (again, always with an attentiveness to how sustainable these encounters might be). In the case of migration, we might focus not just on our sense of sympathy and pity for the obstacles that these migrants have overcome and how we might help them but also on how we benefit from our encounter with them. We might think of the way in which the introduction of new people and new experiences enrich our community and enlarge our world. We might want to move beyond a paradigm of refugees, asylum and economic migration, and move towards a joyous ethic of welcoming, embracing the mission statement of various anti-deportation and refugee movements around the world with their cry of 'No One is Illegal'.

The Transborder Immigration Tool

An example of what this practice might look like, which brings together the multiple strands of our investigation into speed, the body, affect, and politics, is presented by the work of Ricardo Dominguez working with Electronic Disturbance Theater and the b.a.n.g lab electronic arts centre, in the creation of what they term the Transborder Immigration Tool (TBT).[16] The TBT was developed in response to the deaths of migrants trying to navigate the treacherous terrain between Mexico and the US. It consists of a smartphone with GPS locator technology, loaded with maps of the terrain of the border crossing as well as the paths of major navigable hiking routes and the locations of shelter and, most importantly, sources of water. The TBT then serves as a guide that hopefully helps migrants to safely cross the border. The smartphones are transported to Mexico and donated to migrants planning on making the border crossing. The TBT is described by the initiative as a Mexico/US border disturbance art project. Therefore, in addition to providing an invaluable service in helping migrants make the crossing safely, the group also solicited works of poetry, in English and in Spanish, centring around the themes of travelling and welcoming, which are also loaded on to the phone. These poems are then presented to the migrants at various points in the crossing, intending to provide support and a welcoming during the dangerous trip.

What is brilliant about this project is the way in which it deals in a direct and forceful way with the different encounters between speed and the body. It acknowledges the ways in which the bodies of South and Central American migrants are bound up in, and frequently damaged and destroyed by, the flows of global capitalism and colonial violence. These migrants are buffeted by the flows of global capital, pushed out of their home states by underdevelopment and conflicts which leaves them with few economic options, and pulled to the American context, where a desire for cheap labour creates a twilight economy where migrants are used by the state and market but also marginalized and persecuted. The trajectory of this flow of mobility passes through the harsh physical terrain of the Mexican-American border. The encounter between these global flows and the bodies of these migrants frequently results in death. Here we see the most extreme version of the fears of the first two encounters between speed and the body, with a global acceleration destroying the bodies of migrants.

Dominguez, EDT, and b.a.n.g lab's intervention then seeks to take another fast-moving line, that of advanced information and communication devices (premised upon the commercial availability of the military technologies of satellites and GPS locators), and uses them to reorganize the migrants' encounter with the trajectory across the border, helping them to survive it. What is more, by including the artistic expressions, the poems, and the songs of welcoming, the Transborder Immigration Tool shifts the affective disposition of the entire encounter from one of pity and sympathy to one of joyous welcoming.

If one only stuck to the Gibsonian or Rousseauian perspective of speed technologies, the GPS locator and smartphone would be viewed primarily as one of the lines of advanced info-capitalism, which serves to hollow out and grind down human bodies. But by thinking of speed in terms of disparate lines of resonance, Dominguez and b.a.n.g lab were able to think of these technologies as one node in a larger assemblage. As they put it in their mission statement:

> The Transborder Immigrant Tool would add a new layer of agency to this emerging virtual geography that would allow segments of global society that are usually outside of this emerging grid of hyper-geo-mapping-power to gain quick and simple access to GPS system.

In this context, the smartphone serves as a phase modulator, which takes several disparate rhythms and tempos (global capital mobility, transnational migration, the physical travel of any individual migrant, the actions of US academics and artists, satellite communication devices, etc.) and produces a phase shift which stops this encounter from diminishing or destroying bodies, and instead empowers and supports them. It increases the *conatus* of individuals instead of diminishing or destroying it, and in doing so, increases the power of a community. This is a joyful politics of bodies, and a joyful engagement with an accelerating world. There might be resentment and anger here, at the predation of global capitalism, at the callous indifference and calculated exploitation of governments, at the xenophobic drives of racist and reactionary movements. But this politics does not just stay at this level. It does not allow this resentment to calcify into *ressentiment*. It instead looks for a joyful politics of welcoming and productive intervention.

This is the approach we must take in all of our politics. On the democratic left we spend so much time thinking of what it is that we are seeking to destroy, overcome, challenge, smash (capitalism, patriarchy, racism, homophobia, the State, colonialism, etc.) that we can frequently become oriented away from what it is we are trying to build, from the joyful affects of coming together as a community, as a multitude, and the way in which this encounter with and of the multitude increases our power. This joyful affect of cooperation is a crucial one in the context of the *ressentiment* against speed that calls into being despotic and tyrannical drives for certitude. We must therefore develop dispositions that reaffirm our commitment to the joys of cooperation.

Practices, Politics, and Living at Speed

The practices I have discussed earlier might be directed towards oneself, modifying one's own affects and corporeal dispositions, or to others, by trying to inculcate and provoke new dispositions in them. A Spinozistic approach provides us with tools both for maintaining ethical practice in ourselves, as well as trying to encourage it in others. Bill Connolly calls this application of Spinozistic practices more broadly a program of micropolitics, a politics focused not on molar aggregates of state and party but an intervention at the molecular level of bodies and feelings.

> You can think of micropolitics, in the Deleuzian sense, as a cultural collectivization and politicization of arts of the self. Micropolitics applies tactics to multiple layers of intersubjective being. Because it is often practiced in competitive settings, it contains an agonistic element. The assemblage to which such micropolitical tactics are applied might be a small group, a large constituency, or an interdependent constellation of people holding divergent position on issues in need of general resolution. Arts of the self and micropolitics are ubiquitous in cultural life, even though they also stand in a relation of torsion to each other.
>
> *(2002: 108)*

Thus, following from one of the examples earlier, we might think about the micropolitics of creating spaces and media which disseminate the stories of migrants in their own voices. Such a practice could serve the purpose of inculcating new affective dispositions in constituencies who might historically have had no exposure to such stories or experiences. Or we might think of the TBT as a provocation, forcing attention to the dangers and difficulties of the desert crossings, and the network of global flows which make them necessary.

We might feel somewhat uncomfortable with the idea of engaging in a politics of affect. In a political and cultural environment still ruled by the ideas of the enlightenment, with its focus on rational political discourse and eschewing emotions, the use of affect to alter politics feels, at best, sneaky and underhanded. At worst, it seems to link up with the large scale affective and corporeal mobilizations of various fascisms. By attempting to engage people at the affective and corporeal level, aren't we trying to circumvent their rational thought? How does this differ from the sketchy politics of thought control and demagoguery?

Such concerns are valid, and certainly we should be aware of the ways in which various forms of affective and corporeal politics have been deployed in the past (and we should always be concerned with the ethical implications of our political tactics, whatever they may be). However, this argument becomes much less powerful when we reject its major implicit assumption, that there can be political practices that do not have affective or corporeal effects. As

Spinoza tells us, there is always an emotional component to rational thought. The mind is not an autonomous cartesian substance. Rather, mind is only one modal expression of the same substance as the body. If ought implies can, then there can be no moral imperative to avoid engaging politically with the affects and bodies of others because this is impossible. Our encounters will always be affectively charged and corporeally mediated. As such, our only choice is whether we will have these encounters wilfully, thoughtfully, and ethically, or unthinkingly. Furthermore, as Connolly points out earlier, practices of the self and micropolitics are ubiquitous in life. The world is a collection of warring assemblages, each attempting to inculcate different affective and corporeal dispositions and create different composite bodies. If those on the left cede the terrain of affect and the body (not to mention the terrain of speed and technology), we will simply leave more space for those who *are* willing. We have already discussed the way in which the tyrannical state is dependent upon the creation and maintenance of certain affective dispositions, and the capitalist axiomatic long ago learned the importance of micropolitics to maintain its viability. If a democratic, egalitarian, and pluralistic politics is to have any chance, it must be willing to engage in the messy, dangerous but also fruitful politics of the body. It must simply make sure that it does so in a way that is consonant with its ethical principles. Once again, Spinoza's work can guide us. He points out the importance of building a politics of the body which focuses on the joyous affects and avoids the sad affects of fear, anxiety, hatred, or resentment.

Is there the danger of these kinds of interventions lapsing into a paternalistic politics in which we are attempting to act 'in the best interest' of others? Of course. How could there not be? Any engagement with others will always be riven by alternate conceptions of the good life, which might come into conflict. But in attempting to aid and encourage ethical sensibilities in others, we can be guided by Spinoza's conception of *conatus* which carries with it no set model of what the good life looks like. Instead, the conception of *conatus* is always premised upon a question of increasing power, of increasing options. We must seek to encourage affective and corporeal positions that provide agents with more possibilities of affecting and being affected. This means not just increasing their power but also increasing their options and opportunities for articulating their own desires and conceptions of the good life. And such articulations must play a role in setting the agenda for communal activity. Remember, for Spinoza, the most important expression of *conatus* is the creation of a community, a multitude, and that multitude must be constantly engaged in a democratic process of self-definition and self-empowerment. As Sharp puts it,

> Prompted by our more or less accurate notions of the joys and aversions of our fellows, we aim to please them, which, by definitions, comprises an effort to be a source of power for them. If we succeed in generating joy, we contribute to the perfection of others and are in turn enabled by (and

experience love for) them. Thus, according to Spinoza, the very effort to empower oneself is objectively inextricable from enabling others, even if one's subjective purpose is often quite different. Finitude is such that one cannot be powerful without fortifying others as well.

(141)

Such an understanding of *conatus* breaks down the distinction I maintain earlier, that between individual practices of the self and collective micropolitics, as well as the unidirectional flow such a politics seemed to produce. Instead, what we see developing is a communal affective politics in which a multitude attempts to develop a politics of the joyous affects, of love and friendship, and thus increase the *conatus* of all members of the community, even while acknowledging that, in an imperfect world, the ability of political agents to express their *conatus* will be widely varied and hierarchically organized. In such contexts, it is the ethical responsibility of those who find themselves in privileged conditions to do what they can to remove policies, institutions, affective dispositions, etc., which might inhibit the expression of the *conatus* of other members of the community, either current or potential (hence Dominguez's Transborder Immigration Tool). If we do not, then we become unwitting tyrants, with our own power premised upon the sad passions of other members of our community (even members we might not acknowledge as parts of our communities).

I acknowledge that I have provided very little in the way of concrete examples of what these various practices of the self and micropolitics might be (not to mention what kinds of technological 'phase modulators' might be available to us to increase the number of joyous encounters between speed and the body). There are at least two reasons for this. First, these practices will always be singular, seeking to intervene in a particular political issue, and related to a dense network of different assemblages. As such, creating abstract examples before the fact will not necessarily be useful. My goal here has primarily been to encourage us to be attentive to this dimension of politics in an accelerating world. By doing so, we might hopefully become aware of what kinds of affective and corporeal dispositions are politically active in the world, and how we might intervene in them.

And this leads us to the last point that I want to make, mainly that I can't provide too extensive a list of practices for the simple reason that the analysis that I have developed in this chapter speaks to the need for an experimental orientation to a politics of speed and the body. This is because of the twin natures of both speed and the body. If we assume that we understand the 'natural' and absolute tempos of things, and how they must essential interact, we are trapped in the first story of speed and the body, assuming that once human bodies travel beyond a certain velocity, they must surely disintegrate. Now, once again, this is not to say that there can't be harmful encounters between speed and the body. But assuming we know beforehand what these encounters will be, or what the 'natural' tempos of the body are absolutely, ignores the complex networks of composite bodies – the complex relations of motion-and-rest – which bodies are always bound up in. As Spinoza says, 'nobody as yet has learned from experience what the body can and cannot do' (III P2S). Certainly, we can make educated guesses, learn from the past, and seek to predict the future. But we must always be open to the fruitful and unexpected encounters.

And this openness to the future is also called for by the nature of speed. As we said, if we are to live in an accelerating world, we must be open to contingency, futurity, and exteriority which it brings into being. If we become too sure about the 'natural tempos' we are used to, too attached to the narratives we project into the future, too guarded about the boundaries which we feel secure us, we will be primed to lapse into *ressentiment* when these are inevitably challenged. To live ethically in an accelerating world means to adopt an experimental mindset, to be willing to adapt and change, to live at multiple different tempos, and in multiple different spaces. (Notice how this is also Spinoza's conception of what democracy looks like. Never a set of eternal principles, but instead an always self-defining community existing and unfolding in open time.) It is thus a remarkable bit of luck that what is necessary for living ethically in an accelerating world is also what is best for expressing our body's *conatus*. To return once more to Antonio Damasio:

> Fluid life states are naturally preferred by our *conatus*. We gravitate towards them. Strained life states are naturally avoided by our *conatus*. We stay away. We can sense these relationships, and we can verify that in the trajectory of our lives fluid life states that feel positive come to be associated with events that we call good, while strained life states that feel negative come to be associated with evil.
>
> *(2003: 131–2)*[17]

A life which is too constrained, which clings too tightly to one set of circumstances, one rhythm, one trajectory, is bad for *conatus*, bad for the body, bad for ethics, and bad for politics. As I said, a remarkable bit of luck. Or, if we are to pay attention to Spinoza, not really a matter of luck at all. For if ethics is always fundamentally about increasing our power as well as increasing the power of those around us, our openness to speed, to uncertainty, to new possibilities, and to democracy are – like mind and body – simply different aspects of the same substance. No one has yet learned how fast the body can or cannot go. For the sake of our bodies, our politics, and our ethics, we must be willing to take this as a challenge and an invitation.

Notes

1. Hampshire concurs, saying 'Spinoza will not allow any mention of design or of final causes in the study of Nature' (114).

2. As Sharp says,

> Existence for Spinoza is horizontal. The infinite creative force of nature is not separable from the infinitely many beings that exist. Humanity receives no special metaphysical value and no privileged place in nature. Spinoza's naturalism denies human exceptionalism in any form. Like any other thing in nature, humans are corporeal and ideal, ineluctably immersed in a system of cause and effect, and each of us comprises a power that is infinitely surpassed by the totality of other beings.
>
> *(2)*

3. We can see here a strong connection between Spinoza and Nietzsche's metaphysics, something that Nietzsche himself identified (Wollenberg 2013: 617–8).
4. See also her discussion of teleology in (1995: 25–6).
5. Says Michael Mack:

> Teleological thought pitches the telos of one community against that of another. The difference in religious worship thus furthers war between different social units, each of which deifies its specific way of life that goes along with its specific (anthropomorphic) conception of God. Under this teleological – theological constellation, particularity comes into conflict with universality.
>
> *(2011: 112)*

6. See Macherey (2011: 153).
7. We will return to the question of meditation and shaping our orientation to the nature of time in Chapter 5.
8. See (Glezos 2012: Ch. 4).
9. We should not, from this, presume that face-to-face encounters automatically foster empathy. Hall (2007) describes how guards in a British detainment centre for refugee claimants treat the detainees with fear and contempt. At the same time, she also describes how, in what we will see is a very Spinozist way,

> Periodically, the officers have cause to recognise that the detainees – far from being wholly other, dangerous, threatening – are *just like them* (and vice versa). Glimpses of mutuality may be found in a conversation about cricket, excitement at a football match, a shared joke. More than this, the imagination of similarity can 'creep upon' detainees and staff in an emergent fragile empathy.
>
> *(30)*

10. Note, this is not to ignore other factors which might contribute to first world agents rejecting the claims of refugees or other migrants, such as economic incentives, previously existing racist or xenophobic beliefs, etc. It is rather to see how such discourses and structures have an affective dimension, which can potentially be reinforced or disrupted.
11. Although this shouldn't be taken to suggest that there aren't economic reasons driving many, or even most migrants, or that these economic reasons make these migrants somehow illegitimate. Quite the opposite. The need to act in the face of economic necessity is one which we all understand. As Zygmunt Baumann quite eloquently puts it

> The wish of the hungry to go where food is plentiful is what one would naturally expect from rational human beings; letting them act on their wishes is also what conscience would suggest is the right, moral thing to do. It is because of the undeniable rationality and ethical correctness that the rational and ethically conscious world feels so crestfallen in the face of the prospect

of the mass migration of the poor and hungry; it is so difficult, without feeling guilty to deny the poor and hungry their right to go where food is more
plentiful.

(1998: 76)

It is the brilliance of neoliberal discourse and reactionary political orientations to
allow us to do just that, to conceive of this most natural of human behaviours, and
treat it as illegitimate, or indeed even threatening.

12. Putting these encounters in perspective, we can look to Sharp's account of the role
of speech in Spinoza saying,

> Speech is liberating . . . only when we cease to see it as free. When we see
> words as bodily motions caused by our mutual involvement with one another,
> we can discover ourselves, not as individuals, but as situated within a complex
> constellation of causes. We can then, together, endeavour to transform that
> environment and build the conditions of genuine freedom, which will nec-
> essarily be a freedom of degree rather than an absolute power to determine
> ourselves. Deliberation and communication might be interesting . . . not pri-
> marily for the content of the words uttered, but for the affects they uncover
> and the energetic resources they foreclose or offer to a community.
>
> *(52–53)*

13. In many ways these two moves in Spinoza are both attacking the same target, the
twinned concepts of the sovereign god and sovereign 'man' of early modern philosophy. As Montag puts it:

> The God who lies beyond the (material) world and is free to direct it accord-
> ing to his unconditioned will is thus the mirror image of the man who tran-
> scends the physical world and governs his own body with absolute mastery,
> itself a mirror image of god: a vicious theological/ anthropological circle.
>
> *(39)*

14. This list could extend almost infinitely, to include policy choices such as seeking to
ameliorate global climate change and other ecological disasters which tend to have
a greater impact on poorer states in the Global South, rethinking approaches to the
so-called 'war on drugs', etc.

15. Note once again we are not talking about a biological reductionism, where laws
and institutions find their roots in bodies and brains and genes and evolution.
Rather we are discussing the way in which emergent encounters *between* bodies,
brains, affects, ideologies, discourses, institutions, laws, etc., produce particular
outcomes. No one component is determinative, but to ignore crucial components
such as affect and bodies (as much political theory does) is to leave us ill-equipped
to enact the political and ethical commitments which we might hold dear.

16. The following summary was drawn from the original Transborder Immigrant Tool
website at http://bang.calit2.net/xborderblog/. Information about the TBT is now
available at https://faculty.washington.edu/michamc/wordpress-bang/. See, also, the
e-book published by CTheory at http://pactac.net/ctheory-books/blueshift-series/
the-transborder-immigrant-toolla-herramienta-transfronteriza-para-inmigrantes/

17. For a similar claim from a sociological perspective, see (Garhammer 2002).

Works Cited

Bauman, Z. (1998) *Globalization: The Human Consequences*, New York: Columbia University Press.

Brown, W. (1995) *States of Injury*, Princeton, NJ: Princeton University Press.

Connolly, W. (2002) *Neuropolitics: Thinking, Culture, Speed*, Minneapolis: University of Minnesota.

Damasio, A. (2003) *Looking for Spinoza*, New York, NY: Harcourt.

Deleuze, G. (1988) *Spinoza: Practical Philosophy*, Trans. R. Hurley, San Francisco, CA: City Lights Books.

Deleuze, G. (1990) *Expressionism in Philosophy: Spinoza*, Trans. M. Joughin, Brooklyn, NY: Zone Books.

Garhammer, M. (2002) 'Pace of Life and Enjoyment of Life', *Journal of Happiness Studies*, 3(3): 217–56.

Glezos, S. (2011) 'The Ticking Bomb: Speed, Liberalism and Ressentiment against the Future', *Contemporary Political Theory*, 10(2): 147–65.

Glezos, S. (2012) *The Politics of Speed: Capitalism, The State, and War in an Accelerating World*, Abingdon, UK: Routledge.

Hall, A. (2007) '"These People Could Be Anyone": Fear, Contempt (and Empathy) in a British Immigration Removal Centre', *Emotions and Human Mobility: Ethnographies of Movement*, ed. M. Svašek, Abingdon, UK: Routledge.

Hampshire, S. (2005) *Spinoza and Spinozism*, Oxford: Oxford University Press.

Macherey, P. (2011) *Hegel or Spinoza*, Trans. S. M. Ruddick, Minneapolis: University of Minnesota.

Mack, M. (2011) 'Towards an Inclusive Universalism: Spinoza's Ethics of Sustainability', *Spinoza Now*, ed. D. Vardoulakis, Minneapolis: University of Minnesota Press.

Montag, W. (1999) *Bodies, Masses, Power: Spinoza and His Contemporaries*, London: Verso.

Nietzsche, F. (1997) *On the Genealogy of Morality*, Trans. C. Diethe, Cambridge: Cambridge University Press.

Nyers, P. (2003) 'Abject Cosmopolitanism: The Politics of Protection in the Anti-Deportation Movement', *Third World Quarterly*, 24(6): 1069–93.

Sharp, H. (2011) *Spinoza and the Politics of Renaturalization*, Chicago: University of Chicago Press.

Spinoza, B. (1982) *The Ethics and Selected Letters*, Trans. S. Shirley. Indianapolis: Hackett.

Vardoulakis, D. (Ed.) (2011) *Spinoza Now*, Minneapolis: University of Minnesota Press.

Wollenberg, D. (2013) 'Nietzsche, Spinoza and Moral Affects', *Journal of the History of Philosophy*, 51(4): 617–49.

PART II
Speed and Perception

4

DESPISERS OF THE POSTHUMAN BODY

Speed, Perception, and Disembodiment

Speed not only allows us to get around more easily; it enables us above all to see, to hear, to perceive and thus to conceive the present world more intensely. Tomorrow, it will enable us to act at a distance, beyond the human body's sphere of influence and that of its behavioural ergonomics . . .

. . . Doomed to inertia, the interactive being transfers his natural capacities for movement and displacement to probes and scanners which instantaneously inform him about a remote reality, to the detriment of his own faculties of apprehension of the real, after the example of the para- or quadriplegic who can guide by remote control – teleguide – his environment, his abode, which is a model of that home automation, of those 'Smart Houses' that respond to our every whim. Having been first *mobile*, then *motorized*, man will thus become *motile*, deliberately limiting his body's area of influence to a few gestures, a few impulses, like channel surfing.

(Virilio 2008: 12, 15–17)

In Chapter 2 we introduced what we termed the prostheticizing/parasitizing image of speed, the image of speed technologies as prosthetics which, as they are grafted on to the human body, begin to sap its vitality and hollow it out. In that discussion, only passing reference was made to the dominant contemporary theorist of the prostheticizing/parasitizing effects of technology, Paul Virilio. In the quote earlier, Virilio charts the ways in which he believes the acceleration of transportation and communication technologies paradoxically make us more immobile. For Virilio, speed technologies turn the healthy human body into a paraplegic or quadriplegic body, reliant on prosthetics.[1] Note, however, that, in the passage earlier, his focus is not, primarily, upon transportation technologies. Rather, the question of the prostheticization/parasitization of the human body is closely linked to information and communication technologies (ICTs). It is our ability to gain information – to *see* beyond ourselves – that introduces a fundamental gap into the human body; a hole poked in the body, through which the mind drains away. Transportation technologies – even the most accelerated – still physically shift the body in space, forcing us to always take ourselves with us. It is ICTs that allow/require us to leave our bodies behind. Thus, in Virilio's account, it is not a transportation technology that introduces the fateful schism, but an ocular one.

> Just when we were apparently procuring the means to see further and better the unseen of the universe, we were about to lose what little power we had of imagining it. The telescope, that epitome of the visual prosthesis, projected an image of a world beyond our reach and thus another way of moving about in the world, the *logistics of perception* inaugurating an unknown conveyance of sight that produced a telescoping of near and far, a *phenomenon of acceleration* obliterating our experience of distances and dimensions.
>
> *(1994: 4)*

As our communication technologies accelerate, as our eyes roam further (and faster) than our bodies, they become an autonomous force in the world, part of a grander 'Vision Machine' as Virilio puts it.

> *Everything I see is in principle within my reach, at least within reach of my sight, marked on the map of the 'I can'.* In this important formulation, Merleau-Ponty pinpoints precisely what will eventually find itself ruined by the banalization of a certain teletopology. The bulk of what I see is, in fact and in principle, no longer within my reach. And even if it lies within reach of my sight, it is no longer necessarily inscribed on the map of the 'I can'. The logistics of perception in fact destroy what earlier modes of representation preserved of this original, ideally human happiness, the 'I can' of sight.
>
> *(7)*

ICTs are, for Virilio, a fundamentally *disembodying* force. And though this process was inaugurated with the ocular technologies of the telescope and the microscope, digital technologies have only accelerated matters. This is because where previous technologies increased the scope of perception, advanced ICTs carry with them the possibility of increasing the pace of perception. This has to do both with the pace at which information is collected (and therefore the amount of it which is collected), and the speed at which it is analyzed. Virilio points out that data collection and analysis are increasingly automated. Virilio, of course, is concerned with military matters, such as targeting and tracking, but we could just as easily point to technologies which track and analyze any number of phenomena from weather systems, to stock markets, to 'suspicious' persons. In all of these systems, the process of perception isn't just extended in space; it is intensified in time, taking in, and analyzing, information much more quickly than any human could.

> These synthetic-perception machines will be capable of replacing us in certain domains, in certain ultra high-speed operations for which our own visual capacities are inadequate, not because of our ocular system's limited depth of focus, as was the case with the telescope and the microscope, but because of the limited depth of time of our physiological 'take'.
>
> *(61)*

In such a context, it is increasingly not just the body that is left behind but the mind as well, in the sense of that which absorbs and analyzes the information which perception acquires. Mark B. N. Hansen provides a gloss on the previous passage which explains just how radical Virilio views this shift to be; that it describes the final point of the disembodiment of perception, in which the human is completely split off from the perceptual process.

> In contrast to earlier visual technology like the telescope and the microscope . . . which function by *extending* the physiological capacities of the body, contemporary vision machines bypass our physiology (and its constitutive limits) entirely. What is important is not just that machines will take our place in certain 'ultra high-speed operations', but the rationale informing this displacement: they will do so 'not because of our ocular system's limited depth of focus . . . but because of the limited *depth of time* of our physiological "take"'. In short, what we face in today's vision-machines is the threat of *total* irrelevance: because our bodies cannot keep pace with the speed of (technical) vision, we literally cannot see what the machine can see, and we thus risk being left out of the perceptual loop altogether.
>
> *(2006: 103)*

As we saw in Chapter 2, Virilio's perception of advanced ICTs as a fundamentally disembodying and dehumanizing force in the world is one that is shared by a host of other critics.[2]

What is more, we should not be surprised by how widely held this position is, as it is, in many ways, the flipside of what many boosters of those same ICTs maintain. A focus on the disembodying effects of ICTs is just as common amongst technophiles, but here the tale is intended to invoke liberation rather than denigration. Liberation from the awkward constraints of space, from the limitations of the flesh. Adrian Mackenzie gives a lovely account of how these themes play out in a set of ads for Toshiba computers, selling that most liberating of technologies, 'wireless internet'.

> In 2003, Toshiba laptop advertisements showed a man usually alone in remote locations, although he was occasionally at work in a casually stylish office meeting. He stood on a rocky promontory beside a storm-tossed sea, he sat in a treehouse looking down on the children playing in a sun-filled backyard, he looked out from a platform high above a sports stadium, or he lay on the grass in the middle of a park on a fine day. It was hard to tell who was working and who was not since these men were not obviously dressed for work. Each time, he looked at a laptop screen on which some other photographic image had been graphically superimposed: an office full of people, a library stocked with books, a scene from an action film. In each case, the superimposed image was somewhat incongruous with the geographic location. The freedom to connect 'in new places' that intel's promotions refer to recurs across many different corporate promotions of wi-fi. An affirmation of 'freedom' − 'enter the world of free computing' . . . 'lose the wires, be free' . . . is attached to an absence of wires. Not having to plug a computer into a socket in the wall to do e-mail, download files, or surf the Web, means that the screen loses its moorings and begins to float around. The socket in the wall to which screens are tethered dissolves. In other words, for the unwired user, the relation between screen and fixed infrastructure changes. Communication is no longer incarcerated, connectivity become quasi-independent of location, and in this liberated space, others become somewhat invisible.
>
> *(2010: 103)*

This image of ICTs producing a radical disarticulation of space will be unsurprising to anyone even remotely familiar with the tropes of contemporary info-capitalism. In this world, as Virilio has diagnosed, space becomes secondary to time and dromography replaces geography. This process is presented as not just de-spatializing or de-materializing; it is also dis-embodying. Note that, in the narrative earlier, it is not just that there is a disjuncture between the location outside the screen and the location in the screen but also a dislocation between the posture and styling of the body of the screen's owner, and the contents of the screen. This is the significance of Mackenzie's telling insight that 'these men were not obviously dressed for work'. Though the body might be at play, the mind is at work (or vice-versa). The extension of the senses through the digital network is thus also the sheering off of the mind from the body, the radical disembodiment of accelerative technologies. Indeed, this kind of separation is necessary in a world in which business happens − to quote the title of Bill Gates' book − '@ the speed of thought' (1999). This account, of course, doesn't go as far as Virilio's, arguing for human obsolescence in the context of accelerating ICTs. In these accounts, it is exactly human mastery which is promised, through overcoming the limitations of world and flesh, and 'entering the world of free computing'.

This image of ICTs as a disembodying, and therefore liberating, force has deeper roots than contemporary advertisements. In many ways, this narrative entered collective consciousness through William Gibson's landmark cyberpunk work, *Neuromancer* where the term 'cyberspace' was invented.

> Cyberspace. A consensual hallucination experienced daily by billions of legitimate operators, in every nation, by children being taught mathematical concepts. . . . A graphic representation of data abstracted from the banks of every computer in the human system. Unthinkable complexity. Lines of light ranged in the nonspace of the mind, clusters and constellations of data.
>
> *(52)*

Though Gibson can hardly be presented as an unreflective technophile (still less as a shill for late modern infocapitalism), the language of this description – with its invocation of cyberspace as a 'nonspace of the mind' – played a crucial role in providing our culture with a visual imaginary for increasingly prevalent digital networks. Gibson equated the engagement with digital information networks as a process of *disembodiment* and *virtualization*. As N. Katherine Hayles notes, as a society we have responded to these networks with a tendency to think in terms of the primacy and independence of flows of information and perception over the materiality of space and body.

> Especially for users who may not know the material processes involved, the impression is created that pattern is predominant over presence. From here it is a small step to perceiving information as more mobile, more important, more *essential* than material forms. When this impression becomes part of your cultural mindset, you have entered the condition of virtuality.
>
> *(1999: 19)*

To employ this trope of virtuality is almost always to speak in a language of disembodiment (and the liberation or capture that disembodiment brings). Hayles points to a strain of social and scientific thought that 'construct[s] virtuality . . . as a metanarrative about the transformation of the human into a disembodied posthuman' (22). Hayles discusses the fundamentally disembodying assumptions of this metanarrative, noting 'the posthuman view privileges informational patterns over material instantiation, so that embodiment in a biological substrate is seen as an accident of history rather than an inevitability of life' (2).

However, though this narrative has unquestionably intensified with the digital revolution, we should not think that this desire for (or fear of) liberation through disembodiment is a new trend. Laura Ephraim does an exceptional job of noting how, in the 19th century, the telegraph was hailed as a fundamentally disembodying technology. As she puts it,

> With the advent of the telegraph in 1837 and its subsequent expansion and popularization, many Victorian Brits and Americans experienced a new and deepened hybridity between themselves and an electronic instrument. They responded to their real or perceived connections with the telegraph with new and sometimes fantastic visions of human thought's liberation from the limitations of the human body.
>
> *(4)*

Indeed, much of the contemporaneous discourse around the telegraph mimicked the disembodying language which accompanies contemporary accounts of digital technologies, as commentators argued that the

> electronic transmission of messages cut the tie between the communication of thought and the transportation of bodies and objects, and seemed to herald the liberation of human consciousness itself from the material body, stuck as it is in time and space.
>
> *(8)*[3]

Indeed, beyond such particular technological instantiations, the will to disembodiment, to liberation from the constraints of materiality and corporeality is at least as old as Western philosophy itself. We can think here of our discussion of Plato's *Gorgias* in the introduction, with its privileging of the world of being over the world of becoming, and his pursuit of the life of the mind over the bodily pleasures.[4] We should also raise Descartes contribution to modernity, through his ontological division of the world into extended matter and unextended spirit, thus providing the foundations for a model of thought, perception, and *information* untainted by corporeality.

One of the roots of this will to disembodiment can be found in Nietzsche's account of *ressentiment*. In *Thus Spake Zarathustra*, Nietzsche discusses the 'despisers of the body' (146), those so resentful over the suffering they feel that they wish to cast off the constraints of this body. Nietzsche describes this *ressentiment* fuelled rejection of the body, saying that it is a '[d]runken joy . . . for the sufferer to look away from his suffering and to lose himself' (143). While Nietzsche primarily discusses the despisers of the body in relation to metaphysical and theological beliefs, we can also see its technological instantiation articulated in thinkers such as Virilio. Virilio notes how the disembodying tendencies of contemporary technologies serve to soothe the suffering of *ressentiment*, allowing us to escape the bodies that thwart our desires for absolute control – both our own, and others'.

> To prefer the virtual being – at some remove – to the real being – close up – is to take the shadow for the substance, to prefer the metaphor, the clone to a substantial being who gets in your way, who is literally on your hands, a flesh-and-blood being whose only fault is to be there, here and now, and not somewhere else. . . . Mysteriously the science of machines exiles us both from the geophysical world and from the physical body of another who always contradicts my ego.
>
> *(2008: 103–4, 113)*

The technological thus gives us the opportunity of overcoming our suffering exactly to the extent that it virtualizes us, liberates us from the intransigence of world and flesh. In this regard, Nietzsche and Virilio are united in their diagnosis of the roots of this will to disembodiment. However, there is a crucial point of contention between the two. Where Virilio thinks this will to disembodiment is achievable (indeed, given the pace of technological development, it is, for him, almost inevitable), for Nietzsche it is not. Virilio claims that

> the goal of science and technology has indeed now been attained. To eradicate the gap, to put an end to the scandal of the interval of space and time that used to separate man so unacceptably from his objective: all this is well on the way to being achieved.
>
> *(119)*

Conversely, Nietzsche wants to make clear that, as much as the despisers of the body might wish the body away, the body will always be there. Indeed, the will to disembodiment is itself an effect of the body.

> Believe me, my brothers: it was the body that despaired of the body and touched the ultimate walls with the fingers of a deluded spirit. Believe me, my brothers: it was the body that despaired of the earth and heard the belly of being speak to it. It wanted to crash through these ultimate walls with its head, and not only with its head – over there to 'that world.' But 'that world' is well concealed from humans – that dehumanized inhuman world which is a heavenly nothing; and the belly of being does not speak to humans at all, except as a human.
>
> *(1976: 143–4)*

In line with our discussions of Spinoza and Damasio in the previous chapter, Nietzsche too is aware of exactly how much mental activity goes on below the surface of consciousness, aware of the role which somatic affect plays in the thinking process.

> 'Body am I, and soul' – thus speaks the child. And why should one not speak like children? But the awakened and knowing say: body am I entirely, and nothing else; and soul is only a word for something about the body . . . behind your thoughts and feelings, my brother, there stands a mighty ruler, and unknown sage – whose name is self. In your body he dwells; he is your body. There is more reason in your body than in your best wisdom.
>
> *(146–147)*

What this means is that, even as we are struck by the desire to cast off our body, this affective *ressentiment* itself springs from our bodies. Wherever we go, there we are.

> It was the sick and decaying who despised body and earth and invented the heavenly realm and the redemptive drops of blood: but they took even these sweet and gloomy poisons from body and earth. They wanted to escape their own misery, and the stars were too far for them. So they sighed: 'Would that there were heavenly ways to sneak into another state of being and happiness!' Thus they invented their sneaky ruses and bloody potions. Ungrateful, these people deemed themselves transported from their bodies and this earth. But to whom did they owe the convulsions and raptures of their transport? To their bodies and this earth.
>
> *(144–145)*

Indeed, as much as Virilio fears the prostheticization of the body through speed, and as much as capitalist rhetoric, Western metaphysics, and some strains of contemporary techno-science glory in the possibility of casting off the slow and cumbersome constraints of world and flesh, the fact is, the body – materiality, corporeality – simply cannot be left behind. Note, this is not to say that the body cannot be changed – or, perhaps better that patterns of embodiment can't shift and transform in the face of technological (not to mention political, economic, social, and cultural) change. As we discussed in Chapter 2, the emergence and evolution of the body, brain and subjectivity has been co-eval with technological innovation (what Bernard Stiegler calls our 'technogenesis' [1998: 45]). Thus, while technophiles predict our imminent virtualization in ICTs and digital networks, providing succour for those despisers of the body who dream of an end to their suffering, such dreams ignore the fundamental materiality and corporeality of the processes of perception and thought, even in the context of digital acceleration.[5]

Remember, in her comment earlier, Hayles made it clear that 'for users who may not know the material processes involved, the impression is created that pattern is predominant over presence' (1999: 19). What this means is that the technophile's dreams, and Virilio's fears, are premised not on a real disembodiment but rather on a cultural, social, economic, and technological narrative which lets us *imagine* that our bodies have disappeared. But this is really just a case of 'out of sight, out of mind'. Even a cursory glance at the material characteristics of contemporary ICTs and digital networks brings us crashing back to earth (and into our bodies). And this is true from multiple perspectives and at multiple scales.

For example, even as Virilio talks of fundamental changes to human society through ICTs and digital networks, we know that their distribution and penetration is far from universal. Large asymmetries of access exist – both between the global north and south, and within each – in the so-called 'digital divide'. For example, in 2011, in the developing world there were 73.8 internet users for every 100 people; in the developing world that number was 26.3.[6]

But more than this, to speak of virtuality, of a speed that lets you leave behind the body, is only possible by ignoring the materiality of the technologies that make possible the delirious speeds of ICTs and digital networks. Indeed, there is something similar here to Nietzsche's account of the formation of consciousness through the force of 'forgetfulness'. According to Nietzsche, for our consciousness to emerge as a seemingly free, wilful, *unextended spirit*, it must first forget the role that the body plays in cognition, 'shut the doors and windows of consciousness for a while; not to be bothered by the noise and battle with which our underworld of serviceable organs work with and against each other; a little peace, a little *tabula rasa* of consciousness' (1997: 35). Similarly, for us to imagine digital networks as a gateway to virtuality we must forget the vast material infrastructure which is necessary to make such accelerations of perception possible. And to conceive this process as a liberating one we must ignore the ways in which these material infrastructures have just as many constraints built into them as the 'physical spaces' which Toshiba promises to free us from. It is true, Virilio recognizes the constraining effects of digital networks but simply inverts the relationship, pairing off this constrained, automatized, prostheticized body to the free, natural, healthy, non-pathological body. In both cases the mind/perception is independent, but for Virilio it needs a 'pure' vessel within which to function or else it becomes distorted and constrained.[7] In both cases, there is the aura of a *ressentiment* which seeks to posits a state or a space free of struggle, of suffering, a state in which we are no longer constrained, in which we are free. But, understanding the experiences of thought and perception which we call 'virtual' requires an understanding of the materiality of both world and flesh.

On the one hand, we must pay careful attention to the physical infrastructure which makes possible these experiences. The technics and politics of where fiberoptic cables are laid (and, of course, where it is not, as questions of the digital divide so clearly spell out), and what amount of bandwidth is available, and to whom. Mackenzie points out the way in which dreams of ubiquitous connectivity and virtuality are stymied by the so-called 'last-mile' problem, the fact that

> while central infrastructures and network backbones can mostly be con-
> structed speedily and expediently, the sheer number and variety of con-
> nections needed to hook every room, desk, village, chair, building, bag,
> pocket, pole, cabin, footpath, or other place to a telecommunications
> network often entail vast expense, upheavals, or complications.
>
> *(2010: 7)*

Mackenzie also points out that even 'wireless' internet access, the technology which Toshiba (amongst others) claims will allow us to 'lose the wires [and] be free', is itself dependent on a network of antennae that are profoundly 'local' and 'wired'.

> An antenna is a geographic-topographic construct. The very calculations
> that determine how high, how big, and what shape and size it should be,
> all relate to geography and signal propagation. And this is not a geogra-
> phy seen from on high, but a geography lived as landscape or place, since
> it is sensitive to obstacles, barriers, heights, depths, nearness, and distance.
>
> *(2010: 125)*[8]

And this relates not just to the large fixed antennae but also to the smaller, frequently hidden ones in our mobile devices. Indeed, though these devices make us connected to a seemingly virtual and global network, they also make us paradoxically more attuned to our location, as we become aware of spaces which might inhibit our 'signal strength' such as underground park-ing garages, skyscrapers, rural areas, or buildings with heavy electromagnetic interference.[9]

Nor does an attentiveness to the materiality of perception in the context of ICTs stop with questions of hardware. Software too plays a crucial role in shaping and constraining thought and perception. We must be attentive to what kinds of codes and architectures underlie communications networks, and thus who can communicate (not to mention how we can, and who is watching when we do). As Lawrence Lessig points out, 'code is law' (2006). While code might provide for more or less free communication and interaction, it will never allow for 'free' communication and thought. Furthermore, the impact of software exists not just at the layer of invisible protocols and codes, but at the most immediate level of the human-computer interface. Far from freeing our minds through virtual universality and 'absolute speed', these interfaces necessarily shape and constrain perception – and thus thought – in key ways. As Lev Manovitch puts it in his analysis of new media,

> As is the case with all cultural representations, new media representations are also inevitably biased. They represent/construct some features of physical reality at the expense of other, one worldview among many, one possible system of categories among numerous others . . . software interface[s] – both those of operating systems and of software applications – also act as representations. That is, by organizing data in a particular way, they privilege particular models of the world and the human subject.
>
> *(2001: 15–16)*

Note here the invocation of a 'worldview', a particular worldview. The benefits of a virtual nonplace, the advantages of a perception that see at 'absolute speed' is supposed to be its very lack of both 'world' and 'view'. And yet Manovich reminds us that where there is aesthetics (as there surely is in cyberspace) there is always already an embodied perception.

And this brings us to the second sphere of materiality we must be attentive to when investigating the constrained nature of perception and thought in relation to technology: the body. As Manovich points out, it is exactly at the point of an interface – at the point where we can speak of 'aesthetics' – that flesh and world meet. Hayles points out that perception – however 'mediated' or 'immediate' – is always already embodied. As she puts it 'Information, like humanity, cannot exist apart from the embodiment that brings it into being as a material entity in the world; and embodiment is always instantiated, local, and specific' (1999: 48–9). As much as we narrate our experiences with ICTs and digital networks as disembodying, our body is always in play, shaping and being shaped by the process of perception and by our interactions with different technologies. Take Hayles' account of computer use. Although frequently seen as the disembodying technology par excellence, Hayles points out the obvious, and yet ignored, fact that this experience has a distinct corporeality to it.

> The computer restores and heightens the sense of word as image – an image drawn in a medium as fluid and changeable as water. Interacting with electronic images rather than with a materially resistant text, I absorb through my fingers as well as my mind a model of signification in which no simple one-to-one correspondence exists between signifier and signified. I know kinesthetically as well as conceptually, that the text can be manipulated in ways that would be impossible if it existed as a material object rather than a visual display. As I work with the text-as-flickering-image, I instantiate within my body the habitual patterns of movement that make pattern and

randomness more real, more relevant, and more powerful than presence and absence.

(1999: 26)

Note that, in this passage, Hayles acknowledges that there is something unique about writing using a word processor, as compared to a typewriter, or pen. Indeed, she even happily invokes words which technophiliac business writers use when discussing cyberspace; that it is a medium as fluid and changeable as water, that text becomes manipulable flickering electronic images. Neither Hayles, nor I, are claiming that *nothing* has changed in our experience of thinking or perceiving with the rise of ICTs or digital networks. Rather, she wishes to make clear that the change is not from embodiment to disembodiment – from materiality to virtuality – but from one *kind* of embodiment to another. The fluidity of information is experienced not just conceptually, but 'kinesthetically', not just as modes of thought but as 'habitual patterns of movement instantiated within the body'.[10]

What is more, we cannot simply dismiss this as a result of insufficiently advanced technology. It is not that we are on the cusp of true virtualization waiting for the last technological salvo to get us there. Hansen's analysis of virtual reality, mixed reality, and augmented reality makes clear the way in which these most 'virtualized' of technologies and interfaces are still never free of the constitutive role of embodiment in perception. He notes the way in which the most successful 'VR' projects have been those which have emphasized rather than transcended, markers of embodied perception, such as proprioception, tactility, and audility (2006: Ch. 2). Furthermore, he discusses how even the most immersive digital environment will necessarily require, and evoke, an embodied perceptual experience. In any VR encounter,

> there necessarily takes place, within the body of the participant, an embodied experience: a bodily processing of the action that has the effect of 'making it real' for the participant. Indeed, it is precisely this 'hallucinatory' dimension, applied to virtual reality more generally, that explains the capacity for the VR interface to couple our bodies with (almost) any arbitrary space.
>
> *(2006: 41)*

Again, the fact that VR interfaces have the ability (or at least the potential) to 'couple our bodies with (almost) any arbitrary space' ensures that the spatiality of the body, or the world, is not left unchanged. What is clear, however, is that even in 'Virtual' reality neither the world nor flesh is left behind.

This is because perception is always inherently an embodied phenomenon. Contrary to how major Western philosophical figures such as Descartes sought to identify perception as fundamentally allied with thought (with the two of them opposed to – or seeking to overcome the restrictions of – the body), we must think of perception always as a bodily process. Here we can turn to one of the foremost thinkers of embodied perception, Merleau-Ponty (whom we will be dealing with extensively in Chapters 6 and 7), who states:

> the way we relate to the things of the world is no longer as a pure intellect trying to master an object or space that stands before it. Rather, this relationship is an ambiguous one, between beings who are both embodied and limited and an enigmatic world of which we catch a glimpse (indeed which we haunt incessantly) but only ever from point of view that hide as much as they reveal, a world in which every object displays the human face it acquires in a human gaze.
>
> *(2004: 53–4)*

What is more, this ambiguous, embodied, limited character of perception remains, even if we turn from the physical world to virtual worlds (or rather if we engage with the material infrastructures which give rise to experiences of 'virtuality'). This is because this embodied character is an inherent characteristic of our perceptual faculties.[11] Our perception is not a passive recipient of objective sense data, a 'pure intellect' there to provide an accurate representation of the world. Indeed, one of the other major thinkers of embodied perception (who we will be dealing with in the next chapter), Henri Bergson, doesn't even think human beings capable of forming 'representations'. This is because a representation is something that only a passive being could produce, a screen which would receive images, whereas human perceptual faculties developed evolutionarily as part of a *sensorimotor* system, i.e. a fundamentally active system. As he says, 'My body, an object destined to move other object, is, then a center of action; it cannot give birth to a representation' (1991: 20).

Critics and boosters of ICTs alike are able to fear and praise their disembodying effects only because they have an image of human perception and thought which is always already *disembodied*. They speak like Nietzsche's child, who says 'Body am I, and soul'. The technophiliac praises technology for the way in which it frees the soul from the body, while the technophobe fears the way in which technology might capture the soul in a prostheticized body. But for Bergson and Merleau-Ponty, the soul and the body are, if not exactly 'one', at the very least inseparable. And thus, while new technologies might introduce new perceptions, new embodiments, new forms of consciousness, even new bodies, they will never produce a *dis*embodiment proper.

Accepting this point means rejecting the *ressentiment* of the despisers of the body, of those strands of the enlightenment which seek an absolute rationality in a purification of vision allowing us to escape the uncertainty, flux, and confusion of the corporeal world of becoming. Merleau-Ponty says as much, when he makes clear that an awareness of the embodied character of perception is to accept that to be is to be a body in the world – a world which, as he says, 'hides as much as it reveals', a world which is full of other bodies who resolutely refuse to bow down to our desires for mastery.

> In this ambiguous position, which has been forced on us because we have a body and a history (both personally and collectively), we can never know complete rest. We are continually obliged to work on our differences, to explain things we have said that have not been properly understood, to reveal what is hidden within us and to perceive other people. Reason does not lie behind us, nor is that where the meeting of minds takes place: rather, both stand before us waiting to be inherited. Yet we are no more able to reach them definitively than we are able to give up on them.
>
> *(2004: 66–7)*

The question of perception and embodiment (and how we think of both) is then always already an ethical and political issue. As new technologies inaugurate new styles and forms of perception and embodiment, this will have an impact on the ways in which we act in the world. This means that, even as I disagree with Virilio's conclusions about the effects of advanced ICTs and digital networks, I agree with him that they are having a profound impact on politics, society, economics, culture, subjectivity, and affection. And that one of the prominent vectors of these transformations is the acceleration of communication. The next three chapters will therefore seek to understand the effects that acceleration has on the always already embodied process of perception. What are the ethical and political implications of these effects, and what sorts of responses at the global, domestic, and individual levels might we want to enact to ensure that we can continue to struggle for justice, equality, and democracy? In some cases, this will involve resisting, challenging, or attempting to modify dominant communications regimes. In other cases, it will involve availing ourselves of the new possibilities these technologies provide us with. In no case is an outright rejection of these technologies possible. As Hayles says,

> Paul Virilio has observed that one cannot ask whether information technologies should continue to be developed. Given market forces already at work, it is virtually (if I may use the word) certain that we will increasingly live, work, and play in environments that construct us as embodied virtualities. I believe that our best hope to intervene constructively in this development is to put an interpretive spin on it – one that opens up the possibilities of seeing pattern and presence as complementary rather than antagonistic.
>
> *(1999: 48–9)*

For her language of pattern and presence, we can substitute a language of virtuality and embodiment.

Chapters 5, 6, and 7 divide the question of the acceleration of communication and perception between two aspects: intensive and extensive, or, better put, amount and scope (or more abstractly put, time and space). Though at first 'amount' might not seem to be a measure of the acceleration of communication, it becomes so when we think in terms of the speed at which ICTs are able to record, create, and communicate, producing the constant rush of new information which seems to be the hallmark of so many accounts of post-modernity. As every morning we turn on the computer and find more and newer information, we find ourselves forced to navigate this constant avalanche of information and fight the alternating poles of paralysis and distraction which it tends to engender. To investigate this intensive axis of speed and information, in Chapter 5 we will turn to the philosophy of Henri Bergson, whose theories of the automatizing and subtractive character of embodied perception provides us with a way of understanding the effects these new technologies might produce, as well as the ethical, philosophical, and political responses we might wish to enact. In turn, the extensive aspect of the acceleration of perception, refers to the increasing scope of our perception, that 'telescoping of distances' which Virilio describes. What does it mean to have access to information from around the world, even as our bodies remain as resolutely local as ever? How does the rise of mobile devices change our relationship to virtual space? To answer questions such as these, in Chapters 6 and 7 we will turn to the philosophy of Maurice Merleau-Ponty, whose phenomenology includes a nuanced and embodied account of the spatiality of perception. This division of labour is also based on the two thinkers' specific emphases in working with the question of embodied perception, Bergson, the thinker of temporality and Merleau-Ponty, the thinker of spatiality. This is, of course, an arbitrary distinction, as one cannot speak of time without space, and vice versa, but then, the distinction between intensive and extensive effects, too, is an arbitrary distinction. The goal is not theoretical fidelity but a pragmatic and productive engagement with new technologies, new affects, and new perceptions.

Notes

1. We see here the stark ableism Virilio's perspective here, with his valorization of a natural, normal, able body and reciprocal denigration of the apparently pathological *disabled* body. This necessarily suppresses the wide variety of different bodies and abilities, a point raised by Mitchell and Snyder in their introduction to *The Body and Physical Difference* (1997). This is why in what proceeds I will use the language of the 'prostheticization/parasitization' of the body, to make clear that I am employing/critiquing Virilio's ableist conception of prosthetics and disability.

2. As Mackenzie puts it:

   Machine time, it has often been argued in critical thought, is inhuman or nonlived time. Machine time is a relatively abstract, taken-for-granted term that refers to the speed at which mechanisms and devices carry out

> operations. Usually, responsibility for the deleterious and positive effects of technological speed is attributed to the high rate at which movements are carried out. For much critical theory this ever-increasing rate (expressed prosaically, say, in CPU speeds used to advertise computers or in Moore's Law) reduces temporal complexities, memory, and subjective experience to attenuate abstractions, to nonlived spaces and times, to intervals and orderings that are inimical to human lifeworld structures. Adverse reactions to machine time are particularly strong in the domain of media images.
>
> *(2007: 89)*

3. See also Petranker (2007: 175).
4. See also Hannah Arendt's discussion of the privileging of the Vita Contempletiva over the Vita Activa in chapter six of *The Human Condition*.
5. Tomlinson makes a similar point, although from a slightly different perspective, saying,

> It is our *bodies* that mark the key difference between telemediated and other modalities of immediacy. If we want to encapsulate the prime cultural impact of new communications technologies, then, it might be fair to say that they have produced a kind of *false dawn* of expectations of the liberation of human beings from the constraints of both embodiment and place. . . . The existential worry . . . is that we begin to hope and expect that [technology] can.
>
> *(107)*

See also Hassan (2007: 50–1).
6. International Telecommunications Union *ICT Data and Statistics* Last accessed on June 27, 2012 at: www.itu.int/ITU-D/ict/statistics/ To be fair, Virilio is aware of this divide, and of the power and violence implicit in it, saying:

> The global metropolitics of the future electronic information highways in itself implies the coming of a society no longer divided so much into North and South, but into two distinct temporalities, two speeds: one *absolute*, the other *relative*. The gap between developed and underdeveloped countries being reinforced throughout the five continents and leading to an even more radical divide between those who will live under the empire of real time essential to their economic activities at the heart of the virtual community of the *world city*, and those, more destitute that ever, who will survive in the real space of *local towns*, that great planetary wasteland that will in future bring together the only too real community of those who no longer have a job or a place to live that are likely to promote harmonious and lasting socialization.
>
> *(2008: 71)*

And yet, even as he criticizes this new regime of late-modern info-capitalism, he accepts and perpetuates its central mythos, mainly that it is global and virtual. That it has successfully cast off the constraints of locality and corporeality. In this regard, Virilio speaks in the same voice as the Toshiba commercial earlier, even though he says it with a frown instead of a smile. In this regard there is a similarity here between Virilio's treatment of the claims of late-modern info-capitalism and the claims of military omnipotence by first world militaries. I discuss this topic in chapter two of *The Politics of Speed*.
7. Again, here we see the unsettling ableism that haunts Virilio's account of technology and the body, which is also present in the second encounter with speed we discussed in Chapter 2.
8. The use of such technologies is also dependent on the social and economic assemblages to which they are connected. Thus, as Mike Crang says of wireless technologies,

even if one gains locational flexibility, that is not the same as locational indifference. So contrary to predications, and endless commercial advertising, networked or wireless access rarely means working from the top of the mountain. In fact, in most high-tech industries we see massive agglomerations in key urban quarters because copresences with colleagues, suppliers, and clients to interact, brainstorm, and work through issues is, if anything, more vital than ever.

(81–82)

9. We will discuss the spatiality of mobile devices in greater detail in Chapter 7.
10. We see a similar discussion in Galloway who describes how

> I am in a position to identify more clearly the conservatism of Kittler, who on this point finds a confrere in Marshall MacLuhan. By conservative I mean the claim that *techne* is substrate and only substrate. For Kittler and McLuhan alike, media means hypomnesis. They define media via externalization of man into objects. Hence a fundamentally conservative dichotomy is inaugurated – which to be clear was in Plato before it was in Aristotle – between the good and balanced human specimen and the dead junk of the hypomnemata. Contrast this with an alternate philosophical tradition that views *techne* as technique, art, habitus, ethos, or lived practice.
>
> *(2012: 26)*

11. Thus, Virilio's fear, in the quote earlier, that the Merleau-Pontian dictum that 'Everything I see is in principle within my reach, at least within reach of my sight, marked on the map of the "I can"' might be broken or overturned demonstrates that Virilio never really agreed with Merleau-Ponty in the first place. This is because Virilio wants to make this a normative account of 'authentic' human perception, which we must cling to with fidelity (again, shades of Virilio's ableism), when for Merleau-Ponty, it is a description of human perception that is always mobile and adaptive, shaped by the technological context in which it finds itself.

Works Cited

Arendt, H. (1998) *The Human Condition*, Chicago, IL: University of Chicago Press.

Bergson, H. (1991) *Matter and Memory*, Trans. N. M. Paul and W. S. Palmer, Zone Books: New York.

Crang, M. (2007) 'Speed=Distance/Time: Chronotopographies of Action', *24/7: Time and Temporality in the Network Society*, ed. R. Hassan and R. E. Purser, Stanford, CA: Stanford Business Books.

Ephraim, L. (2011) '"An Electric Union Blest": Post-Humanist Visions from the Age of the Telegraph', *Unpublished Paper Presented at APSA 2011*, Seattle, WA.

Galloway, A. R. (2012) *The Interface Effect*, Cambridge: Polity Press.

Gates, B. (1999) *Business @ the Speed of Thought*, New York: Grand Central Publishing.

Gibson, W. (1984) *Neuromancer*, New York: Ace Science Fiction.

Hansen, M. B. N. (2006) *New Philosophy for New Media*, Cambridge: MIT Press.

Hassan, R. (2007) 'Network Time', *24/7: Time and Temporality in the Network Society*, ed. R. Hassan and R. E. Purser, Stanford, CA: Stanford Business Books.

Hayles, N. K. (1999) *How We Became Posthuman*, Chicago: University of Chicago Press.

Lessig, L. (2006) *Code: And Other Laws of Cyberspace, Version 2.0*, New York, NY: Basic Books.

Mackenzie, A. (2007) 'Protocols and the Irreducible Traces of Embodiment: The Viterbi Algorithm and the Mosaic of Machine Time', *24/7: Time and Temporality in the Network Society*, eds. R. Hassan and R. E. Purser, Stanford, CA: Stanford Business Books.

Mackenzie, A. (2010) *Wirelessness: Radical Empiricism in Network Culture*, Cambridge, MA: MIT Press.

Manovich, L. (2001) *The Language of New Media*, Cambridge: MIT Press.

Merleau-Ponty, M. (2004) *The World of Perception*, Trans. O. Davis, London: Routledge.

Mitchell, D. and Snyder, S. (1997) *The Body and Physical Difference*, Ann Arbor: University of Michigan Press.

Nietzsche, F. (1976) 'Thus Spoke Zarathustra', *The Portable Nietzsche*, Trans. W. Kaufmann, New York: Penguin Books.

Nietzsche, F. (1997) *On the Genealogy of Morality*, Trans. C. Diethe, Cambridge: Cambridge University Press.

Petranker, J. (2007) 'The Presence of Others: Network Experience as an Antidote to the Subjectivity of Time', *24/7: Time and Temporality in the Network Society*, eds. R. Hassan and R. E. Purser, Stanford, CA: Stanford Business Books.

Stiegler, B. (1998) *Technics and Time, 1*, Trans. R. Beardsworth and G. Collins, Stanford, CA: Stanford University Press.

Tomlinson, J. (2007) *The Culture of Speed: The Coming of Immediacy*, London: Sage Publications.

Virilio, P. (1983) *Pure War*, Trans. M. Polizzotti, New York: Semiotext(e).

Virilio, P. (1994) *The Vision Machine*, Trans. J. Rose, Bloomington: University of Indiana Press.

Virilio, P. (2008) *Open Sky*, Trans. J. Rose, London: Verson.

5

EMBODIED VIRTUALITY

Speed, Perception, and New Media in Bergson

Introduction: Drowning in Information

One of the central issues that emerges when discussing accelerating information and communication technologies (ICTs) is the problem of the amount of information. As the speed with which information can be captured, produced, analyzed, and communicated increases, we find ourselves awash in data. As Howard Rheingold explains:

> In August 2010, Google CEO Eric Schmidt dropped a mind-boggling statistic at a high-tech conference: every two days, humans produce as much information as we did from the era of cave paintings up to 2003. . . . SMS messages were up to seven trillion annually by 2011. Facebook displayed a trillion ads in 2010. According to a study done at the University of California at San Diego, the Average American consumes thirty-four gigabytes of information on an average day.
>
> *(2012: 98–9)*

It is a problem that Mark Andrejevic terms 'Infoglut', the idea that 'the amount of *mediated* information . . . has surely increased dramatically, thanks in no small part to the proliferation of portable, networked, interactive devices' (2013: 3). The result of this condition is that

> [w]e have all become intelligence analysts sorting through more data than we can absorb with . . . what are proving to be inadequate resources for adjudicating amongst the diverse array of narratives. We have become, in a sense, like the intelligence analysts overwhelmed by a tsunami of

information or the market researcher trying to make sense of the explod-
ing data 'troves' they have created and captured.

(3–4)

This reference to a 'tsunami' of information is representative of a lot of commentary around accelerating ICTs. Natural disaster metaphors abound, as
writers talk about 'floods' and 'tidal waves' of information, 'tsunamis' and 'ava-
lanches' of data. These natural disasters frequently put our bodies in harm's
ways, threatening to 'drown' us in data, to 'crush' us beneath the weight of
information. Here we see a version of the discourses which developed in the
first encounter we discussed in Chapter 2, in which speed threatens and over-
whelms the human body.

The anxious (and at times apocalyptic) tone of such commentary is not surprising. Many in the first world (and elsewhere) have experienced the traumas
of 'infoglut' – the shock at opening our email in the morning and seeing the
number of messages awaiting our attention, the panic of trying to keep up
with the unfolding of a 24/7 news cycle, the paralysis of trying to choose from
amongst a million search results. The visceral nature of these experiences is not
just due to the increasing amount of information but also the feeling that it is
constantly being pushed on us by mobile devices, Wi-Fi internet, and satellite
news. As Douglas Rushkoff puts it:

> Our broadband connection – whether in our homes or in our phones –
> keeps our applications on, updating, and ready at every moment. Any-
> time anyone or anything wants to message, email, tweet, update, notify,
> or alert us, something dings on our desktop or vibrates in our pocket.
> Our devices, and by extension our nervous systems are attached to the
> entire online universe all the time.
>
> *(34)*

This visceral feeling of being crushed under a flood of information gives rise
to two interrelated sets of issues. The first circulates around the problem of
attention – the idea that in a world of accelerating information flows, we
will be unable to effectively apply sustained attention to necessary objects
of information. Such concerns tend to organize around the twin poles of
paralysis and distraction. Paralysis is the fear that we will become overwhelmed by the impossibility of absorbing all of this information, and thus
fail to absorb anything whatsoever. The political concern is that this sense
of paralysis will fuel apathy. On the other hand, where paralysis is marked
by an inability to absorb *anything*, distraction is marked by a pathological
attempt to absorb *everything*, a neurotic flitting from one thing to the next,
always being drawn to the latest post, tweet, video, story. This condition
has the same effect as that of paralysis, ultimately making us incapable of

meaningfully understanding a phenomenon, connecting with an event, or feeling along with others.

The second set of issues infoglut produces relates to the strategies we frequently turn to to deal with this crushing wave of information. More often than not, this boils down to the problem of filtering, picking out those pieces of information that are useful to us, and discarding the rest. As Eriksen puts it 'A crucial skill in information society consists in protecting oneself from the 99.99 per cent of the information offered that one does not want (and, naturally, exploiting the last 0.01 per cent in a merciless way)' (2001: 17). The political problem, of course, lies in how we filter and in who is doing the filtering. Numerous political commentators (discussed later) have raised the problem of 'echo chambers', the danger of people retreating into a bubble in which they only encounter information, experiences, and individuals, that confirm what they already believe. The problem of echo chambers is exacerbated in a world of accelerating ICTs, as the explosion of informational offerings allows us to almost always find sources that fit our preconceived notion. The existence of these echo chambers is politically dangerous, say critics because they polarize political beliefs, inhibit critical thinking, and diminish our sense of a shared public sphere. As Eli Pariser says '[d]emocracy requires citizens to see things from one another's point of view, but instead we're more and more enclosed in our own bubbles. Democracy requires a reliance on shared facts; instead we're being offered parallel but separate universes' (5). The problem of the echo chamber is further exacerbated by what Pariser terms the 'filter bubble'. This is the fact that, when it comes to choosing what information to expose ourselves to, it is not just a problem of human bias. Rather, as our pursuit of information is increasingly mediated by digital platforms such as Google, Facebook, and Twitter, the information we are exposed to is chosen by algorithms which seek to automatically present us with information we will like. In this regard, the human propensity to seek out information that confirms our pre-existing worldview is enabled by digital structures that seek to present us with such information, even without us explicitly asking for it (and thus giving the impression that we are receiving a neutral, unbiased set of information rather than one tailor made for us).

The problem, of course, is that some form of filtering is necessary, and as the flood of information increases beyond the abilities of humans to effectively filter it, automated algorithms will increasingly play the role of filtering agents, separating the wheat from the chaff. This, according to many critics of speed, is the greatest danger of all. Andrejevic asks, 'What happens when we offload our 'knowing' onto the database (or algorithm) because the new forms of knowledge available are 'too big' for us to comprehend' (16)? We can see how this resonates with the concerns raised by Virilio in the previous chapter, of a technological vision in which the human is taken 'out of the loop' completely. Indeed, here we see a resonance with the second encounter with speed discussed in the second chapter, in which prostheticizing/parasitizing technologies hollow out human bodies and cognition, making us mere appendages to the machines which do the actual thinking.

It is, however, at this point, that we might wish to push back against these criticisms and framings, much as we did in the previous chapter. While it is certainly the case that the dramatic increase in the amount of information poses various political and personal challenges, we should be wary of assuming that we are entering a unique era of information saturation that is making traditional modes of perception and politics impossible. As we discussed in the previous chapter, concerns about the 'capturing' effects of digital technologies are frequently based on Cartesian assumptions which already imagined a disembodied human consciousness somehow trapped (or freed) by new information technologies. Fears about the way in which new information technologies might filter, bias, or control humans, start from a vision of cognition and perception which is neutral, objective, and passive. These accounts (similar to the Rousseauian account of the body in Chapter 2) assume a neutral, unbiased, and attentive human mind, which can be captured and distorted by forms of technological perception. In contrast, in Part 1, I wish to develop a theoretical approach rooted in the work of Henri Bergson which rejects these Cartesian assumptions, instead presenting a vision of human perception and cognition which is always already biased, filtered, and automated. Having developed this theoretical framework, I will return to the problems raised earlier, attempting to tackle the very real issues they raise, without resorting to a nostalgia for a fictional 'slow' past, or assuming a Cartesian account of human cognition which technological perception can't help but distort and subvert. Thus, in Part 2 I will turn to the question of attention, in Part 3, echo chambers, and in Part 4, filter bubbles.

Part 1: Bergson

Bergson and Embodied Perception

To maintain that accelerating ICTs and media have a distorting, controlling, or capturing effect on human perception and cognition is to assume that human perception and cognition are, at root, objective, neutral, and autonomous. As discussed, such an account is based in a Cartesian vision of the mind as unextended spirit, and perception as a kind of neutral conduit between it and the world of extended matter. Contrary to this, in Bergson we get an account of perception which is always already biased, partial, and active. As Hansen puts it, for Bergson, perception is always '*impure*' (2006a: 4). This is because Bergson conceives of perception as action oriented rather than representational. Bergson rejects accounts of perception that presume it to be a fundamentally passive and 'knowing' faculty. Indeed, Bergson criticizes the major philosophical doctrines of his day – realism and idealism – on the grounds that both share this same passive and objective conception of thought, saying:

> [i]f we now look closely at the two doctrines, we shall discover in them a common postulate, which we may formulate thus: perception has a wholly speculative interest; it is pure knowledge . . . to perceive means above all to know.
>
> *(1991: 28)*

This is to misunderstand the very nature of perception, which is not, says Bergson, to *know*, but *to act*. This explains the quote which I introduced in the previous chapter: 'My body, an object destined to move another object, is, then a center of action; it cannot give birth to a representation' (20). This means that rather than perception being a question of passively and objectively acquiring knowledge, it is an active process in which perception is conditioned according to the needs of action. Perception is impure precisely because it is not objective. It is prejudiced, it acts in our favour, seeks out aspects of the world which might help us to survive (or at least have in the past – our past and in the distant evolutionary past). Perception is not fundamentally about knowing; it is about acting, surviving, and living.[1] What this means then is that the content of the images that we perceive will be conditioned by the needs of survival. To fulfil this duty, perception is, for Bergson, simultaneously subtractive and additive.

It is subtractive in that, of the vast amount of potential information in the world, of the countless 'images' that might be 'presented' to the mind, our perceptual faculties only pick out certain ones. The vast plenum of the world is strained through the sieve of our perception. Bodies 'allow to pass through them, so to speak, those external influences which are indifferent to them; the others, isolated, become "perceptions" by their very isolation' (Bergson 1991: 20). This filtering process happens most obviously in terms of the fundamental limitations of our perceptual faculties. Thus, out of the continuum of electromagnetic radiation, our eyes can only pick out a very narrow band of frequencies, (and it is the same for our ears and soundwaves, etc.). Infrared and ultraviolet light bypass our eyes because, in the evolutionary struggle, perception of the 'visible' spectrum proved adequate to ensure survival. In this regard, the criteria that determine which images are perceived and which aren't (or rather, the criteria which allowed certain configurations of the perceptual faculties to endure, such that they only perceive certain types of images) is not 'truth' or 'knowledge' but action and survival. We might know more about the world if we could see gamma rays whizzing through the air, but such an ability was not particularly important for our primary evolutionary needs, namely finding edible food and avoiding sabretooth tiger attacks.

Here we see the first resonance between Bergson's account of perception, and the problem of accelerating ICTs, namely the problem of filtering, or extracting pertinent information from a 'tsunami' of data. For Bergson, perception is always already such a filtering mechanism. As Deleuze puts it in his book on Bergson:

> a being can retain from a material object and the actions issuing from it only those elements that interest him. So that perception is not the object *plus* something, but the object *minus* something, minus everything that does not interest us.
>
> *(1988: 24–5)*

We will return to this issue in the third and fourth parts of this chapter related to the question of filtering. For now, however, we need to discuss that, for Bergson, this is not the only way that perception is impure. For perception is also *additive*. That is to say that content is added by the body to the images produced by the world in two ways: 1) via affection, and 2) via memories.

Affect and Memory

This vision of perception as inherently additive is, again, to reject an account of perception as neutral, unbiased, or passive in relation to its object. As Deleuze puts it in his book on Bergson:

> We assumed that the body was a like a pure mathematical point in space, a pure instant, or a succession of instants in time. All that is left now is to ask ourselves what fills up the cerebral interval, what takes advantage of it to become embodied. Bergson's response is three-fold. First, there is affectivity, which assumes that the body *is* something other than a mathematical point and which gives it volume in space. Next, it is the recollections of memory that link the instants to each other and interpolate the past in the present. Finally, it is memory again in another form, in the form of a contraction of matter that makes the quality appear.
>
> *(1988: 25–6)*

We must now take each of these additions in turn. Bergson's conceptions of affections are similar to the definitions we provided in Chapters 2 and 3, which is to say various corporeal shifts in response to particular stimuli (whether externally or internally generated) happening at a generally non-conscious level (although having conscious effects in the form of emotions, feelings, moods, behaviours, thoughts, etc.). As Hansen puts it, for Bergson, 'Affectivity, in short, names the body's agency over itself' (2006a: 226), i.e. the body's ability to produce and give rise to certain corporeal states in response to stimuli. Affects occur exactly insofar as perception is an embodied process (Bergson

1991: 56). Affects are additive to perception for Bergson, in ways similar to those we discussed in Chapters 2 and 3 – they colour and shape our perceptions in non-conscious ways, as well as spark actions and responses faster than conscious thought can achieve.

The way in which affects play an additive role in perception is paralleled by (and in many ways intertwined with) the role that memory plays. According to Bergson, we can think of memory in two different respects: memory images and embodied habit (although these are better thought of as opposed poles on a continuum rather than completely separate phenomenon). Bergson explains the distinction between the two through the example of learning a section of text by heart. He says we can compare the way in which we 'remember' the text once we've learned it, (saying it automatically without thinking about it), versus us 'remembering' the experience of learning (i.e. the different times we spent staring at the text, practicing it). The former constitutes memory in the form of habit, the latter, in the form of a memory-image (79–80). Each of these modes of memory have their own way of shaping perception and thought according to our past experiences and preconceived notions.

In terms of the memory-image, Bergson argues that when we perceive the world, we rarely perceive it as it actual is. Rather, for the sake of speed, we tend to 'overlay' our perception with memory images, filtering out what we presume will be the same, allowing us to focus on the new and important things. Our assumptions about what the world is like, drawn from memory images, paper over our immediate perceptions.

> In fact, there is no perception which is not full of memories. With the immediate and present data of our sense, we mingle a thousand details out of our past experience. In most cases these memories supplant our actual perceptions, of which we then retain only a few hints, thus using them merely as "signs" that recall to us former images.
>
> *(33)*

Or as he says elsewhere, 'Your perception, however instantaneous, consists then in an incalculable multitude of remembered elements; in truth, every perception is already memory' (150). This is the core of what Deleuze calls the 'Bergsonian revolution' in perception: 'We do not move from the present to the past, from perception to recollection, but from the past to the present, from recollection to perception' (1988: 63). This role that memory plays in supplementing, and sometimes supplanting, 'pure' perception is also tied to questions of speed and the body, and the constraints of action and survival. If we had to meet each image anew, grasp it in its absolutely singularity and novelty, perception and cognition would be painfully slow, barely able to keep up with the onrush of new images to be decoded. The ability to bring forward memories from the past in response to a particular detail or stimuli, and thus deal not with a completely new image, but one already known and understood, carries with it tremendous advantages. On our usual walk home from the bus stop, we do not need to slow down to perceive every car in every parking space, or every new billboard to navigate our way home. Says Bergson,

> The body is indeed for us a means of action, but it is also an obstacle to perception. Its role is to perform the appropriate action on any and every occasion; for this reason it must keep consciousness clear . . . of objects over which we have no control.
>
> *(1977: 314)*

This means, of course, that we are never dealing with a pure, objective perception. Instead our perception frequently functions on a 'good enough' principle in which specificities and singularities are smoothed out, elided, or just ignored. Indeed, in many cases this will result in us simply misperceiving what is actually happening. As Bergson puts it, 'The convenience and the rapidity of perception are bought at this price; but hence also springs every kind of illusion' (1991: 33). We have all, I suspect, had the experience of looking for some lost object, only to find that it is resting on a table we've inspected multiple times. The object was there before our eyes, but our perception – not expecting to see it where it normally wasn't – simply didn't.

Here, again, is a resonance with our earlier discussion of the impacts of accelerating ICTs. There we saw a concern over the development of echo chambers which simply reflected back to us our preconceived beliefs. But we can see that, in Bergson's account, we are frequently not perceiving the world as it is but rather *as we remember it to be*. The impure mixture of perception and memory means that we have a tendency to present ourselves with a world always already familiar to us. We have an innate antipathy to novelty insofar as our sensorimotor system is primed to draw on established templates, to overlay the newness of the future with the familiarity of the past. And once again, this is a function of the need to respond rapidly to a world of accelerating information.

Thus, we see that the problem of infoglut, and the need to filter, although certainly exacerbated in our present day, are by no means 'new'. This problem of navigating an accelerated, information rich environment, is one as old as human perception itself. What is more, the fact that the need to filter our perception in the context of accelerating information can run the risk of blinding us to novelty, is also not simply an artefact of the digital present, but an ongoing element of cognition.

We will discuss this issue more in Parts 2, 3, and 4, but first we must continue to tease out the implications of Bergson's account of this central role of memory in perception and cognition.

Automatism and Habit

For Bergson, the persistence of the past, and its activation in relation to an emerging future, is also present in the other pole of memory discussed earlier, the bodily acquisition of habits. Habit is another way in which we transport the past into the future, storing up the patterns and activities of the past in our bodies. Habit is essentially bodily insofar as it is action that I am able to do and repeat without subjecting it to conscious intentionality. Indeed, as Bergson points out, in most habitual activities we have trained our bodies to do, if we had to consciously think about each action and sub-action, we wouldn't be able to act quickly enough to be effective.

> The true effect of repetition is to decompose and then to recompose, and thus appeal to the intelligence of the body. At each new attempt it separates movements which were interpenetrating; each time it calls the attention of the body to a new detail which had passed unperceived; it bids the body discriminate and classify; it teaches what is the essential; it points out, one after another, within the total movement, the lines that mark off its internal structure. In this sense, a movement is learned when the body has been made to understand it.
>
> *(1991: 111–12)*

Thus, as Grosz describes,

> Habit . . . is memory accumulated in order to act. Memory-proper is contemplation, reverie, the slowing down, arrest or simplification of movement: habit is the complexification of movement through its routinization. Habit is a form of accumulation of memory and repetition in the body. Where memory represents and imagines the past, habit acts and repeats it.
>
> *(2013: 228)*

This habitual intelligence of the body shapes the corporeal process of perception as well. Thus, the example that Bergson gives of how to form a habit is learning a new language. He points out how this habit actively changes our perceptions as what was previously experienced as a string of gibberish becomes comprehensible language. It is not just that words that were meaningless acquire meaning; rather it is that we actively hear differently, as phonemes that were indistinct now resolve as independent words. This example shows us both the power of habit, as well as the profoundly impure and corporeal nature of human perception. Once again, if we had only a pure perception, which objectively received information, and then compared it to a pure memory system to derive its meaning, the process of learning and understanding a language would take far too long to be of any use. If, however, it is a bodily habit, occurring at non-conscious levels through the interpenetration of past and present, the task becomes feasible.

> The difficulty would be insuperable if we really had only auditory impressions on the one hand, and auditory memories on the other hand. Not so, however, if auditory impressions organize nascent movements, capable of scanning the phrase which is heard and of emphasizing its main articulations. These automatic movements of internal accompaniment, at first undecided or uncoordinated, might become more precise by repetition; they would end by sketching a simplified figure in which the listener would find, in their main lines and principle directions, the very movements of the speaker. Thus would unfold itself in consciousness, under the form of nascent muscular sensations, the *motor diagram*, as it were, of the speech we hear.
>
> *(Bergson 1991: 110–11)*

And though we have so far been speaking of intentional attempts to acquire new habits, it's important to realize that habit forming is not just something that happens in response to a conscious effort. Our bodies are habit-forming machines, as we constantly absorb repetitive movements, actions, perceptions, experiences, breaking them down and storing them to be deployed in the future.

> It is true that the example of a lesson learned by heart is to some extent artificial. Yet our whole life is passed among a limited number of objects, which pass more or less often before our eyes: each of them, as it is perceived, provokes on our part movements, at least nascent, whereby we adapt ourselves to it. These movements, as they recur, contrive a mechanism for themselves, grow into a habit, and determine in us attitudes which automatically follow our perception of things.
>
> *(84)*

Thus, we might return to the example of racial profiling which we developed in Chapter 3. Here we can think about the way in which the perception of racist police officers is trained (both actively through formal training, and passively, through ingesting a racist culture) to seek out and perceive the bodies of people of colour as threats while allowing white bodies to fade into the background. Here we see a tension around habit similar to the subtractive qualities of perception discussed earlier. On the one hand, the human propensity towards habit (and its role in organizing perception) is valuable insofar as it introduces a useful speed into our actions and reactions but in doing so introduces the danger of unreflective errors and biases being layered into our perceptions (we will return to this ambivalence of habit later).

Regardless of its value, habit and automatism are in the nature of human beings. While we unquestionably are capable of (relatively) free and autonomous behaviour in life such behaviour always kicks against our inherent tendency towards automatism:

> Our freedom, in the very movements by which it is affirmed, creates the growing habits that will stifle it if it fails to renew itself by a constant efforts: it is dogged by automatism. The most living thought becomes frigid in the formulae that expresses it. The word turns against the idea. The letter kills the spirit.
>
> *(Bergson 1998: 127–8)*

Bergson traces the way in which human beings are 'dogged by automatism'; the role that habit and memory play in shaping not just our actions but also our very perceptions and thoughts. Thus, contrary to the concerns raised by thinkers such as Virilio and Andrejevic, we see that human perception and action are marked by automatism not insofar as we are 'technological' but precisely insofar as we are 'natural'. As Alexandre Lefebvre puts it 'habits constitute the very stuff of our personality. . . . These routines not only determine the vast majority of our conduct; they also make us into who we are' (2013: 59). Now this is not to say that we are not also capable of creativity, of breaking the repetition of the past. However, we must understand that the question is not freedom or constraint, creativity or repetition, liberation or automation. We are always-already both at the same time. The question then is what kind of freedom and what kind of constraints (and what mixture of the two)? And perhaps more importantly, when, why, and how we should struggle against the constraints of habit, whether they be internal or external, technological, corporeal or always-already both. What is more, we should be careful not to go too far here, or to treat this tendency towards habit and automatism as if it were 'bad' in comparison to more reflective or 'wilful' thoughts and actions. As described these tendencies towards habit and automatism play a crucial role in maintaining our viability as organisms in the world.[2]

The Open and the Closed

If the forces of habit and automatism constitute one pole of Bergson's thought on psychology and biology, freedom and creativity constitute the other. Bergson says that we are – to a limited degree and in a relative way – able to break the habitual cycle of the repetition of the past. Indeed, not only can we, but we must if we are to live full and ethical lives.

The connection between habit, creativity, and ethics is laid out in Bergson's *Two Source of Morality and Religion*. There he begins by noting that the human proclivity towards habit driven perception and action isn't just useful in terms of the survival of the individual but also the community.

> From this first standpoint, social life appears to us a system of more or less deeply rooted habits, corresponding to the needs of the community. Some of them are habits of command, most of them are habits of obedience, whether we obey a person commanding by virtue of a mandate from society, or whether from society itself, vaguely perceived or felt, there emanates an impersonal imperative. Each of these habits of obedience exerts a pressure on our will.
>
> *(1977: 10)*

Thus, for Bergson, the age-old question of what it is that provides morality with its obligation is solved by reversing the order. It is not the moral law which comes first, and the obligation that follows. Humans are creatures of habit prone to feel obligation. The moral law comes second and provides it with a content. Notice that this is not an attempt to discern the biological or evolutionary roots of morality per se. Bergson is not here making any comments about the specific *content* of the moral law. What he is discerning is the human *habit of forming habits*. This is the root of obligation, and a crucial one in terms of the sustainability of a community, since it 1) renders humans relatively stable and predictable and 2) allows for habits of obedience which inclines us to put the interest of others before our own. Alex Lefebvre thus argues that 'Bergson is and is not a biological determinist' (50). Bergson is a biological determinist insofar as, for him, 'the source of morality is biology' (15). But,

> [h]e is most definitely not a biological determinist if that means he believes particular obligations and duties can be read off our biological nature. All rules, habits, mores, customs, manners, and morals are historically contingent and open-ended.
>
> *(50)*

Thus, as much in the 'social' animal as in the 'natural', our tendency towards automatism – our 'habit of contracting habits' – is a central mechanism in the survival of the species. However, just as the 'convenience' and 'the rapidity of perception' is brought at the price of 'every kind of illusion' (1991: 33), the social cohesion which our habitual nature allows comes with a price tag. That price is a social form of being which is ill-equipped, both intellectually and ethically, to deal with the radically new. A society or morality founded solely upon principles of habit and obedience constitutes what Bergson terms the 'closed society', i.e. closed off spatially and temporally, rejecting both that which is foreign and that which is new. From such roots comes all manner of violence and atrocity, justified under the banner of an established morality, a deeply felt but unquestioned sense of obligation.[3] An ethics worthy of the name, for Bergson, needs to be more than mere automatism. Closed morality is the morality of those individuals and societies

> whose activity ran indefinitely in the same circle, whose organs were ready-made instruments and left no room for the ceaselessly renewed invention of tools, whose consciousness lapsed into the somnambulism of instinct instead of bracing itself and revitalizing itself into reflective thought.
>
> *(1977: 209)*[4]

Contrary to this, Bergson posits an open morality, an open society, and an open soul.

> The other attitude is that of the open soul. What, in that case, is allowed in? Suppose we say that it embraces all humanity: we should not be going too far, we should hardly be going far enough, since its love may extend to animals, to plants, to all nature. And yet no one of these things which would thus fill it would suffice to define the attitude taken by the soul, for it could, strictly speaking, do without all of them. Its form is not dependent on its content. We have just filled it; we could as easily empty it again. 'Charity' would persist in him who possesses 'charity', though there be no other living creature on earth.
>
> *(1977: 32)*

Open morality takes the form not of morality as law, which is to say a check-list of individuals who deserve moral respect or a set of duties to be definitively achieved. Rather open morality takes the form of an internal disposition of charitable openness to the new, new moral claims, and new moral agents (Bergson speaks of 'pioneers in morality' [40]). As Bergson says of moral history '[e]ach development was a creation, and indeed the door will ever stand open to fresh creations' (76). Openness, therefore, is reflective and critical, capable of breaking with the cyclicality of habit, and asking who, and what, is being elided in the automatism of perception and habit. This is, of course, no easy task, not just because attempting to break from social norms and habits leaves one open to marginalization and oppression but because our habit-forming habit is just as good at suppressing novel thoughts and perceptions as it is at pre-empting self-centred behaviour.

However, luckily, humans are not purely unthinking automatons. In the struggle against habit and repetition we are aided by the equally human capacity of engaging in free and creative action. Consciousness, for Bergson, is one end point of a process of evolutionary development which introduced greater variety, complexity, and *indeterminacy*, into sensorimotor responses. This introduction of indeterminacy is, for Bergson, a natural characteristic of life, and the counterpart to the instinct towards repetition and automatism.

> the role of life is to insert some *indetermination* into matter. Indeterminate, *i.e.* unforeseeable, are the forms it creates in the course of its evolution. More and more indeterminate also, more and more free, is the activity to which these forms serve as the vehicle.
>
> *(Bergson 1998: 126)*

This move to indetermination is no less inspired by, related to, and maintained through its benefit towards the body.

> The will of an animal is the more effective and the more intense, the greater the number of mechanisms it can choose from, the more complicated the switchboard on which all the motor paths cross, or, in other words, the more developed its brain. Thus, the progress of the nervous system assures to the act increasing precision, increasing variety, increasing efficiency and independence.
>
> *(252)*

As Bergson says, this introduction of indeterminacy into matter is the role of life, and hence all living things do it to a greater or lesser extent. For Bergson, however, it is in the human that this tendency reaches its highest point, bringing with it the possibility of a decisive break from the automatism of mere matter.

> The human brain is made, like every brain, to set up motor mechanisms and to enable us to choose among them, at any instant, the one we shall put in motion by the pull of a trigger. But it differs from other brains in this, that the number of mechanisms it can set up, and consequently the choice that it gives as to which among them shall be released is unlimited. Now, from the limited to the unlimited there is all the difference between the closed and the open. It is not a difference of degree, but of kind.
>
> *(1998: 263)*

This difference in kind is, according to Bergson, what separates humans from animals, and what makes the former as marked by intelligence, as the latter is by instinct. That being said, these should only be viewed as tendencies, not absolute types, as, says Bergson, there is always some intelligence mixed into instinct, and always some instinct mixed into intelligence (263–264).

It is this capacity for indeterminacy that makes possible a breaking of the cycle of habit, an opening of the soul to new moral agents and claims. As

Lefebvre puts it 'obligation, unlike the necessity of instinct, is a force with which we can argue. Human beings are not tied to their duties in the way that ants are' (64). However, we should note the limitations that Bergson places on this trend of indeterminacy. For, as mentioned, this indeterminacy always happens in the context of a thoroughly embodied system of perception, thought, and action. As such, even as it may pull against the constraints of habit and obligation, they too pull back. Thus, as he says later,

> consciousness is essentially free; it is freedom itself; but it cannot pass through matter without settling on it, without adapting itself to it: this adaptation is what we call intellectuality; and the intellect, turning itself back toward active, that is to say free, consciousness, naturally makes it enter into the conceptual forms into which it is accustomed to see matter fit. It will therefore always perceive freedom in the form of necessity; it will always neglect the part of novelty or of creation inherent in the free act; it will always substitute for action itself an imitation artificial, approximate, obtained by compounding the old with the old and the same with the same.
>
> *(1998: 103)*

This is why the much-vaunted intelligence which Bergson assigns humans to differentiate them from animals is just as much prone to habit and the repetition of the past as instinct. Indeed, as Bergson points out, habits are nothing so much as intelligence turned into a pseudo-instinct.

What this means is that, like Spinoza, morality is not the result of a moment of enlightenment, of intellectually grasping the moral law. Rather it is an embodied struggle to open ourselves up to new ethical possibilities. Now, obviously, many moral philosophies acknowledge that being a moral person is a struggle. However, such struggle is for the purpose of living up to an already grasped and understood code of moral behaviour. Bergson breaks from this, arguing that, when we presume that we have grasped the moral code in its entirety, is exactly when we are closed up in the circularity of habit and automatism. Now, such closed moralities are not necessarily bad, and indeed, play a crucial role in maintaining the stability and cohesion of societies. But they are not, in themselves, sufficient for achieving a moral behaviour and outlook. This is because of the durational, creative nature of time itself. We cannot predict in principle what kind of moral claims the future will place on us. As Marrati puts it in her discussion of Bergson:

> What is particularly misleading in a vision of knowledge that claims to possess in advance the necessary elements for encountering all possible objects and events is that it blinds itself to the challenge of the new. It cannot admit, even in principle, that new objects may require new

concepts and methods of thinking, that something in the world simply might not fit peacefully into old intellectual habits and categories.

(7)

We thus must attempt to become 'pioneers of morality' and open ourselves up to new moral agents, claims, and outlooks.

Achieving such openness is more than an attempt to struggle against the 'heteronomy of the will' or the 'innate depravity of man'. Rather it is a matter of fighting against our tendency towards automatism and habit and opening ourselves to the idea that the moral law which we take as absolute and transhistorical is instead limited and contingent, subject to constant reappraisal and reformation. And because of the embodied roots of this tendency towards automatism, such a struggle must be both intellectual as well as affective, engaging both the mind and the body.

> We do not deny the utility, the necessity even, of a moral instruction which appeals to reason alone, defining duties and connecting them with a principle of which it follows out in detail the various applications. It is on the plane of intelligence, and on that plane alone, that discussion is possible, and there is no complete morality without reflexion, analysis and argument with others as well as with oneself. But if instruction directed to the intelligence be indispensable to give confidence and delicacy to the moral sense, if it makes us fully capable of carrying out our intention where our intention is good, yet the intention must exist in the first place, and intention marks a direction of the will as much as and more than of intelligence.
>
> *(Bergson 1977: 97)*

Marrati interprets this idea by saying, 'To look at the processes that bring about novelty does not come spontaneously to us at all but, rather, requires something like a conversion of attitude, a constant effort of attention' (4).

Thus, we must turn to a mode of philosophy that actively attempts to break from the becoming-instinct of the intellect, to which we are all prone. To properly remain attentive to the unfolding novelty of time, Bergson says 'we must do violence to the mind, go counter to the natural bent of the intellect. But that is just the function of philosophy' (1998: 30). To do this, we must become attentive to the singularity and novelty of the present, which is to say, reject the automatizing movements of perception, affect, and memory which seek to layer the image of the past over the dynamism of the present and future. As Bergson puts it,

> The more we succeed in making ourselves conscious of our progress in pure duration, the more we feel the different parts of our being enter into

each other, and our whole personality concentrate itself in a points, or rather a sharp edge, pressed against the future and cutting into it unceasingly. It is in this that life and action are free.

(201)

Of course, this is never fully possible, exactly because our perception is never pure. But the indetermination which consciousness introduces into the human mind allows for the possibility of matching the indetermination in the flow of durational time, at least in a limited way. We can do this by turning our tendency towards habit against itself, building habits premised on openness and critical reflection, through a process of 'training, in the highest meaning of the word' (Bergson 1977: 97). Bergson speaks of 'the superiority of [man's] brain, which enables him to build an unlimited number of motor mechanisms, to oppose new habits to the old ones unceasingly, and, by dividing automatism against itself, to rule it' (1998: 264–5). This ability to divide automatism against itself is interesting because, once again, we see the role of embodiment and training in matters of morality and politics. Indeed, this can very fruitfully be connected up with the Spinozist ethical program we discussed in the previous section. There we noted the way in which repetition or 'practice' of moral beliefs and viewpoints could serve to embed moral behaviours and viewpoints which will be ready-to-hand as we navigate moral dilemmas in a fast-moving world, a point which is true of Bergson's moral theory as well. Says Lefebvre about Bergson:

> What is the benefit of such repetition? It is twofold: first, by drilling maxims into ourselves, we are provided with a set of ready-made responses to whatever life throws at us; and second, through constant repetition, these maxims become integrated into our personality. They cease to be merely true or acceptable propositions and come instead to shape the whole of our being.
>
> *(79–80)*

Ultimately what is crucially about our account of perception, speed, ethics, and politics in Bergson is an account of how human life is marked by a tension between the open and the closed, at both the individual and the social level. At the individual level, human perception and cognition tend towards automatism and habit, in the movement 'from the past to the present, from recollection to perception' (Deleuze 1998: 63). However, despite this we still have the possibility of free creative action which chooses from 'unlimited' options, even though

> it will always neglect the part of novelty or of creation inherent in the free act; it will always substitute for action itself an imitation artificial, approximative, obtained by compounding the old with the old and the same with the same.
>
> *(Bergson 1998: 103)*

However, crucially that same habit-forming-habit that humans possess can be turned against itself, as we inculcate habits of seeking out the new.[5] At the social level, societies and moralities tend towards closedness, even as there is always the possibility of 'pioneers of morality' who shock or challenge people out their ingrained habits, opening up their minds to unacknowledged moral claims and actors. These two accounts are interrelated, as the individual tension reinforces the social, and vice versa. Ultimately, it is this tension that we will be discussing in the next three parts as we return to the central question of a world of accelerating flows of information. These sections will argue that the problems of attention and filtering are essentially about how individuals, and societies, can work to navigate these fault lines between the open and the closed in ways which are ethically and socially sustainable.

Part 2: Attention

Paralysis and Distraction

As discussed in the introduction, the new pace of information acquisition, processing, and communication manifests as an increase in the amount of information to which we are subject, the tidal wave that manifests every time we turn on our TVs, boot up our laptops, or check our smartphones. This sense of being overwhelmed gestures, once again, at Brown's Paradox. This new flow of information provides us with opportunities that past generations could only dream of, and yet it leaves us feeling all the more powerless. As Andrejevic puts it:

> The paradox of an era of information glut emerges against the background of this new information landscape: at the very moment when we have the technology available to inform ourselves as never before, we are simultaneously and compellingly confronted with the impossibility of ever being *fully* informed.
>
> *(2)*

As discussed, one of the ways in which anxieties over this infoglut manifests is as concerns over the problem of attention – how will we maintain focus on what is important, without being overwhelmed. This problem of infoglut and attention can be understood through the Bergsonian problem of the new, and therefore conceived of under the problematique of the closed and the open (i.e. a closed or open disposition to the emergence of the new). In Bergson, one of the central problems for human perception is how to deal with the constant rush of new information which the world generates. It does this through the various subtractive and additive processes discussed earlier, filtering, blocking, or replacing much of the information we might be receiving for the sake of being able to effectively (and quickly) navigate the world. Such tactics serve, ultimately, to 'close off' perception enough that it is not overwhelmed. However, at the same time, human perception and cognition needs to maintain enough 'openness' to effectively engage with the new when it is encounter. This tension, between the open and the closed, is exacerbated in a world of accelerating flows of information. From this perspective we can understand the two poles of 'broken attention' which we discussed in the introduction – paralysis and distraction – as two maladaptive responses to an information rich environment constantly demanding we pay attention to the new. Indeed, we can see them hypertrophies of human responses to the new, with paralysis constituting a kind of pathological closedness, and distraction a kind of pathological openness.

Paralysis is one pole of our encounter with information overload, as we simply freeze up, incapable of taking action in the face of the torrent of new information to which we are subject. This has profound implications for political and ethical action. While in principle being informed about important political issues and injustices can be a spur to action, in practice, the media's constant deluge of stories of corruption, disaster, and horror can leave us not only unsure of where and how to start. Andrejevic describes how the result of information overload is a kind of paralysis: 'The psychological reaction to such an overabundance of information and competing expert opinions is to simply avoid coming to conclusions' (7). This inability to come to conclusions, this paralysis in the face of an onrush of new information, can have several political consequences. Political apathy – frequently interpreted as an expression of laziness or self-centredness amongst citizens – can perhaps be sometimes understood simply as a manifestation of paralysis, a fatalism brought on by an endless crushing wave of (frequently bad) news. As David Loy says, 'doesn't infinite possibility likewise imply paralytic indecision? How do I decide what to do, what should have priority, when nothing is more present than anything else, physically or temporally?' (2007: 204). We might also here see the phenomenon of echo chambers – a retreat into social and informational spaces which present us not with new information, but with information which by and large reinforces our previous understanding of the world – as a defence mechanism against this paralytic inability to engage with newness. In either case what we see is a kind of pathological rejection of the new, a closing off of the perception, either through collapse or through retreat.

If paralysis is one pole of our potential reaction to information overload, distraction provides the other. Where paralysis constitutes a kind of pathological fixing of attention, distraction constitutes an inability to fix our attention on any one thing for long. When paralyzed we cannot focus on anything; when distracted, we try to focus on everything. The political implications of this are as potentially devastating as paralysis, as James Der Derian spells out:

> We are all familiar with the contemporary production and transformation of multimedia by networked information technologies, from

increased CPU speeds and broadband access, to realtime cable news and CNN effects, to embedded journalists and network-centric warfare. The global networking of multi-media has become unstoppable, and I believe that its effects may well have accelerated beyond our political as well as theoretical grasp. A public attention deficit disorder leaves little time for critical inquiry and political action by a permanently distracted audience.

(2003: 445)

In a Bergsonian framework, we can think of distraction as the opposite problem to paralysis. Where paralysis was a rejection of newness, distraction is a kind of pathological pursuit of newness at the expense of being able to integrate this newness into our patterns of thought and behaviour. As Loy puts it:

> The cyberpresent results from slicing time so thinly that our sense of duration disappears, replaced by accelerating speed. Our awareness usually hops from one perch to the other, but now it hops so quickly that the sensation is more like running on an accelerating treadmill. This is possible, however, only because now-moments – our treadmill steps – are denuded of meaningful content. Each step is no different from the last, or the next. Whatever content there is, is immediately replaced by different content. Without a relationship to previous and following moments, the present becomes dehistoricized, autonomous, fungible, and interchangeable with the next moment – which denudes it of extended meaning.
>
> *(2007: 207–8)*

This is the failure of the system of filtering and shaping perception through affect and memory to pay attention only to important elements to avoid being overwhelmed by the new.

What is extra dangerous about the kind of world of accelerating flows of information that contemporary ICTs makes possible, is the way in which it might actively inculcate these habits of distraction. Matt Richtel, a science writer for the New York Times, argues that digital media is making us not just increasingly distracted but distract*able*.

> Scientists say juggling e-mail, phone calls and other incoming information can change how people think and behave. They say our ability to focus is being undermined by bursts of information. These play to a primitive impulse to respond to immediate opportunities and threats. The stimulation provokes excitement – a dopamine squirt – that researchers say can be addictive. In its absence, people feel bored. . . . The nonstop interactivity is one of the most significant shifts ever in the human environment, said Adam Gazzaley, a neuroscientist at the University of California, San Francisco.' We are exposing our brains to an environment and

asking them to do things we weren't necessarily evolved to do,' he said. 'We know already there are consequences.'

What we see here is a problem, ultimately, of memory and habit. The new information and experiences that distracted humans are exposed to are not integrated into our sense of self. Instead, the only habit that is really cultivated here is the pursuit of newness, even if that newness does not go on to produce anything. Thus, the outrage we feel at a news story about an atrocity committed somewhere is immediately supplanted and replaced by outrage at a different atrocity. The concern raised by a politically astute tweet is given the same time and consideration as a joke tweet, or a comment on a recent TV show. None of these interactions are given enough sustained attention to give rise to new habits or behaviours. To put it another way, none of these encounters are engaged with substantively enough to open us up to a new world. Rather we remain closed up within the cycle of a continual pursuit of newness which never actually changes anything for us. Here once again we can see another potential root of political apathy. It is not that we are lazy, or indifferent to corruption, atrocities, or injustices. It is rather that our media move so quickly from one thing to the next, that we have no time for in-depth consideration, or long-term planning. In this regard, we can see how the floating attentionality of distraction can, when stretched thin enough, turn into the frozen attentionality of paralysis. (We should also note that, while these difficulties of attention might have been an inevitable consequence of human perception interacting with these accelerating information flows, it is also the case that they are the result of concerted efforts by platform owners and media creators, to make their content and platforms as 'sticky' and 'distracting' as possible, and thus that they play a role in consciously trying to make their audience more 'distractable', a point to which we will return in our discussion of filter bubbles.)[6]

However, as much as new technologies introduce new difficulties, these problems of attention speak to the fundamental issues that human perception struggles with. How to engage with an information dense environment in which we are constantly encountering newness, in a way which allows us to take measured, effective, and timely action? A world of accelerating information certainly exacerbates this problem, but it does not introduce it. As Marrati stated in the previous section: 'To look at the processes that bring about novelty does not come spontaneously to us at all but, rather, requires something like a conversion of attitude, a constant effort of attention' (4). From this perspective, the problem of attention ultimately speaks to the problem of the relationship between the open and the closed. How do we remain open enough to encounter the genuinely new but closed enough to ensure that what we do encounter can be incorporated into a stable and sustainable state of affairs (whether this be at the level of individual perception, or at the level of society)? Crucially, Bergson notes that our tendency towards habit, automatism, and closure can itself be fought and managed through habit, through 'training, in the highest meaning of the word' (1977: 97). In this regard, Marrati's 'constant effort of attention' can relate to the inculcation of new habits and attention.

This raises an important point. That our patterns of attention, our habits of relating to new information, can be shaped over time. As Duke University's Cathy Davidson puts it, 'We learn attention as infants and that means we can unlearn attentional patterns and relearn new ones'. Thus, insofar as we might be rightly worried about tendencies towards distraction and paralysis, we can begin to learn habits and behaviours to fight these tendencies. Indeed, this is the flipside of the neuroplasticity which Richtel fears for its ability to weaken our attention. As Rheingold puts it,

> Human thinking processes are neither wired nor rewired, although it is convenient to think of them in that way. Even if the probability that a specific set of brain cells will fire in synchronization does resemble fixed circuitry, the brain works in a more dynamic way than the wiring meta-phor implies. [Professor of child development at Tufts University] Wolf emphasizes that groups of neurons create new connections and strengthen pathways between them in specific networks whenever a person acquires a new skill. 'Thanks to this design', Wolf notes, 'We come into the world programmed with the capacity to change what is given to us by nature, so that we can go beyond it.'
>
> *(59)*

Here we can see how this carries with it the echoes of Bergson's indetermina-tion of the intellect, or 'the superiority of [man's] brain, which enables him to build an unlimited number of motor mechanisms, to oppose new habits to the old ones unceasingly, and, by dividing automatism against itself, to rule it' (1998: 264–5). Though there are a variety of potential habits that can be developed in response to a world of accelerating information, in the next sec-tion I wish to focus on one which has received increasing attention in political theory: mindfulness.

Habit and Mindfulness

The habit that Rheingold, and many others, recommend to help engage with our accelerating informational environment is 'mindfulness'. In a special issue of *New Political Science*, Michele Ferguson explains:

> Since the turn of the millennium, there has been an explosion of research in psychology, neurobiology, education, and business demonstrating a wide range of benefits of . . . 'mindfulness.' Mindfulness has been shown to reduce stress, depression, and anxiety; to increase impulse control,

attention spans, and worker productivity; to improve interpersonal and workplace relationships; and to reduce reactive, conflictual, and violent behavior.

(201)

Hölzel et al., in a frequently cited article from *Perspectives on Psychological Science*, defines mindfulness as a 'nonjudgmental attention to experiences in the present moment', describing

> a two-component model of mindfulness, where the first component is the regulation of attention in order to maintain it on the immediate experience, and the second component involves approaching one's experiences with an orientation of curiosity, openness, and acceptance, regardless of their valence and desirability.

(538)

Although there are a variety of different forms of mindfulness meditation (drawing from multiple traditions, most prominently Buddhism and Hinduism, although more contemporary secular traditions have emerged), one of the most common involves sitting quietly and focusing attention on one's breath. As the mind wanders, the meditator draws the attention back to the breath (depending on the tradition the meditator might be encouraged to identify or catalogue the thoughts which distracted their attention). In doing so, one begins to train and strengthen one's attention. As the Hölzel et al. article notes

> Illustrating the effects of repeated practice of focused attention meditation, meditators report that the regular practice enables them to focus their attention for an extended period of time . . . and distractions disturb this focus less frequently during formal meditation practice and in everyday life. In accordance with such self-reports, a number of studies have empirically documented enhanced attentional performance in meditators.

(540)

Returning to our discussion in the previous section, mindfulness meditation thus constitutes a practice which helps us to strengthen and develop certain modes of attention. In a Bergsonian light, it is the inculcation of a habit which serves to shape our cognition and perception, in ways which, paradoxically, leave us potentially less subject to the unconscious conditions of paralysis and distraction and shift our relationship to encounters of the new.[7]

To get deeper into this idea, and to grapple explicitly with the temporal dimensions of thought and perception which it develops, we might turn to an account by science writer David Rock, summing up research by neuroscientists Farb et al., which argues:

> people have two distinct ways of interacting with the world, using two different sets of networks. One network for experiencing your experience involves what is called the 'default network' . . . This network is called default because it becomes active when not much else is happening, and you think about yourself. If you are sitting on the edge of a jetty in summer, a nice breeze blowing in your hair and a cold beer in your hand, instead of taking in the beautiful day you might find yourself thinking about what to cook for dinner tonight, and whether you will make a mess of the meal to the amusement of your partner. This is your default network in action. It's the network involved in planning, daydreaming and ruminating. . . . This default network also become active when you think about yourself or other people, it holds together a "narrative". A narrative is a story line with characters interacting with each other over time. The brain holds vast stores of information about your own and other people's history. . . . When you experience the world using this narrative network, you take in information from the outside world, process it through a filter of what everything means, and add your interpretations.

We can see immediately the parallel between this image of thought and the habitual closed image Bergson presents of 'impure' perception. Here our perceptions of the present are always bound up in memories of the past, and projections into the future. We apply a filter of already existing meanings and interpretations. Most importantly, temporally we see how this mode of thought begins from the 'vast stores of information about your own and other people's history', using these stores of knowledge to filter and interpret our experience of the world. Here we see the Bergsonsian revolution in perception described by Deleuze, in which 'We do not move from the present to the past, from perception to recollection, but from the past to the present, from recollection to perception' (1998: 63).

This 'default network' of experience is contrasted with what the researchers called the 'direct experience network'.

> When this direct experience network is activated, you are not thinking intently about the past or future, other people, or yourself, or considering much at all. Rather, you are experiencing information coming into your senses in real time. Sitting on the jetty, your attention is on the warmth of the sun on your skin, the cool breeze in your hair, and the cold beer in your hand. . . . Experiencing the world through the direct experience network allows you to get closer to the reality of any event. You perceive more information about events occurring around you, as well as more accurate information about these events. Noticing more real-time

information makes you more flexible in how you respond to the world. You also become less imprisoned by the past, your habits, expectations or assumptions, and more able to respond to events as they unfold.

(Rock)

Here once again, we see a direct parallel to Bergson's account of an open state of mind, in which we perceive the novelty and singularity of the present, and grasp the creative, durational unfolding of time rather than papering over it with memories and presuppositions. We 'break the chain' of habit, as Bergson says, and are able to respond flexibly to the singularity of the situation (note, therefore, that this is a way of encountering the durational unfolding of time without lapsing into a neurotic, distracted pursuit of the new). As Rock describes, when experiencing the world via the direct experience network. 'You also become less imprisoned by the past, your habits, expectations or assumptions, and more able to respond to events as they unfold'. We might compare this with the passage in Bergson in which he describes how

> The more we succeed in making ourselves conscious of our progress in pure duration, the more we feel the different parts of our being enter into each other, and our whole personality concentrate itself in a point, or rather a sharp edge, pressed against the future and cutting into it unceasingly. It is in this that life and action are free.
>
> *(1998: 201)*

In terms of the 'default network', Rock makes clear that 'There's nothing wrong with this network', much as Bergson also accepts that our habitual behaviour and impure perception play a crucial role in survival. However, Rock argues, 'the point here is you don't want to limit yourself to only experiencing the world through this network'. For Bergson this is even more crucial as such an open frame of mind is a necessity for pursuing an open morality.

This loosening of the hold the default network – of the habits of closedness – is no easy task since, as Rock points out that 'The default network is active for most of your waking moments and doesn't take much effort to operate', an insight which Bergson would thoroughly agree with. However, the good news is that, as Davidson pointed out, 'We learn attention as infants and that means we can unlearn attentional patterns and relearn new ones'. The Farb study points to the fact that people can learn to become attentive to the mode of attention they're employing, a kind of metacognition where we think about how we're thinking (hence 'mindfulness'). From this attentiveness stems the ability to choose which network of experience we wish to employ.

> In the Farb experiment, people who regularly practiced noticing the narrative and direct experience paths, such as regular meditators, had

stronger differentiation between the two paths. They knew which path they were on at any time, and could switch between them more easily. Whereas people who had not practiced noticing these paths were more likely to automatically take the narrative path.

(Rock)

What this means is that those who have cultivated this sense of mindfulness, through bodily practices of meditation, find themselves better able to fight off distractions, as they are attuned to where their attention is focused and how they are experience the world. They know when they are navigating by habit and when they are acting intentionally and flexibly. More importantly, they can better choose when to do so. The result of this is potentially something like what Bergson describes as the process by which 'we succeed in making ourselves conscious of our progress in pure duration' wherein 'life and action are free'. O'Sullivan notes this connection between a meditation and an ethics of creativity and duration in his comparative study of Bergson and Buddhism, saying:

> Meditation, at least in one of its forms (samadhi), is simply the cultivation of awareness of this point, this moment of 'decision' – and the prolonging of a certain pause, a dwelling 'in' the gap. Again, for Bergson, it is also through this gap (Bergson calls it a 'hesitancy') that memory, this time in the sense of the 'pure past' (or, again, a virtuality), pours in. In itself this allows for a certain creativity to replace our more reactive modes of behaviour; a kind of liberation from the (utilitarian) concerns of the organism.
>
> *(2014: 260–1)*[8]

Mindfulness and Politics

This cultivation of mindfulness, especially through meditation, is gaining mainstream acceptance. Michele Ferguson describes how mindfulness

> has also been absorbed into corporate and military contexts. General Mills runs a 'Mindful Leadership' program for its executives; Google offers its employees a mindfulness course called 'Search Inside Yourself'; the US Marine Corps has offered service members Mindfulness-based Mind Fitness Training prior to deployments.
>
> *(202)*

In turn Matt Richtel reports that '[a]t an Army base on Oahu, Hawaii, researchers are training soldiers' brains with a program called "mindfulness-based mind fitness training"'.

Note here that the invocation of corporate and military training raises a crucial point. Frequently these calls for 'mindfulness', and the exhortation of the benefits of mindfulness training to navigate our newly hypermediated environment, are justified by claims to improved productivity. Such tactics, it is claimed, can make us more focused students, workers, and soldiers. As such, these techniques can be seen as simply a new set of tactics in contemporary capitalist biopolitics, in which we try to shape behaviour, thought, and perception, to be as productive and efficient as possible. Ferguson describes how 'mindfulness practices have seamlessly integrated into Western neoliberal capitalism, in a form we could call the Mindfulness Industrial Complex' (202).[9]

And it is absolutely true that these techniques can be (and are) employed in such a way as to provide state and capital with more 'flexible' workers and more focused soldiers. However, we should not therefore think that this is the only thing that they can do. Indeed, if we accept as given that corporate- and state-owned media structures have an interest in maintaining and encouraging distraction and paralysis, then the ability to resist these forces, and intentionally shape our attentional patterns, is a crucial one. As we discussed earlier, this shift towards a maximum of distraction in networked environments is not arbitrary, but linked to the business models of many major online businesses (Carr 2008). In this context, it is all the more crucial to develop and teach tools to respond to information overload. There is the tendency to treat the effects of different media and technologies as determinative – that they have necessary effects on human nature. This ignores the way in which we develop responses to these innovations, responses which can be improved and taught. As Edwin Ng says:

> In order to expose attentional traps, it is important to interrogate the propaganda function and political economic influence of transnational media. But the liberation of attention also requires receptivity towards the ways in which the audience may actively resist or subvert the power asserted by the media or other institutional forces.
>
> *(378–379)*

More importantly, if we are worried about the ways in which mindfulness meditation can be useful at training more productive soldiers and workers, then ultimately we are accepting the idea that such tactics might work – work to make us more attentive in a distraction rich environment, to give us greater control over our own sense of cognition and perception. If this is the case, we would be foolish to cede such techniques solely to corporations and militaries. Such techniques can also be put towards efforts for political acts of resistance. In the *New Political Science* symposium, Ferguson provides an overview of some of these political mobilizations of mindfulness:

> In 2011, Sit Down, Rise Up led meditation in Zuccotti Park as part of Occupy Wall Street. The Prison Yoga Project began in 2001 to teach embodied mindfulness practices to at-risk youth and inmates in the

California prison system, aiming to reduce reactivity and encourage non-violence. In 2007, Mindful Schools started to train public school educators in mindfulness techniques, to reduce toxic stress particularly among underprivileged students, and burnout among public school teachers. . . . Many activists and policy-makers have determined that mindfulness is relevant to their politics.

(201–202)

James K. Rowe conducted ethnographic research on activists in New York and San Francisco who integrate mindfulness meditation into their political work, describing how

social justice activists are busily experimenting with how mind/body practices can support collective liberation. While their efforts remain below the public radar, several organizations now work at the fold between subjective and social change. This intersection is increasingly called 'transformative social change.' The Movement Strategy Center, generative somatics, and the Center for Transformative Change are leading organizations in what I call the 'transformative movement-building current': the growing number of organizations integrating personal and social transformation practices.

(208)

Rowe interprets these practices by arguing they indicate ways in which 'techniques of the self and micropolitics can support Left macropolitics' (209). (Note again, we can see similarities between this account of techniques of the self and our discussion of ethical practice and repetition in Spinoza in Chapter 3.) Ng agrees:

Amidst all the attempts by dominant structures of power to colonize attention, it seems that mindfulness can function as a countervailing force . . . to . . . advocates of a micropolitics of perception, this embodied practice of attuning ourselves to the affective forces of everyday life would serve as the basis for a stronger ethos of engagement and social responsibility.

(380)

Now, we might worry at the potentially individualizing nature of mindfulness as a solution to the problem of accelerating information; that this ultimately offloads the systemic problem of infoglut onto individual actors. Indeed, we might point out that in an increasingly fast-paced world, it gives actors one more task they have to accomplish in an already busy day.[10] While we should be attentive to these kinds of concerns, ultimately my argument is not that mindfulness is the sole *solution* to the problem of infoglut, or that it is sufficient absent broader systemic changes (which will be discussed later). Rather, I view mindfulness as one potential technique – one habit which can be inculcated – that can allow individuals to better navigate an information rich environment, and potentially contribute to political engagement (and combat burnout) in ways which will help contribute to movements for systemic political change. Most importantly, from a Bergsonian point of view, it encourages a disposition of openness to the new which is crucial for maintaining our ethical and political commitments in an accelerating world.

Part 3: Echo Chambers

Though mindfulness provides a potential habit that can aid in our navigation of an information rich environment, it is not, in and of itself, sufficient. While working on our attention can help us to be thoughtful about how we relate to the unfolding of the new, it is still the case that the world is saturated with far too much information for us to effectively absorb and use. In this case, the basic human perceptual strategy of filtering is necessary to seek out only those pieces of information that we need or want. This kind of filtering process is already at work in regard to information overload in new media, in both technological and social forms. Search engines provide the most basic filtering mechanism, zeroing in on specific information within the infinite sea that is the internet. RSS feeds which allow us to quickly skim through articles we wish to read in full do the same, as do aggregator blogs on topics we are interested in, curated by people whose taste we trust. Even our social networks serve as filters, as, for example, the newsfeed of social media accounts becomes collections of articles posted by our friends, or sent to us specifically, frequently applying to our interests. Although many of these are specific technologies, they are also practices, as we learn to use them effectively to filter the stream of information, ensuring that we are able to take advantage of the power of digital networks without drowning under a tidal wave of knowledge.

However, these filters carry with them the same dangers as the subtractive and additive qualities of human perception, namely, the possibility of ensuring that you only see what you expect to see. Numerous commentators have pointed to the rise of the so-called 'echo chamber' effect, in which any information which might clash with our current viewpoints is filtered out. Now, of course, there is nothing new with people seeking out news sources and encounters which reconfirm their viewpoint and affirm their beliefs. As we discussed, for Bergson, the closure of the mind such that we only encounter that which we are already familiar with (whether this be a result of internal perceptual processes, or external social processes) is a perhaps an inherently human tendency. However, in a world of accelerating ICTs, one's choice of information sources has expanded so immeasurably, that one can now find access to resources which match one's political/social/cultural leanings exactly. Contrary to the days of the 'mass media' in which media artefacts had to appeal to a wide variety of viewers and listeners, and thus could not appeal perfectly to any of them, the so-called 'narrowcasting' which cable and the internet provide fragments the audiences into countless indexed niches. As Mark C. Taylor puts it:

> The more sophisticated the technology and the faster the connectivity, the more these fragments are fragmented until the horizon disappears and each person becomes sealed in a bubble where it is difficult if not impossible to hear anything but the echo of one's own voice or the voices of those who are just like oneself. The result of this fragmentation is the loss of common knowledge and shared values that are the basis of every community.
>
> *(2014: 208)*

In this regard we can (paradoxically) navigate a world of infinitely varied information and experiences while never being surprised or challenged. Again, at root here is Bergson's account of the open and the closed, and their relation to the new. According to Bergson, at both the individual and the social level, humans have a tendency to close themselves off to the new, preferring to run 'indefinitely in the same circle' (1977: 209). Elsewhere, Bergson describes how perception function as a

> filter or a screen . . . it helps us to see straight in front of us in the interests of what we have to do; and, on the other hand, it prevents us from looking to the right and left for the mere sake of looking.
>
> *(314–315)*

This tendency to 'see straight in front of us' only, to run 'indefinitely in the same circle', produces distinct ethical and political problems.

Cass Sunstein agrees with this diagnosis, arguing that the rise of echo chambers is a fundamentally dangerous phenomenon for a democracy. This is because echo chambers undermine two key features he thinks are necessary to maintain a democratic system in a heterogenous society:

> First, people should be exposed to materials that they would not have chosen in advance. *Unanticipated encounters*, involving topics and points of view that people have not sought out and perhaps find irritating, are central to democracy and even to freedom itself. Second, many or most citizens should have a range of *common experiences*. Without shared experiences, a heterogeneous society will have a more difficult time . . . understanding one another.

Sunstein goes on to argue that mass-media provided the possibility of such common experiences and unanticipated encounters.

> If you tune into the evening news, you will learn about a number of topics that you would not have chosen in advance. Because of their speech and immediacy, television broadcasts perform these public forum-type functions more than general interest intermediaries in the print media. The 'lead story' on the networks is likely to have a great deal of public salience; it helps to define central issues and creates a kind of shared focus of attention for millions of people. And what happens after the lead story – dealing with a menu of topics both domestically and internationally – creates something like a speakers' corner beyond anything imagined in Hyde Park. As a result, people's interest is sometimes piqued, and they might well become curious and follow up, perhaps changing their perspective in the process.

Sunstein's concern is that absent both 'unanticipated encounters' and 'common experiences' we see the emergence of a kind of group polarization, wherein our interactions with others only serves to secure, and never challenge, our worldviews. Andrejevic shares Sunstein's concern, looking at the way, for example, Fox news builds their brand around exploiting this tendency towards echo chambers.

> The success of Fox news . . . is, in part, a result of its willingness to embrace what Sunstein terms 'balkanization' by ensuring that audience members consistently receive information, analysis, and rhetoric that reinforces their worldview. . . . Sunstein describes the resulting logic of divergence and polarization as a technologically driven one: in a world in which audiences can customize their information consumption, they will, though the force of selective exposure and selective retention, become increasingly fragmented and polarized in their worldview.
>
> *(49)*

In such contexts, we experience our worldview as fundamentally secure and objective and perceive those who disagree with us as wilfully absurd or stubborn (after all how can they ignore what's right in front of their/our eyes?)

However, in considering Sunstein's claims, there are at least two mitigating factors which must be considered. First, this concern over the seeming paradox that an increase of communicational freedom can lead to us experiencing less rather than more, divergent viewpoints is, as mentioned, not a new one. This is the central concern of, for example, John Stuart Mill's *On Liberty* (which, to his credit, Sunstein mentions as well). Indeed, what is being described here is exactly Bergson's description of the tendency towards closure, in which we shut ourselves off from experiences, constituencies, and changes which might challenge our understanding of the world and require us to change our mode of engagement with it. According to Bergson, this is a consistent tendency of human societies and individuals across all times and cultures. This is not to say that this should not be a concern of ours. But it is to say that we should be careful about pinning it on a particular (and recent) change in our media environment.

The second point is that, even as we might become concerned about the 'echo chamber' effect, we should not do so at the expense of lionizing the mass media which came before it as 'general interest intermediaries' discussing issues of 'public salience'. We need only a brief perusal through Chomsky and Herman's *Manufacturing Consent* to question whether the interest which the mass media serviced was truly 'general'. While in principle, Sunstein acknowledges the potentially biased nature of mass media, his desire for a 'common experience' seems to override this concern. As he says:

> None of these claims depends on a judgment that general interest intermediaries are unbiased, or always do an excellent job, or deserve a monopoly over the world of communications. The Internet is a boon partly because it breaks that monopoly. So too for the proliferation of television and radio shows, and even channels, that have some specialized identity. . . . All that I am claiming is that general interest intermediaries expose people to a wide range of topics and views and at the same time provide shared experiences for a heterogeneous public.

What is missing from Sunstein's account, however, is any discussion at all of power and representation. Whether, and how much, you had unanticipated experiences of heterogeneous viewpoints in the mass media over the last century would depend greatly on whether or not you were white, male, straight, cisgendered, able bodied, etc. The unanticipated experiences of the mass media which Sunstein extols were never experienced symmetrically. Indeed, in a clear example of missing the point, Sunstein invokes the following example.

> If you take the ten most highly rated television programs for whites, and then take the ten most highly rated programs for African Americans, you will find little overlap between them. Indeed, more than half of the ten most highly rated programs for African Americans rank among the ten *least* popular programs for whites. With respect to race, similar divisions can be found on the Internet. Not surprisingly, many people tend to choose like-minded sites and like-minded discussion groups.

The implications of this being that this is more dangerous and potentially undemocratic state of affairs then one in which the same shows end up in the top ten choices of both white American and African-Americans. This, of course, misses the point that such 'common experiences' were only achievable because there were few shows which were marketed to African-Americans. What Sunstein portrays as group polarization, and the fragmentation of the public, is in many ways nothing more than the development of a cultural apparatus which provides content and information to more than just one hegemonic demographic group.

Sunstein is right that 'the Internet is a boon partly because it breaks that monopoly' of mass broadcasters. What he misses is that it is not the same boon to everybody. The choice between mass media and new media is not the choice between the 'general public' and the 'echo chamber'. It is the choice between a more general or a more fine-grained hegemony. To say that one is better than the other is, at best, premature, and at worst, ignores the historical marginalizations of any numbers of peoples in favour of a fictitious nostalgia for a unified 'public'. Indeed, as we will discuss, this apparent plea for openness to the unexpected actually demonstrates a stronger anxiety over the collapse of a stable 'closed' world.

Useful here is Nancy Fraser's critique of the concept of the 'public sphere' as developed in the work of Habermas and other late Critical Theorists. Fraser notes the way in which these accounts valorize the existence of a unitary 'public sphere', marked by a 'common experience' of the 'public good', and critique the 'fragmentation' or 'splintering' of that unitary public sphere. As Fraser notes, this assumes that everyone has equal ability to participate in this public sphere, and that the experiences, arguments, and needs of different groups are equally capable of being articulated in this public sphere. In terms of the mass media of the last century this is manifestly untrue. Our society is riven by a variety of social inequalities across axes of race, class, gender, sexuality, gender orientation, religion, etc. This has serious consequences for nostalgic attempts to valorize the 'shared public space' of previous media environments. As Fraser says:

> it is not possible to insulate special discursive arenas from the effects of societal inequality; and . . . where societal inequality persists, deliberative processes in public spheres will tend to operate to the advantage of dominant groups and to the disadvantage of subordinates. Now I want to add that these effects will be exacerbated where there is only a single, comprehensive public sphere. In that case, members of subordinated groups would have no arenas for deliberation among themselves about their needs, objectives, and strategies.

(66)

Against this unitary vision of the public sphere, Fraser argues for the value of what she calls 'subaltern counterpublics', which she describes as 'parallel discursive arenas where members of subordinated social groups invent and circulate counterdiscourses, which in turn permit them to formulate oppositional interpretations of their identities, interests, and needs' (67). The fragmented media landscape that Sunstein laments also provides opportunities for subaltern groups to share relevant information, organize, and strategize rather than simply having to make do with a hegemonic media culture focused on the interests and experiences of a dominant group. Fraser thus rejects 'the assumption that the proliferation of a multiplicity of competing publics is necessarily a step away from, rather than toward, greater democracy, and that a single, comprehensive public sphere is always preferable to a nexus of multiple publics' (62–63). Instead, she argues that 'the proliferation of subaltern counterpublics means a widening of discursive contestation, and that is a good thing in stratified societies' (67). From a Bergsonian perspective, we might describe this as a rejection of a larger closed world in favour of a world that allows a variety of worlds to proliferate, increasing opportunities for the emergence of new worlds and new encounters.

What we see then is that, for all of his concern around 'unanticipated encounters' and 'common experiences', Sunstein fails to recognize ways in which these two phenomena are in tension. Unanticipated encounters represent the open, and common experiences represent the closed. While it is true that a world of accelerating flows of information fundamentally disrupts the balance between these two forces in certain ways, Sunstein ignores the opposition and instead imagines a unified, nostalgiafied past where they were united under the closed rubric of 'the public sphere'. He fails to grapple with the fact that the lost common experiences he laments were only really common amongst a certain group in society, and the unanticipated encounters he desired tended to consistently exist within certain limits that left many perspectives and experiences hidden and unexpressed. In other words, for all of his concern for an 'open mindset', what Sunstein is really lamenting is the increasing challenge to the closed world and mindset which felt (to him) as if it encompassed everyone effectively. The 'balkanization' of information which would seem to provide individuals with *more* opportunities for unanticipated encounters is lamented exactly for the fact that it erodes the dominance of the common experiences (Sunstein's) which were taken as the only ones necessary.

Indeed, it is worth noting the way in which the process of 'balkanization' does not function symmetrically across social groups. Let us look again at Andrejevic's account of Fox News:

> Fox is tapping into the reactions – the intense sense of anxiety, fear, indignation, superiority, or anger that they feel or want to feel. Its viewers are seeing themselves, perhaps, more as discriminating consumers choosing the brand of impassioned (and outraged) "news" than as citizens enduring the outdated ritual of listening to a dispassionate accounting of the facts, as determined in some distant newsroom.
>
> *(48)*

This tendency – to seek out a brand that represents one's identity – is presented as a kind of universal experience of the desire to turn to echo chambers. But this ignores the fact that there is a radical difference between older white Americans turning to Fox News, and, say, people of colour turning to proliferating channels and websites which provide content written by and for them. In the latter case you have individuals who are ill-served by the traditional 'mainstream' media sources seeking out 'common experiences' that actually reflect their lives. In the former, you have individuals retreating to increasingly narrow media out of anger and outrage at having to occasionally encounter experiences that are not their own. Thus, we see that the retreat into media 'echo chambers' is primarily a phenomenon of the political right. For example,

> According to a new Pew Research Center survey, Americans who say they voted for Trump in the general election relied heavily on Fox News as their main source of election news leading up to the 2016 election, whereas Clinton voters named an array of different sources, with no one source named by more than one-in-five of her supporters.
>
> *(PEW 2017)*

Benkler et al. find similar results in their studies of online news sources, saying, 'Unlike on the right, on the left there is no dramatic increase in either the number of sites or levels of attention they receive as we move to more clearly partisan sites'.

Thus, rather than a shift from a world of 'common experiences' marked by 'unanticipated encounters' to one of 'balkanized echo chambers', we have one in which hegemonic groups seek out echo chambers exactly because they are uncomfortable with an increasingly diverse world in which they are forced to experience 'unanticipated encounters'. And conversely, in which subaltern groups are able to actually seek out discursive spaces which reflect *their* common experiences rather than simply having to make do with hegemonic accounts. Absent these counterpublics, subaltern groups would be

> less able than otherwise to articulate and defend their interests in the comprehensive public sphere. They would be less able than otherwise to expose modes of deliberation that mask domination by absorbing the less powerful into a false 'we' that reflect the more powerful.
>
> *(Fraser 1990: 66–7)*

Thus, we should neither think that this tendency towards 'group polarization' and 'echo chambers' is a new problem, nor one that can be solved through a rejection of new media. As Benkler et al. put it:

> Our analysis challenges a simple narrative that the internet as a technology is what fragments public discourse and polarizes opinions, by allowing us

to inhabit filter bubbles or just read 'the daily me'. If technology were the most important driver towards a 'post-truth' world, we would expect to see symmetric patterns on the left and the right. Instead, different internal political dynamics in the right and the left led to different patterns in the reception and use of the technology by each wing. While Facebook and Twitter certainly enabled right-wing media to circumvent the gatekeeping power of traditional media, the pattern was not symmetric.

We must therefore understand these political phenomenon not just as a response to technological innovation (although obviously this plays a role) but also through more political questions of collective organization by marginalized groups and growing resentment amongst previously hegemonic majorities who see their privileges and status challenged. Attentiveness to these more 'political' dimensions doesn't mean that we should ignore the impact these technologies have, or the danger of seeking out information environments that reinforce our pre-existing assumptions and worldviews. But it does mean that we should think about such tendencies in the context of those oh-so-human tendency towards automatism and closedness, to see only what we expect to see, to seek out only those things we have already decided are part of the world (as well as the specific politics of *ressentiment* that shape reactionary politics in an accelerating world, as discussed in Chapter 1).

Part 4: Filter Bubbles

And yet, even as we should be leery of nostalgia, and recognize continuities in a human tendency towards closedness and habit, we should also acknowledge that there are some new aspects to our accelerating technological world. In the case of filtering, while in the past one had to actively seek out information sources which agreed with you (in the process of which you necessarily had to encounter ones that didn't), now this can happen without you even knowing. This is because various search and aggregation applications are based on algorithms which seek to provide you with content that most closely fits your wants. As a result, when searching through Google, looking at news on Facebook or Twitter, or searching for books on Amazon, you can find yourself in a situation in which you aren't being given a 'neutral' result (whatever that might mean) but one tailored to reflect your individual interests and needs. This is a concept which Eli Pariser terms the 'filter bubble'.

> The new generation of Internet filters looks at the things you seem to like – the actual things you've done, or the things people like you like – and tries to extrapolate. They are prediction engines, constantly creating and refining a theory of who you are and what you'll do and want next. Together, these engines create a unique universe of information for each

of us – what I've come to call a filter bubble – which fundamentally alters the way we encounter ideas and information.

(9)

In one way this is a good, and potentially even necessary, practice. As discussed, we now exist in world of ever accelerating amounts of information, and technological processes which can help to filter out unnecessary information for our purposes can be dramatically helpful. If I search for 'Dentists in Victoria' it is useful if I am automatically given results for Victoria, Canada, where I live, and not Victoria, Australia. The problem is that this process happens invisibly, through applications which we might presume to be neutral. Thus,

> Most of us assume that when we google a term, we all see the same results – the ones that the company's famous Page Rank algorithm suggests are the most authoritative based on other pages' links. But since December 2009, this is no longer true. Now you get the result that Google's algorithm suggest is best for you in particular – and someone else may see something entire different. In other words, there is no standard Google anymore.
>
> (2)

This is dangerous because it can lead to a kind of hypertrophy of the echo chamber effect. In the echo chambers described earlier we sought out a world that fit our preconceived notions, while here we are presented with one ready-made and which we are therefore all the more likely to take as neutral and objective. As Pariser says,

> In polls, a huge majority of us assume search engines are unbiased. But that may be just because they're increasingly biased to share our own views. More and more, your computer monitor is a kind of one-way mirror, reflecting your own interests while algorithmic observers watch what you click.
>
> (3)

He goes on to say:

> Left to their own devices, personalization filters serve up a kind of invisible autopropaganda, indoctrinating us with our own ideas, amplifying our desire for things that are familiar and leaving us oblivious to the dangers lurking in the dark territory of the unknown.
>
> (15)

In this regard, we see an externalization of the Bergsonian process whereby our perception returns to us that which we were already expecting to see. And the fact that it happens without us knowing about it means that we are more likely to simply take whatever information we are given as a neutral image of the world. This means that 1) we might be less likely to interrogate our already held assumptions, and 2) we might be less inclined to give the perspectives of others the benefit of the doubt.

And this is the case even if we only presume a relatively benign effort on behalf of technologies and platforms to more efficiently deliver us the information that we are seeking out. As discussed earlier, platforms, social media sites, search engines, and content sites are all interested in making themselves as 'sticky' and distracting as possible. In this regard, their algorithms are not just designed with the relatively neutral goal of providing you with the most appropriate information for your interests. They are interested in providing you with the information that is mostly likely to make you continue engaging with them. As has been shown social media apps and websites are more likely to provide you with information that is shocking, provocative, enraging, etc. Work has even been done to show the way in which recommendation algorithms on sites such as YouTube lead to radicalization of viewers by presenting them with increasingly extreme videos around issues such as White Supremacy, conspiracy theories, alt-right politics, etc. Paul Lewis, in *The Guardian*, describes how the YouTube 'play next' algorithm

> has been found to be promoting conspiracy theories about the Las Vegas mass shooting and incentivising, through recommendations, a thriving subculture that targets children with disturbing content such as cartoons in which the British children's character Peppa Pig eats her father or drinks bleach.
>
> *(2018)*

Lewis interviewed former YouTube employee and whistleblower Guillaume Chaslot, 'a 36-year-old French computer programmer with a PhD in artificial intelligence'.

> During the three years he worked at Google, he was placed for several months with a team of YouTube engineers working on the recommendation system. The experience led him to conclude that the priorities YouTube gives its algorithms are dangerously skewed. 'YouTube is something that looks like reality, but it is distorted to make you spend more time online', he tells me when we meet in Berkeley, California. 'The recommendation algorithm is not optimising for what is truthful, or balanced, or healthy for democracy.'

Such tendencies interact with the echo chamber effects discussed earlier, making consumers more partisan, more enraged, and more radical (although crucially, and following our discussions earlier, such effects don't exist symmetrically across the political spectrum [Alfano et al.: 310]).

The danger of this historical technological moment, then, is one in which our innate perceptual tendency towards a closed filtering process, which presents us with what we already expect to see, becomes integrated into external technologies in ways which don't just replicate but amplify these tendencies in forms which are intended to benefit tech monopolies rather than consumers. It is specifically the externalization of these processes which critics of accelerating ICTs frequently point to. We discussed in the previous chapter Virilio's concern about the way in which acceleration removes humans from the process of perception and cognition. Andrejevic's makes a similar critique in *Infoglut* noting that as the flood of information accelerates, more and more of the processing, filtering, sorting, and analyzing of that information will be done through external ICTs, saying:

> The challenge to comprehension, sense-making, and referentiality posed by information glut leads to the offloading of knowledge-generating processes onto the figure of the sorting machine or the allocating market. We no longer have to take responsibility for making sense of the data – the apparatus does this for us.
>
> *(14–15)*

Throughout much of his text, Andrejevic's concern is with the asymmetry of access to both these big data stores and to the techniques of data mining. I agree with this critique and think that the question of who controls these technologies and to what ends is a crucial question, which I will return to at the end of this chapter. But in passages like these we see slip out indications (as we see in Virilio) that the concern is ultimately not solely about who owns these technologies, or how specifically they function, but that they exist at all. These critiques seem to be founded on the belief that such forms of knowledge making and perception are illegitimate, perhaps inhuman. We see Andrejevic remark that much of our contemporary information environment involve an 'offloading of knowledge-generating processes onto the figure of the sorting machine'. He follows this up elsewhere by saying: 'It is hard to even conceive of the magnitude of the data being collected, imagine trying to *make sense* of its contents. This process will, of necessity, become the province of automated forms of data mining, sorting, and analysis' (34). Implicit in this is a fundamental distinction between a natural human cognition/perception which happens internal to the human body, and an unnatural, inhuman cognition/perception which is done through external technologies, seemingly regardless of who is in charge of these technologies and how they operate. Again, here we see a prostheticizing/parasitizing vision of speed in which technology parasitically drains the full, unitary, natural human body. To respond properly to this vision, we must return to Bergson's account of embodied perception and see how he envisions the role of so-called 'external' technologies.

Bergson and Technology

Bergson is a particularly useful philosopher for discussing the intersection between the human and the technological because, in ways similar (though not identical) to Spinoza, his work frequently breaks down binary oppositions such as the human and the animal, the human and the technological, and even the animal and the vegetable. He develops a sort of tendential ontology in which the differences between things are more often than not ones of degree rather than kind. As Bergson puts it, 'the group must not be defined by the possession of a certain characters, but by its tendency to emphasize them' (1998: 106). As Marrati put it, '[l]ife, Bergson argues, is nothing but a tendency to change that expresses itself along divergent lines of evolution; what all those lines have in common, though, is that they are different, but equally elegant, solutions to problems' (9).[11] This means that the best way to understand the relationship between the human and the technological is, first, to understand the relationship between these divergent lines of evolution.

We've already discussed what is, for Bergson, the distinction between humans and animals, that humans are marked by intelligence and animals by instinct; again, with the understanding that these are merely tendential, and that there is always some intelligence in instinct, and some instinct in intelligence (not to mention the ways in which intelligence turns into a pseudo-instinct through habit). Earlier, we identified the distinction between intelligence and instinct as primarily related to the amount of indetermination they introduced into the sensorimotor system. However, Bergson also produces an alternate definition, that instinct functions through bodily organs, whereas intelligence functions through found or created tools.

> As regards human intelligence, it has not been sufficiently noted that mechanical invention has been from the first its essential feature, that even today our social life gravitates around the manufacture and use of artificial instruments, that the inventions which strew the road of progress have also traced its direction.
>
> *(1998: 138)*

Going on to say:

> If we would rid ourselves of all pride, if, to define our species, we kept strictly to what the historic and prehistoric period show us to be the constant characteristics of man and of intelligence, we should say not *Homo Sapiens*, but *Homo Faber*. In short *intelligence, considered in what seems to be its*

original feature, is the faculty of manufacturing artificial objects, especially tools to make tools, and of indefinitely varying the manufacture.

(138–139)

In contrast to this ability to manufacture an infinite variety of tools, instinct is defined in terms of the perfected knowledge of how to use those pre-given tools, the organs of the body. 'Now, does an unintelligent animal also possess tools or machines? Yes, certainly, but here the instrument forms a part of the body that uses it; and, corresponding to this instrument, there is an *instinct* that knows how to use it' (139–140).

Marrati raises the crucial point here that this distinction between instinct and intelligence parallels that between technology and organs.

> In Bergson's account nothing essential differentiates organs and machines; what distinguishes them is just the 'stuff' of which they are made. Organs are 'organic tools,' while machines are 'inorganic tools'; that is to say, they are different chemical formations, but they serve analogous purposes and have analogous functions.
>
> *(11)*

What is more, if we do look at tools as 'external organs', then given the 'variable manufacture' to which they are susceptible, that means that the human body can be changed, depending on how these tools are changed. Says Bergson, 'The workman's tool is the continuation of his arm, the tool-equipment of humanity is therefore a continuation of its body. Nature, in endowing us with an essentially tool-making intelligence, prepared in this way a certain expansion' (1977: 309). Marrati expands on this by saying:

> The importance granted to technology is accompanied in Bergson by an insight that largely anticipates many contemporary developments in philosophy and anthropology, namely, the idea that tools and machines open up the possibility of new functions, within and beyond the scope they were originally created for, and thus react back on humans, to provide them with what Bergson does not hesitate to call – and let us remember that *Creative Evolution* was published in 1907 – 'new organs' that prolong and expand the 'natural' organism.
>
> *(11)*

Thus, the ability to use technology is directly related to the indetermination which intelligence introduces into the sensorimotor system, since both technology and intelligence increase the variety and creativity of human thought and action in the world. In comparing the 'unorganized instrument' of the intellect to the 'organized instrument' of instinct, Bergson notes that it is true that the latter is, at least in the earlier stages, invariably better adapted and constructed than the former.

> The instrument constructed intelligently, on the contrary, is an imperfect instrument. It costs an effort. It is generally troublesome to handle. But, as it is made of unorganized matter, it can take any form whatsoever, serve any purpose, free the living being from every new difficulty and bestow on it an unlimited number of powers. Above all, it reacts on the nature of the being that constructs it; for in calling on him to exercise a new function, it confers on him, so to speak, a richer organization, being an artificial organ by which the natural organism is extended. For every need that it satisfies, it creates a new need; and so on, instead of closing, like instinct, the round of action within which the animal tends to move automatically, it lays open to activity an unlimited field into which it is driven further and further, and made more and more free.
>
> *(1998: 140–1)*

More than just fulfilling a pre-existing need then, technology actually shapes and changes our bodies, introducing new functions, needs, and experiences. Bergson can therefore be seen as a thinker of technogenesis, of the evolution of the body via technology (similar here to the third encounter with speed which we saw in the second chapter). That we have a static and essentialized image of our bodies (and of human nature) is, says Bergson, a result of our automatism, our insistence on sticking to habit rather than perceiving the novel nature of the durational present (1998: 138).

Given the essentially technological nature of the human body according to Bergson, and its susceptibility to change, Marrati argues we can describe Bergson as a thinker of the cyborg.

> Now, if cyborgs – these creatures that populate fiction, theory, and, according to some, social reality – are a hybrid of machine and organism, it is fair to say that, from a Bergsonian perspective, we living beings are all natural cyborgs. And humans, in particular, are natural cyborgs.
>
> *(13)*

This is therefore an added way in which perception is 'impure'. It is not just that the perceptions are mixed with, and shaped by, memories and affects; technology too affects the senses. Technologies contribute to both the subtractive and additive characteristics of perception. Sunglasses filter out light, making other elements of the visual plane clearer; telescopes, microscopes, and hearing aids focus, amplify, and manipulate light and sound waves to focus our attention on different aspects of the world. These technologies 'mediate' our encounter with the world in ways similar to the body. Says Bergson 'if our organs are natural instruments, our instruments must them be artificial organs' (1977: 309). Note, it is this last point which shows how this account goes against the prosthetic/parasitic account of technology. There, the technology-as-external-organ replaces the human, emptying out the body. Here the body is always already in flux, capable of radical changes and shifts.[12] This is because, as mentioned earlier, there is no radical ontological distinction between the animal and the human for Bergson, and thus no radical distinction between the natural and the artificial. All have their roots in an evolutionary drive to achieve survival. Again, for Marrati:

> there is no clear-cut line that divides organisms and machines, 'artificial' devices and 'natural' organic functions: only different cognitive strategies and material formations for the purpose of coping with and modifying the environment – strategies that run through, although at different degrees, all animal forms of life, human and nonhuman alike, and that expand and transform the boundaries of experience.
>
> *(12)*

Underlying the criticisms of Virilio and Andrejevic (as well, as Rousseau, Descartes, etc.) is a normative image of the body and cognition, which presumes an essential pace of the body allowing for the free, undistorted processes of perception and cognition. Given such a set of assumptions, technologies (especially accelerative technologies) constitute a threat to the integrity, cohesion, and 'natural-ness' of these processes. If, however, we start from 'how Bergson conceives of technology – as the preeminent means by which human beings employ intelligence to extend their perceptual grasp over matter, to enlarge their own living duration' (Hansen 2006a: 258), then the difference begins to be one of degree. The human body was always already technological, a cyborg body. Furthermore, perception – rather than becoming successively corrupted, suspect, and eventual superfluous due to 'optical technologies' – was always impure from the beginning well before any 'technological' elements were brought into the mix. We know that Virilio's major concern is the *speed* by which these technologies function, both in terms of the speed with which they deliver images to us, as well as the speed with which they collect and analyze them. This constitutes the power that the technological has over us, that they can work at a pace faster than our natural 'physiological take'. Because our perception cannot keep pace with technology, we necessarily become its slave. But we know from our discussion that the human body and perception are always happening at multiple paces, and that much of our thought and perception happens too fast for conscious, wilful control. The fact is, perception is always subject to countless interventions, subtractive and additive, internal and external. We are subject to innate drives and unconsciously developed habits. As we saw earlier, human beings are 'naturally' marked by extensive automatism. We neither transparently perceive the world nor do we act purely wilfully and intentionally.

This is not to say that there isn't a difference between the automatism of our organic body and the automatism of our inorganic body, between the effects of our 'organized instruments' and 'unorganized instruments'. But the difference is not simply that one is bad and the other is good (or, to say the same thing, that one is 'natural' the other 'unnatural'). The major difference is that our technological body is far more subject to intervention than our organic body. This has, of course, its dangers, insofar as powerful forces can shape our technological bodies in ways that make us more pliable. But, as Bergson would point out, it also has its possibilities, as it allows us to shape ourselves in powerful, reflective, and thoughtful ways. Virilio is right to turn our attention to these technologies. If, as Bergson thinks, new technologies shape the nature of the human body, if they provide us with new needs, new 'ideas and feelings', if they are the primary drivers of social change, then we must be deeply attentive to which technologies we choose to employ and how. But they are not 'unnatural', and therefore not fundamentally bad for that reason. We therefore accept the challenge that Virilio (and others like him) puts to us, of being attentive to the ethical and political effects of perceptual technologies, while rejecting the answer that he already gives, namely that those effects are, inherently, *inhuman*.

From a Bergsonian perspective, our ethical responsibility in relating to the technological is, in other words, the same as our responsibility in relating to our bodies. We must learn to work with them in ways which incline us most towards an ethical openness to the world. As Marrati puts it:

> In the domains of politics, morality, and religion, Bergson's position is interesting insofar as he rejects any form of naturalism or naturalization without falling to the opposite position, to what we nowadays would call some unrestricted form of social constructionism. Instead of ignoring or denying the constraints of nature, Bergson calls for a strategy that aims at countering nature, so to speak, from within – looking for ways to go against 'natural tendencies', to change and modify their direction with the help of other tendencies that are already available to us or that we can create with our 'natural' organic and inorganic tools. In short, Bergson's strategy is to counter nature with its own weapons.
>
> *(16)*

Thus, just as we have to develop practices, habits, policies, ideas, and affects to open ourselves up moral requirements, we must do the same with our technological bodies. The tactics and techniques might be different (although as we will see, there is a surprising – or perhaps not – overlap between the two), but the goal is the same.

What [Bergson] hopes to see is the emergence of a new alliance between mysticism and technology. Mysticism (which in his view is nothing but an aspiration to open up the limits of the present) could divert science and technology from the commodity-oriented quest and false needs of industrial societies, while the unprecedented power of science and technology could create the tools, organic and inorganic, for further pursuing the experiment of an open society.

(17)

Practical Responses to an Accelerating World

Following from Bergson's belief that science and technology should be directed in ways that serve the cultivation of an ethical and political openness (and not merely the interests of corporations), we might look to policies that could serve to shape ICTs in ways that limit the tendencies towards closure and radicalization discussed earlier. As a more minor starting point, Pariser argues that companies such as Google and Facebook should have much greater transparency around how their filtering algorithms work (90–91), as well as potentially allowing greater intervention in how those algorithms are applied. This call for greater transparency is linked to a call for greater responsiveness on behalf of increasingly powerful tech companies. Pariser notes that 'Appointing an independent ombudsman and giving the world more insight into how the powerful filtering algorithms work would be an important first step' (231). Additionally, tech companies and platforms might recognize the limitations of filter bubbles and seek to develop algorithms more interested in introducing the unexpected into our search results and feeds. 'There's one more thing the engineers of the filter bubble can do. They can solve for serendipity, by designing filtering systems to expose people to topics outside their normal experience' (235).[13]

The problem with such suggestions is that '[t]his will often be in tension with pure optimization in the short term, because a personalization system with an element of randomness will (by definition) get fewer clicks' (235). What is more, this presumes companies that are willing to make such technological and organizational changes, potentially at the cost of power and profit. As Lanier says, 'If owning everyone's attention by making the world terrifying happens to be what earns the most money, that is what will happen' (2018: 34). This caveat directs us to more major interventions we might make into the corporations and organizations that own and operate the platforms, sites, and technologies that play a central role in our accelerating information environment. While the filtering and organizing of information streams might be a necessity in an era of accelerating ICTs, and while this filtering and organizing might parallel similar processes that happen internally to human perception and cognition, in our current system technical decisions around this filtering and organizing are concerned not with optimizing human perception (or democracy, or truth), but with profit. In this regard, responses to many of the dangers discussed earlier might turn to 1) policies which seek greater control over increasingly powerful tech companies and platforms, and 2) open source and open hardware programs which provide greater transparency and greater control for individual users.[14] We might especially push for policies which seek to break up technology and media monopolies, more heavily regulate their actions, and cultivate public options of various stripes. As Alfano et al. describe:

> While it may be possible to rely on well-intentioned and well-resourced firms to implement such design principles when given the chance, not all firms have sufficient good will and resources. For reckless and malicious actors, regulation with sufficient enforcement power will be needed. For well-intentioned firms that lack the technological skills or the resources to put those skills to use, a taxpayer-funded repository of code-reviewed open-source algorithms that embody best practices may be the optimal solution.
>
> *(318)*

At the same time as we push for these more systemic changes, we will continue to have to navigate an accelerating information environment that will continue to reinforce and amplify natural human tendencies towards perceptual, ethical, and political closure. This means that, as discussed in Part 2, we should look to individual level tactics which can help to open ourselves up ethically and politically, and cultivate more open communities (even as we recognize the insufficiency of purely individual tactics). We might, therefore, seek to reflect upon the ways in which we seek out information sources which reflect back to us our own pre-existing beliefs, and therefore we can also think about ways in which we might inculcate habits which seek to break us out of these echo chambers and filter bubbles. Again, the necessity of seeking out information, experiences, and perceptions which might surprise or even challenge us is a long running theme in discussion of the public sphere and free speech. What is crucial here is the recognition that such necessity is not something that can be achieved simply through sheer force of will but rather must be sought out through the development of embodied habits. Thus, just as we noted how our attention might be trained and developed through the repetition of mindfulness techniques, here we might look to practices which might serve to break up habits that make us susceptible to echo chambers and filter bubbles. As a starting point, we might, when we seek out news, make a habit of seeking out one piece of information that we wouldn't normally find (either by looking at sources we would normally eschew, or looking at topics, or sections, that we normally wouldn't be interested in). Though a small thing, over time this sort of practice can help to produce the 'unexpected encounters' which are important to our engagement with the public sphere. Additionally, we might seek to foster a critical response to information which reinforces our pre-existing beliefs, reminding ourselves of the way in which filter bubbles work and being suspicious of information which seems too seamless in its reflection of our worldviews. Such practices are especially necessary for those of us who find ourselves members of privileged demographics who are more likely to be catered to by hegemonic popular culture. While these may seem like small gestures, the point is the development of habits over time that serve to break up the tyranny of habit itself – habits of seeking out novelty and difference (and yes, challenge and disappointment) and habits of suspicion over the too-smooth reading of a world that reflects back only what we expect.

Interestingly, the attempt to break old habits serves to reshape not just the filtering algorithms in our heads but also the ones in our computers. As discussed, filter bubbles function by developing profiles of our behaviour, and if we vary our behaviour more, our profile algorithms will produce more varied and unexpected results. Pariser describes the way in which our personal nonconscious habits and online algorithms can produce positive feedback loops as we try to stretch our interests.

> Habits are hard to break. But just as you notice more about the place you live when you take a new route to work, varying your path online dramatically increases your likelihood of encountering new ideas and people. Just by stretching your interests in new directions, you give the personalizing code more breadth to work with. Someone who shows interest in opera and comic books and South African politics and Tom Cruise is harder to pigeonhole than someone who just shows interest in one of those things. And by constantly moving the flashlight of your attention to the perimeters of your understanding, you enlarge your sense of the world.
>
> *(223–224)*

This point makes us aware that, in trying to change our encounters with the online world, it is not enough to simply change our own behaviour. We must also be knowledgeable about the structure of accelerating ICTs if we are going to effectively intervene in these processes. Just as the development of books and newspapers required the development of a certain amount of media literacy, the impact of accelerated ICTs means that being an informed, critical citizen means understanding, at least somewhat, the ways in which these digital networks function. As Pariser says,

> it's becoming more important to develop a basic level of algorithmic literacy. Increasingly, citizens will have to pass judgement on programmed systems that affect our public and national life. And even if you're not fluent enough to read through thousands of lines of code, the building-block

concepts – how to wrangle variables, loops, and memory – can illuminate how these systems work and where they might make errors.

(228)

Douglas Rushkoff makes a similar point in his book *Program or Be Programmed* when he says,

> Understanding programming – either as a real programmer or even, as I'm suggesting, as more of a critical thinker – is the only way to truly know what's going on in a digital environment, and to make wilful choices about the roles we play.

(8)

At its simplest, this call for digital literacy can mean understanding the specific options available to us in the different platforms and applications we use to fight against filter bubbles and the like. So, for example, Pariser notes how filter bubbles frequently rely on the use of 'cookies' which track users' behaviour, allowing them to develop profiles which shape and constrain what we're shown. Thus, 'regularly erasing the cookies your Internet browsers uses to identify who you are is a partial cure. Most browsers these days make erasing cookies pretty simple – you just select Options or Preferences and then choose Erase cookies' (224). When using social media such as Facebook and Twitter, we can investigate how to change our settings to ensure that we are given a wider set of information More broadly, as we learn more about the way in which filtering algorithms work, we can seek out platforms, applications, and information sources that 'give users more control and visibility over how their filters work and how they use your personal information' (224–225). And in some cases, we might decide that the dangers outweigh the benefits, and unplug from specific platforms or services which seem particularly predatory (Lanier 2018).

My suggestions here are intentionally general, as they will have to change with changing technological environments, and respond to particular social, political, and economic contexts. However, what is necessary in being able to productively develop such policies and tactics is a framework for analysis that does not rely on a vision of a free, objective, undistorted human perception, and a unitary, normative human body. Bergson is useful for us exactly because he gives us a human perception and body that is always already impure. In doing so, he gives us the tools to engage productively with an uncertain future rather than retreating into a fictional nostalgic past.

Notes

1. As Paola Marrati puts it:

   > Calling for a deep awareness of the reciprocal belonging of life and knowledge, Bergson goes against a long and powerful tradition that sees an

> unbridgeable gap between the supposedly pure, disembodied, and disinterested procedures of reason that produce knowledge, on the one hand, and the supposedly obscure and irrational force of life, on the other hand.
>
> *(8)*

2. See Grosz (2013).
3. See Worms (2012).
4. Note that Bergson's account of open and closed societies is shaped by certain colonial and racist assumptions. I discuss these limitations in Bergson's thought, and possible ways of overcoming them, in Glezos (2019).
5. See Grosz (2013: 225).
6. See, for example, Chiang and Hsiao (2015); Lewis (2018), and Alfano, Carter and Cheong (2018).
7. It's worth noting that there is a surprisingly extensive secondary literature on the relationship between Bergson and Buddhism, by both his contemporaries such as Nishida Kitaro (1986) and Kuki Shuzo (1978), as well as more recent work by O'Sullivan (2014), Bunnag (2017), Yapp (2014), Ng (2014), Jones (2002), and Botz-Bornstein (2000).
8. See also Shuzo (1978: 73).
9. See also Zizek (2001).
10. See also Purser and Loy (2013).
11. Or, in the words of Clare Colebrook:

> In some respects Bergson could be *the* philosopher of a posthuman future. He does, after all, locate the human intellect within a broader trajectory of life and creative energy. And the intellect, far from being the reason and telos of life, is a stultifying pause in an otherwise greater and greater expansion of complexity.
>
> *(75)*

12. Indeed, such changes are not always the result of technological shifts. In an example that very strongly parallels contemporary work on neuroplasticity, Bergson notes how, when someone loses a sense, they don't therefore have 'less of a body'. Rather they develop a *different* body.

> But the truth is that the character of movements which are externally identical is internally different, according as they respond to a visual, an auditory or a tactile impression. Suppose I perceive a multitude of objects in space; each of them in as much as it is a visual form, solicits my activity. Now I suddenly lose my sight. No doubt I still have at my disposal the same quantity and the same quality of movements in space; but these movement can no longer be coordinate to visual impressions; they must in future follow tactile impression, for example, and a new arrangement will take place in the brain.
>
> *(1991: 45–6)*

This account also has the benefit of rejecting Virilio's insistence on a normative body, with its ableist implications.

13. Alfano et al. provide a complementary set of technical suggestions (2018: 317–18).
14. For a discussion of open source technology, see Hassan (2007: 56–7), Stallman (2002), and Glezos (2012: Ch. 3).

Works Cited

Alfano, M.; Carter, J. A.; and Cheong, M. (2018) 'Technological Seduction and Self-Radicalization', *Journal of the American Philosophical Association*, 4(3): 298–322.

Andrejevic, M. (2013) *Infoglut: How Too Much Information Is Changing the Way We Think and Know*, New York, NY: Routledge.

Benkler, Y.; Faris, R.; Roberts, H.; and Zuckerman, E. (2017) 'Study: Breitbart-Led Right-Wing Media Ecosystem Altered Broader Media Agenda', *Columbia Journalism Review*, March 3. Available at: www.cjr.org/analysis/breitbart-media-trump-harvard-study.php (Accessed July 9, 2019).

Bergson, H. (1977) *The Two Sources of Morality and Religion*, Trans. R. Ashley Aura and Cloudesley Brereton, Notre Dame, IN: University of Notre Dame Press.

Bergson, H. (1991) *Matter and Memory*, Trans. N. M. Paul and W. S. Palmer, Zone Books: New York.

Bergson, H. (1998) *Creative Evolution*, Dover: Toronto.

Botz-Bornstein, T. (2000) 'Contingency and the "Time of the Dream": Kuki Shūzō and French Prewar Philosophy', *Philosophy East and West*, 50(4): 481–506.

Bunnag, A. (2017) 'The Concept of Time in Philosophy: A Comparative Study between Theravada Buddhist and Henri Bergson's Concept of Time from Thai Philosophers' Perspectives', *Kasetsart Journal of Social Sciences*, 30: 1–7.

Carr, N. (2008) 'Is Google Making Us Stupid?', *The Atlantic*, July/August. Available at: www.theatlantic.com/magazine/archive/2008/07/is-google-making-us-stupid/306868/ (Accessed July 22, 2019).

Chiang, H. and Hsiao, K. (2015) 'YouTube Stickiness: The Needs, Personal, and Environmental Perspective', *Internet Research*, 25(1): 85–106.

Colebrook, C. (2012) 'The Art of the Future', *Bergson, Politics, and Religion*, eds. A. Lefebvre and M. White, Raleigh, NC: Duke University Press.

Connolly, W. (2002) *Neuropolitics: Thinking, Culture, Speed*, Minneapolis: University of Minnesota Press.

Davidson, C. (2010) 'Here's How the Brain Science of Attention Really Works', *HASTAC Weblog*, October 9. Available at: http://hastac.org/blogs/cathy-davidson/heres-how-brain-science-attention-really-works (Accessed June 20, 2012).

Deleuze, G. (1988) *Bergsonism*, Trans. H. Tomlinson and B. Habberjam, New York, NY: Zone Books.

Der Derian, J. (2003) 'The Question of Information Technology in International Relations', *Millennium: Journal of International Studies*, 32(3): 441–56.

Eriksen, T. H. (2001) *Tyranny of the Moment: Fast and Slow Time in the Information Age*, London, UK: Pluto Press.

Ferguson, M. L. (2016) 'Symposium: Mindfulness and Politics', *New Political Science*, 38(2): 201–5.

Fraser, N. (1990) 'Rethinking the Public Sphere: A Contribution to the Critique of Actually Existing Democracy', *Social Text*, 25/26: 56–80.

Glezos, S. (2012) *The Politics of Speed: Capitalism, The State, and War in an Accelerating World*, Abingdon, UK: Routledge.

Glezos, S. (2019) 'Bergson *Contra* Bergson: Race and Morality in *The Two Sources*', *European Journal of Political Theory*. Available at: https://journals.sagepub.com/doi/full/10.1177/1474885119834760 (Accessed August 1, 2019).

Grosz, E. (2013) 'Habit Today: Ravaisson, Bergson, Deleuze and Us', *Body & Society*, 19(2/3): 217–39.

Hansen, M. B. N. (2006a) *New Philosophy for New Media*, Cambridge: MIT Press.

Hassan, R. (2007) 'Network Time', *24/7: Time and Temporality in the Network Society*, eds. R. Hassan and R. E. Purser, Stanford, CA: Stanford Business Books.

Hölzel, B. K.; Lazar, S. W.; Gard, T.; Schuman-Olivier, Z.; Vago, D. R.; and Ott, U. (2011) 'How Does Mindfulness Meditation Work? Proposing Mechanisms of Action From a Conceptual and Neural Perspective', *Perspectives on Psychological Science*, 6(6): 537–59.

Jones, C. S. (2002) 'A Lost Tradition: Nishida Kitarō, Henri Bergson and Intuition in Political Philosophy', *Social Science Japan Journal*, 5(1): 55–70.

Kuki, S. (1978) 'Bergson in Japan', *Shuzo Kuki and Jean-Paul Sartre: Influence and Counter-Influence in the Early History of Existential Phenomenology*, ed. S. Light, New York, NY: Journal of the History of Philosophy.

Lanier, J. (2018) *Ten Arguments for Deleting Your Social Media Accounts Right Now*, New York, NY: Henry Holt and Company.

Lefebvre, A. (2013) *Human Rights as a Way of Life: On Bergson's Political Philosopher*, Stanford, CA: Stanford University Press.

Lewis, P. (2018) '"Fiction Is Outperforming Reality": How YouTube's Algorithm Distorts Truth', *The Guardian*, February 2. Available at: www.theguardian.com/technology/2018/feb/02/how-youtubesalgorithm-distorts-truth (Accessed July 9, 2019).

Loy, D. R. (2007) 'Cyberlack', *24/7: Time and Temporality in the Network Society*, eds. R. Hassan and R. E. Purser. Stanford, CA: Stanford Business Books.

Marrati, P. (2010) 'The Natural Cyborg: The Stakes of Bergson's Philosophy of Evolution', *The Southern Journal of Philosophy*, 48(Spindel Supplement): 3–17.

Ng, E. (2014) 'Towards a Dialogue between Buddhist Social Theory and "Affect Studies" on the Ethico-Political Significance of Mindfulness', *Journal of Buddhist Ethics*, 21: 353–77.

Nishida, K. (1986) *Intuition and Reflection in Self-Consciousness*, Trans. V. H. Viglielmo, T. Toshinori, and J. S. O'Leary, Albany, NY: State University of New York Press.

O'Sullivan, S. (2014) 'A Life between the Finite and Infinite: Remarks on Deleuze, Badiou and Western Buddhism', *Deleuze Studies*, 8(2): 256–79.

Pariser, E. (2011) *The Filter Bubble: What the Internet Is Hiding from You*, New York, NY: The Penguin Press.

PEW Research Centre (2017) 'Trump, Clinton Voters Divided in Their Main Source for Election News: Fox News Was the Main Source for 40% of Trump Voters', January. Available at: www.journalism.org/2017/01/18/trump-clinton-voters-divided-in-their-main-source-for-election-news/ (Accessed August 1, 2019).

Purser, R. and Loy, D. (2013) 'Beyond McMindfulness', *The Huffington Post*, August 31. Available at: www.huffpost.com/entry/beyond-mcmindfulness_b_3519289 (Accessed July 22, 2019).

Rheingold, H. (2012) *Net Smart: How to Thrive Online*, Cambridge, MA: MIT Press.

Richtel, M. (2010) 'Attached to Technology and Paying a Price', *The New York Times*, June 6. Available at: www.nytimes.com/2010/06/07/technology/07brain.html?_r=3&ref=matt_richtel&pagewanted=all (Accessed June 20, 2012).

Rock, D. (2009) 'The Neuroscience of Mindfulness', *Psychology Today*, October 11. Available at: www.psychologytoday.com/blog/your-brain-work/200910/the-neuroscience-mindfulness (Accessed June 20, 2012).

Rowe, J. K. (2016) 'Micropolitics and Collective Liberation: Mind/Body Practice and Left Social Movements', *New Political Science*, 38(2): 206–25.

Rushkoff, D. (2011) *Program of Be Programmed: Ten Commands for a Digital Age*, Berkeley, CA: Soft Skull Press.

Stallman, R. M. (2002) *Free Software, Free Society: Selected essays of Richard M. Stallman*, ed. J. Gay, Boston: Free Software Foundation.

Sunstein, C. (2001) 'The Daily We', *Boston Review*, Summer. Available at: http://bostonreview.net/BR26.3/sunstein.php (Accessed Jun 20, 2012).

Taylor, M. C. (2014) *Speed Limits: Where Time Went and Why We Have So Little Left*, New Haven, CT: Yale.

Worms, F. (2012) 'The Closed and the Open in *The Two Sources of Morality and Religion*: A Distinction that Changes Everything', Trans. A. Lefebvre and P. Ravon, *Bergson, Politics, and Religion*, eds. A. Lefebvre and M. White, Raleigh, NC: Duke University Press.

Yapp, H. (2014) 'Chinese Lingering, Meditation's Practice: Reframing Endurance Art beyond Resistance', *Women & Performance: A Journal of Feminist Theory*, 24(2–3): 134–52.

Zizek, S. (2001) 'From Western Marxism to Western Buddhism', *Cabinet*, Issue 2. Available at: www.cabinetmagazine.org/issues/2/western.php (Accessed August 2, 2019).

6

IN THE FLESH OF AN ACCELERATING WORLD

Merleau-Ponty, Technology, and the Encounter With the Other

Introduction: From Intensity to Extensity

In the previous chapter we engaged with the acceleration of ICTs, and their impact on human perception. There we approached the question from the perspective of the intensive acceleration of information – the dramatic increase in the amount of information which people are exposed to on a daily basis – and the way in which this produces struggles over attention. In the next two chapters, we will approach the question of speed and perception from the perspective of extensive acceleration, the increased scope or distance over which information is now being conveyed. This question is not entirely separate from the intensive acceleration of information. This is because the extensive acceleration of information is, in many ways, a relatively old phenomenon. It was really with the introduction of the telegraph, and the acceleration of information to the speed of electrons (if not quite the speed of light), that we saw a true example of the 'annihilation of distance by time' (Marx 1973: 524). The expansion of the telegraphy network around the world, and its steady replacement by telephone lines and then fiberoptic cable certainly extended the scope of that annihilation, but ultimately by increments that could, in many ways, never match up to that first moment of peerless acceleration.

However, although telegraphy allowed information to accelerate at hitherto unheard speeds, it maintained a thin bandwidth, providing very little information. In this regard, the steady advancement in communication technologies did more than just increase the scope of that first acceleration. Increases in bandwidth did not just quantitatively increase the scope over which the 'annihilation of distance by time' took place but qualitatively changed the nature of that annihilation. The proliferation of high-bandwidth fiberoptic cable has allowed for the proliferation of realtime audio and video communication, as well as telerobotic control, allowing for increasingly robust telepresence technologies.[1] To continue using Marxist terminology, if the telegraph was a kind of formal subsumption of perception into a regime of the 'annihilation of distance by time', contemporary ICTs bring us ever closer to its real subsumption.

While this isn't to ignore the impact of the initial acceleration of the telegraph, it is to say that an analysis of the current scope of accelerating ICTs must take into consideration the density of the information which can now be communicated all over the globe. This density – and the new auditory, visual, and enactive interfaces through which we engage with it – means that we need to be able to discuss the effects of the acceleration of information not just in terms of the intellectual ability to absorb and manage information – which we discussed in the last chapter – but also the embodied experience of perception in a world of 24-hour satellite news, Skype, Facetime, texting, telerobotics, reachback drone operators, telepresence suites, and telecommuting. This is why in this chapter, and the next, we will turn to the work of Maurice Merleau-Ponty, whose phenomenological approach provides us with a nuanced account of embodied perception. This, coupled with his engagements with the question of technology (and the way that these brief engagements have been taken up by contemporary new media theorists), provides a framework through which to understand the effects of an accelerating global media network on embodied perception.

This kind of approach is especially important since, as we discussed in Chapter 4, there is a tendency to view acceleration, and accelerating ICTs, as fundamentally disembodying forces. In discussions of the spatiality of contemporary information networks, this frequently manifests as twin concerns over an increasing isolation or alienation of digitally enhanced bodies, and a concern over the rootlessness of digitally extended perception. Critics of contemporary ICTs – and acceleration more generally – view perception as increasingly sheared off from the body, absorbed into the no-place of cyberspace, alienated from other humans and separated from the material realities of space and place. The experience of accelerated perception is, on this account, a *dislocating* phenomenon, with consequences for our ability to form political solidarity with, and feel moral responsibility for, others.

Conversely, I will argue that perception is always already embodied and embedded in a material context. This is not to say that new information and communication technologies do not produce new forms of embodiment and materiality, or that they don't shape the emergent global nature of spatiality. Nor does it mean that we should uncritically accept these new forms of embodiment and spatiality, or that we will not need to develop new tactics, technologies, and politics to live with them ethically. What it does mean is that rather than being *dislocating*, accelerating perception would be better understood as *translocating*. Rather than leaving us location-less, or dematerialized, these new technologies introduce novel experiences of location and spatiality, suturing together previously distant spaces, without therefore introducing a homogenous distancelessness. Such an account of speed and spatiality also leaves open the possibility of authentic human encounters via the medium of accelerating ICTs. A proper understanding of the impacts of the acceleration of information requires, therefore, that we start from an account of perception which is always already embodied. To do otherwise is to limit our ability to understand the present. The stakes of such a shift in analytic framework is the ability to better understand a variety of political phenomena. For example, in our opening case study, we will look at the question of drone warfare, and the way in which many initial responses turned out to be insufficient, driven as they were by the assumption that accelerating perceptual technologies were inherently alienating and dislocating. The inadequacy of these assumptions will help explain the necessity of a different framework of analysis, rooted in an embodied, phenomenological account of perception.

Drones and Perception

Though initially shrouded in secrecy – and still obscured by claims to national security and executive privilege – since the second half of the George W. Bush administration, the US government's targeted killing programs in Pakistan and Yemen have been heavily discussed, in both popular journalism and academic circles. Although some of this attention has been prompted by debates over the legality and morality of extrajudicial killing, such issues are not unique to US actions in Pakistan and Yemen. Rather, what seems to have prompted the lion's share of the attention, has been the specific use of Unmanned Aerial Vehicles (UAVs) or Drones to conduct the killing. In principle, the use of drones is not wildly different from the use of traditional piloted bombing runs, or even special forces units (such as, for example, the unit which killed Osama Bin Laden). However, the concern is that the use of drone technology constitutes a fundamental shift in the nature of warfare, in that by physically removing humans from the battlefield, it makes killing more likely, both by decreasing the potential loss of lives (on the side deploying the drones) and, more importantly for our purposes, by fundamentally mediating the relationship between killer and victim.

The New Yorker describes the technical set up of the drone system:

> The Predator [drones] in the C.I.A. program are 'flown' by civilians, both intelligence officers and private contractors . . . Within the C.I.A., control of the unmanned vehicles is split among several teams. One set of pilots and operators works abroad, near hidden airfields in Afghanistan and Pakistan, handling takeoffs and landings. Once the drones are aloft, the former counterterrorism official said, the controls are electronically

'slewed over' to a set of 'reachback operators', in Langley. Using joysticks that resemble video-game controls, the reachback operators – who don't need conventional flight training – sit next to intelligence officers and watch, on large flat-screen monitors, a live video feed from the drone's camera. From their suburban redoubt, they can turn the plane, zoom in on the landscape below, and decide whether to lock onto a target.

(Mayer 2009)

The concern is that this mediated relationship to the battlefield, in which 'reach back operators' relate to their potential victims only via computer screens and 'video-game controls', will result in a derealization of the horrors of warfare. Critics assert that drone operators will fail to treat the battlefield as a real space, and their potential victims as human beings, as opposed to just flickering images on a screen. As Caroline Holmqvist puts it,

> an intuitive response to news about the increased reliance on technologies that allow for 'killing at distance' is that it renders war 'virtual' for one side of the conflict. . . . The drone operator, sitting in the safety and comfort of his control room in Nevada, no longer experiences war, goes the argument, and killing as a result becomes casual.
>
> *(2013: 541)*

A repeated theme in critiques of drones is the concern that it turns war 'into a video-game', and thus that the interface itself produces an effect (and an affect) of virtuality and unreality. Fitzsimmons and Sangha do a good job of summing up this criticism:

> Reflecting the sentiments of a number of scholars who are critical of the USAF's use of [Remote Piloted Aircraft (RPA)], Laurie Calhoun assumes that, because operators tend to be located far from the battlefield, they remain psychologically detached and unaffected when they kill human targets during their missions. Framed in this manner, operators appear to be little more than 'adept videogame players', who are entirely removed from the horrors of war.
>
> *(1–2)*

and

> Referring to operators as people who, 'kill in the manner of sociopaths with no feelings whatsoever for their victims', Calhoun argued that . . . for RPA operators, 'the visceral quality of warfare has been altogether removed from the experience of killing. The emotions associated with the activity of killing and risking death have been progressively muted with

distance and now eliminated from the act altogether in summary execu-
tions effected by RPAs and managed by desktop warriors.' Linda Johansson
argued, similarly, that RPA, 'enable, more than any other weapon, a form
of 'numbed killing' . . . due to the fact that combatants are able to maintain
an emotional distance by using this more or less autonomous technology'.

(4)

Here we see the implication that images translated through the video screen
of the drone controls are inherently unreal, virtual, disembodied, resulting in
an experience that is 'detached', 'unaffected', 'surreal', 'muted with distance',
and 'numbed'. Implicit in this analysis, then, is the assumption that this kind of
mediated and distantiated interface lessens the user's sense of moral responsibility to the other, making killing both easier and less impactful.

At the centre of this debate is a concern about speed. Without the dramatic
acceleration of information flows – both in terms of the bandwidth of information and the distance over which that information can travel with relatively
little delay – this kind of 'reach-back' operation of drones would be impossible.
It is not just the video interface that leads critics to worry about the 'surreal-
ity' of the experience but also the physical separation between the space of the
operator and the space of the victim. A repeated theme of critiques is the extent
to which the drone operators are physical distant from the field. Part of the
concern here is the asymmetry of danger between the killer and the victim,
but the other part is the idea that, insofar as the drone operator is fundamentally distant from the killing, he is *distanced*. We might, for example, readily
acknowledge that a fully equipped US soldier – connected to a wide array of
satellite imagery, air support, etc. – is already vastly more powerful than guer-
rilla fighters (not to mention innocent civilians) and thus that there is already
a profound asymmetry of danger between the two, and yet still believe that
there is something important in the soldier physically *being there*, whatever the
distribution of relative danger.

This privileging of *being there* over technologically mediated perception and
action is part of a longer tradition which views perception via mediating technologies as inherently 'less than' 'unmediated' perception – where 'less' can
mean less embodied, less material, less real, less affective, less authentic, or simply less real. Petranker describes the variety of thinkers for whom 'the rise of
the network destroys presence rather than enables it, substituting a weakened,
watered-down "telepresence" for our "concrete presence" in the world' (181).
By way of example, we might look to Hubert Dreyfus' concern over the inau-
thenticity of mediated experiences in his critique of 'telepresence' technologies.
Dreyfus asserts that

> Telepresence . . . call[s] our attention to the way that things and people
> are normally *directly* present to us and we . . . sense that this direct form of

> presence [is] basic and that *mediated* telepresence [is] at best a poor imita-
> tion. If people experienced 'presence' on the screen as a kind of privation
> of direct contact, the kind of washed out telepresence tele-technologies
> provide might well lead to an appreciation of our everyday robust relation
> to things and people.
>
> *(56)*

This sort of dismissal of technologically mediated perception is unsurprising
given Dreyfus' commitment to Heideggerian phenomenology, which, as Cath-
erine Wilson nicely sums up '[tries] to posit a rupture between an original mode
of awareness and interaction, and the artificial one of technology' (67–68).
Heidegger's work is marked by a profound anxiety over the way that the acceleration of both bodies and perceptions serves to alienate and dislocate human
existence. In his essay 'The Thing', Heidegger explains how 'All distances in
time and space are shrinking', and yet 'the frantic abolition of all distances
brings no nearness' (1971: 163). For Heidegger, 'nearness' is something that
can only be equated with the immediate. As a result, mediated perception (or
even distance mediated by accelerated transportation) produces spaces which
are neither near nor distant. As he says, 'The failure of nearness to materialize
in consequence of the abolition of all distances has brought the distanceless
to dominance' (179). The acceleration of bodies and perception thus serves to
dislocate human existence, placing it in a distanceless and inauthentic no-place.[2]

This critical take is by no means restricted to Heideggerian traditions.
Phenomenological ecologist David Abrams presents a similar critique saying
that mediated experience is inherently alienating, separating us from natural
experiences.

> Direct sensuous reality, in all its more-than-human mystery, remains
> the sole solid touchstone for an experiential world now inundated with
> electronically-generated vistas and engineered pleasures; only in regular
> contact with the tangible ground and sky can we learn how to orient and
> to navigate in the multiple dimension that now claim us.
>
> *(1996: ix–x)*

In turn, Hansen notes the conservatism of critics such as 'Baudrillard and Kit-
tler for whom the abstract generality of digital code marks a fundamental and
irremedial departure from the phenomenological ratios governing human
experience' (2006: 37). Nor is this scepticism about mediated perception solely
a philosophical concern, as popular discourse is full of anxieties over the unreality of mediated experiences (older concerns over video images can be seen
in films such as *Videodrome* or *Max Headroom*, while in contemporary culture,
it is digital environments that focus our attention, in films such as *eXistenZ* or
The Matrix, or TV shows like *Black Mirror*). In all of these accounts there is,

implicitly or explicitly, the assumption that this kind of dislocation has an alien-ating effect, making us incapable of connecting with others, losing our capacity for solidarity, empathy, identification across difference, or simply recognizing our moral responsibilities to others. In this context, concerns that the drone pilots would experience their controls and videoscreens as nothing other than a very realistic videogame would seem to be quite natural. There is something disturbing about the idea of killing through a videoscreen, in a way that seem-ingly other forms of killing – whether up close and personal, or from 15,000 feet via a traditional piloted aircraft – are not.

This is why it was so startling for those observing the drone program when reports first emerged that drone operators were showing signs of significant combat stress, indeed, stress in greater numbers than those who were deployed in traditional warzones. As Fitzsimmons and Sangha report,

> data collected by USAF mental health specialists during the past decade have revealed that RPA operators actually experience considerable stress from performing their duties. For example, a recent survey of Predator and Reaper operators in the USAF revealed that 46 percent of pilots, 41 percent of SOs, and 39 percent of MICs reported experiencing high levels of stress, at least some of which was due to their participation in combat operations.
> *(3)*[3]

The reason for this is that, contrary to the narrative which views drone opera-tor interfaces as 'distancing' and 'detached', they actually provide vivid and up-close images of the deaths the drone operators cause.

> Operators may be located far from the battlefields that their aircraft fly over, but they can see the consequences of their actions, including their victims being thrown about and torn apart by explosions, in real time high definition through the monitors that make up their virtual cockpits. As one operator put it, 'You are 18 inches away from 32-inch, high-definition combat. . . . You are there. . . . It's not detached. It's not a video game. And it's certainly not 8,000 miles away.' An operator described the experience of watching his missiles slam into human targets as 'very vivid and went on to state that the video feeds he and his fellow operators saw made the trauma unfolding before their eyes seem, 'right there and personal'.
> *(4–5)*

As Holmqvist puts it:

> Contrary to common perception, drone warfare is 'real' also for those staring at a screen and, as such, the reference to video games is often

simplistic. It is the immersive quality of video games, their power to draw players into their virtual worlds, that make them potent – this is precisely why they are used in pre-deployment training. The video streams from the UAV are shown to have the same immersive quality on the drone operator – they produce the same 'reality-effect'.

(541–542)

This is not to say that operating drones is identical to being in combat. Unlike most soldiers, drone operators can return home to their families at the end of the day's 'combat'. However, many commentators have pointed out that this radical disjuncture between the parts of their day spent 'in combat', and the parts of their day spent in civilian life actually exacerbates the stress the drone operators experience. As Fitzsimmons and Sangha put it,

> the fact that most USAF RPA units are based in the United States means that most operators commute between their family homes and operating stations each day, forcing them to undergo traumatic, rapid shifts between war fighter and civilian mentalities. Returning home at the end of each work day, these operators also typically lack a supportive social environment where they can discuss and alleviate their pent up feelings of combat stress during off-duty hours.
>
> *(2)*

Thus, ironically, for the drone operators themselves, the problem is not that their experiences are numbed or unreal but rather that they are too real, and that the reality of these experiences doesn't match up with the reality of the rest of their lives. They are, in essence, split in two, straddling two radically different lives, and spaces, without any effective means to integrate them. Chamayou quotes a drone operator who, in response to his partner's concern that he is 'a million miles away', says 'Sorry, Not quite that far away. Sometimes it's hard to keep switching on and off. Back and Forth. It's like living in two places at the same time. Parallel universes' (114). The problem for the operators is therefore not one of too little reality (the feared 'less than') but rather of too much.[4]

We should be careful, however, that when we discuss drones we do not just focus on the operators. It is vitally important that the victims of American drone strikes be part of our analysis as well. This is because assumptions of the mediated nature of distanciated and disembodied nature of drones also serves to minimize and marginalize the suffering experienced by those who live under drones.

Part of the justification provided by those who argue in favour of drones is that exactly because of the distanciated nature of their operators, they can ensure a 'precision' and 'certainty' which soldiers on the ground, or piloted aircraft, are incapable of. Even if this were true (and there is ample evidence to suggest that it is not) it ignores the broader social implication of drone use. The impact of drones in the FATA region cannot be limited to the specific, isolated moments of killing. Rather it is the constant presence of the drones, the always present threat of death, which has had the most enduring effect on life in the Waziristani region.

> US drone strike policies cause considerable and under-accounted for harm to the daily lives of ordinary civilians, beyond death and physical injury. Drones hover twenty-four hours a day over communities in northwest Pakistan, striking homes, vehicles, and public spaces without warning. Their presence terrorizes men, women, and children, giving rise to anxiety and psychological trauma among civilian communities. Those living under drones have to face the constant worry that a deadly strike may be fired at any moment, and the knowledge that they are powerless to protect themselves. These fears have affected behavior. The US practice of striking one area multiple times, and evidence that it has killed rescuers, makes both community members and humanitarian workers afraid or unwilling to assist injured victims. Some community members shy away from gathering in groups, including important tribal dispute-resolution bodies, out of fear that they may attract the attention of drone operators.
>
> *(International Human Rights 2012: vii)*

These sorts of broad social effects become apparent only if one takes a holistic account of drone warfare, paying attention to the way the presence of drones shapes the behaviours, minds, and bodies of those who are subject to their violence. Proponents frequently de-realize drone warfare in similar ways to critics, narrowing the presence of drones to brief, punctual encounters between killer and killed. Such an approach denies and ignores the thick materiality of drones; omnipresent menaces, hovering overhead, radiating threat and insecurity. Chamayou quotes *New York Times* journalist David Rohde: 'The drones were terrifying. From the ground, it is impossible to determine who or what they are tracking as they circle overhead. The buzz of a distant propeller is a constant reminder of imminent death' (44). A phenomenology of drone use needs to take into account the physicality of the drone, and observe how it reorganizes the space and bodies of all who are brought into their force field, whether killer, victim, or bystander. Such an approach recognizes that the look (and the missile) do not 'come from nowhere' but rather are always embodied, and subject to the returning gaze of the perceived (and targeted) subject. As Chamayou states,

> Drones are indeed petrifying. They inflict mass terror upon entire populations. It is this – over and above the deaths, the injuries, the destruction,

the anger, and the grieving – that is the effect of permanent lethal surveillance: it amounts to a psychic imprisonment within a perimeter no
longer defined by bars, barriers, and walls, but by the endless circling of
flying watchtowers up above.

(45)

This case study of drones shows how badly we can be misled when we take
as our starting assumption the disembodying and dematerializing effects of
so-called 'virtual' technologies. Virtual perceptions are always already embodied and material because *perceptions* are, by their nature, always already embodied
and material. Hayles points out that 'our interactions with digital media are
embodied, and they have bodily effects at the physical level' (2012: 3). As Laura
U. Marks nicely puts it, the problem 'lies not with virtuality itself but with
the assumption that what is virtual must be immaterial, transcendent' (2002:
178). Such assumptions – that 'virtual' perceptions are immaterial, transcendent, disembodied, nonmaterial, alienating – are, as we discussed in Chapter 4,
based on a Cartesian worldview which takes perception itself as a disembodied process, connecting a non-material mind with the material phenomenon
of the world. The ability to present digital perceptions as disembodying is to
already assume that *it is possible* to sheer off perception from body, mind from
materiality. To properly understand the nature of digitally mediated perception we need to continue the investigation we began in the previous chapter,
developing a philosophy which starts from the essentially embodied nature of
that perception. This is why, in this chapter and the next, we are turning to the
work of Maurice Merleau-Ponty.

Merleau-Ponty's phenomenology of perception starts by rejecting an image
of perception in which 'mind soars over' a 'pure object' (1968: 114). Instead
Merleau-Ponty conceives of perception as an inherently bodily process, in
which the perceptual field is organized in relation to a bodily schema. In turn,
our sense of spatiality is constituted with relation to the orientation, posture,
and virtual capabilities of the body. It is an account of perception in which we
don't see a binary duality between extended matter and unextended mind but
rather a chiasmal intertwining of 'the visible and the invisible', which is to say
the (almost) simultaneity of the body as sensing and the body as sensed. What
is more, in his later work, Merleau-Ponty attempts to break down the binary
duality of subject and object, self and world, through the inherent intermin-
gling of the 'flesh of the body' and the 'flesh of the world'.

Such a phenomenological approach is helpful in avoiding the kind of mis-
takes which frequently accompany attempts to understand contemporary ICTs.
It helps us to understand the embodied nature of perception, even when mediated through technologies. Or rather, to put it in a more extreme manner, it
recognizes the way in which our perception is always already mediated via
both the flesh of the world and the flesh of the body. Indeed, we can push this

point even farther to note that Merleau-Ponty's account of perception makes us aware of the way in which we bring the flesh of the world into the flesh of the body, incorporating human artefacts into our body schema. Under this rubric, we can no more maintain the distinction between the human and the artificial than we can that between 'mind' and 'body'. This helps us avoid a knee-jerk tendency to assume that 'mediated' perceptions are somehow less authentic, real, or important than 'immediate' perceptions. Merleau-Ponty's account of the flesh also provides a foundation for what he believes is the fundamentally intersubjective character of perception. When connected with his account of technologically extended perception, this provides us with a framework for thinking through the question of whether accelerating ICTs fundamentally inhibit our ability to connect with others.

Merleau-Ponty's phenomenology does not just help us understand the nature of technologically mediated perception. It is also crucial in helping us understand the contemporary spatiality of speed. For Merleau-Ponty space cannot be properly understood as the objective spatiality of Cartesian coordinates. As he says, the world of perception 'lacks the rigid framework once provided by the uniform space of Euclid' (2004: 39). In the world of perception,

> space is no longer a medium of simultaneous objects capable of being apprehended by an absolute observer who is equally close to them all, a medium without point of view, without body and without spatial position – in sum, the medium of pure intellect.
>
> *(2004: 41)*

Rather, the embodied nature of human perception warps and bends the absolute Euclidian lines of space, organizing it in relation to the body, and constituting its material in line with the virtual space of the body's potential actions.

> It is of the essence of space to be always 'already constituted', and we shall never come to understand it by withdrawing into a worldless perception. We must not wonder why being is orientated, why existence is spatial, why . . . our body is not geared to the world in all its positions, and why its co-existence with the world magnetizes experiences and induces a direction in it. The question could be asked only if the facts were fortuitous happenings to a subject and an object indifferent to space, whereas perceptual experience shows that they are presupposed in our primordial encounter with being, and that being is synonymous with being situated.
>
> *(1962: 293–4)*

Such an approach views spatiality with a human eye, noting the way in which the space of the world – the space of *our* world – warps and bends in response to human thought, perception, and action. This is especially important in the context of accelerating perception via global ICTs. As humans increasingly interact with accelerating ICTs, the 'situation' of our bodily perceptions changes in ways which 'constitute' space in new and unexpected ways. Thus, for example, an approach which starts from the presumption of objective, static space would take the drone operator as situated physically in Arizona, distant – and thus distan*ced* – from the killing fields of Pakistan. Such an approach would miss the way in which the two spaces are sutured together via the perception of the drone operator. As Caroline Holmqvist says in her own Merleau-Pontian investigation of drones:

> What is of interest to us in examining the interaction of the virtual, material and human here . . . is that this occurs not through the experience (on the part of the drone operator) of distance, remoteness or detachment, but rather through the 'sense of proximity' to ground troops inculcated by the video feeds from the aerial platforms.
>
> *(542)*

In a world of accelerating ICTs which allow us to observe, communicate with, and affect places all around the globe, a philosopher such as Merleau-Ponty is crucial. Merleau-Ponty, although writing before most such technologies came into play, provides us with a platform for understanding the way in which distant spaces can be linked together by a 'sense of proximity', and how the human body can incorporate technological artefacts, and streams of perception, in ways which challenge the human/nonhuman, natural/technological, embodied/disembodied binaries which reign in so many other philosophies of technology. Crucially this affects not just relations between spaces but also between people, providing opportunities for connection, identification, solidarity, and ethical responsibility.

This discussion will proceed in two phases, then, over the course of this chapter and the next. In the remainder of this chapter, we will engage with Merleau-Ponty's embodied philosophy of perception, looking specifically at Merleau-Ponty's theory of technology, how we can incorporate technological artefacts into our body, and how this shapes both our sense of embodiment, and our relationship to others. Having developed this framework of analysis, in the next chapter we will turn to Merleau-Ponty's account of spatiality, looking at how contemporary ICTs, such as mobile phones, computers, telepresence suites, telerobotics, and 24-hour satellite news mold body and world simultaneously, producing new senses of spatiality and proximity. In both chapters, then, what is at stake is whether the acceleration of perception leaves us dislocated and alienated, or whether in an accelerating world there is still the possibility of connection.

Perception and Embodiment

Although different in a variety of ways, Merleau-Ponty's account of perception begins with the same insight as Bergson's, rejecting the image of perception as passive, objective, neutral, and representative. Merleau-Ponty specifically rejects an account of perception in which an objective eye apprehends and synthesizes sense-data taken in from the world. Rather, he says, when we actually study our own perceptions, what we find is that the world presented to us has undergone a profound act of organization, and thus that the perceived world is always already bursting with meaning. Sense data never comes to us isolated or meaningless, raw perceptual material for intellectual investigation and analysis. Rather, objects, sensations, and sense-data always find themselves embedded in a perceptual field, ordered and given meaning.

> The perceptual 'something' is always in the middle of something else, it always forms part of a 'field'. . . . The pure impression is, therefore, not only undiscoverable, but also imperceptible and so inconceivable as an instant of perception. . . . An isolated datum of perception is inconceivable.
>
> *(1962: 4)*

Such an insight is crucial as it rejects an image of perception which is passively receptive. Rather, perception becomes an active process of ordering. Perception

> must be understood as a process of integration in which the text of the external world is not so much copied, as composed. And if we try to seize 'sensation' within the perspective of the bodily phenomena which pave the way to it, we find not a psychic individual . . . but a formation already bound up with a larger whole, already endowed with a meaning.
>
> *(10)*

Merleau-Ponty investigates this constitutive function of perception via multiple examples, from the way our perception parcels out sense data into figures and backgrounds; the way it attributes relative distance to different objects; or, the way it modifies colours on the basis of lighting. In all of these examples, perception acts to ascribe meaning to sense data according to the broader context in which they are found (or rather, it is the way perception *constructs* a broader context which imbues objects with meaning). In this regard,

> perception is just that act which creates at a stroke, along with the cluster of data, the meaning which unites them – indeed which not only discovers the meaning which they have, but moreover sees to it that they have a meaning.
>
> *(42)*

It does not do so infallibly (otherwise, we would never be confused by what we see, or tricked by optical illusions, etc.), but this is exactly the point.

This process of constitution does not occur arbitrarily, but neither is it eternal, unchanging, or transcendent. Rather, the process by which perception organizes the matter of the world is the result of both nature and nurture, a combination of the physical aspects of the body, the human artefacts and practices which shape and mold that body, and the culture, history, and education in which that body is situated. Or, as Merleau-Ponty puts it:

> Reflection can never make me stop seeing the sun two hundred yards away on a misty day, or seeing it 'rise' and 'set', or thinking with the cultural apparatus with which my education, my previous efforts, my personal history, have provided me.
>
> *(71)*

Central to this account of perception, then, is the body. It is insofar as we are embodied that we perceive and thus it is the body that plays the primary role in shaping our perception, and in constituting the phenomenal world. As Elizabeth Grosz puts it:

> Insofar as I live the body, it is a phenomenon experienced by me and thus provides the very horizon and perspectival point which places me in the world and makes relations between me, other objects, and other subjects possible. It is the body as I live it, as I experience it, and as it shapes my experience that Merleau-Ponty wishes to elucidate. Phenomenological reflection on the body reveals that I am not a subject separated from the world or from others, a mind somehow cut off from matter and space.
>
> *(1994: 86)*[5]

Our body is the element that 'magnetizes' the world, 'inducing a direction', constructing a perceptual field in a way that is meaningful *for our body*.

> The pure *quale* would be given to us only if the world were a spectacle and one's own body a mechanism with which some impartial mind made itself acquainted. Sense experience, on the other hand, invests the quality with vital value, grasping it first in its meaning for us, for that heavy mass which is our body, whence it comes about that it always involves a reference to our body.
>
> *(Merleau-Ponty 1962: 60–1)*

Again, here we have an approach similar to Bergson's, in which perception is organized from the biased perspective of the interests and characteristics of our body. Thus, by way of example, Merleau-Ponty discusses how

A body at rest because no force is being exerted upon it is again for sight not the same things as a body in which opposing forces are in equilibrium. The light of the candle changes its appearance for a child when, after a burn, it stops attracting the child's hand and becomes literally repulsive.

(60)

These in-principle identical pieces of sense data take on different meanings given the specific character, and histories, of the body experiencing them.

Part of this constitution of meaning in the phenomenal world relates simply to the bare facts of physiology. The simple organization of a body – the placement of eyes, ears, head, body, legs – serves to provide the world with meaningful spatial orientations ('in front of/behind', 'on top of/under', 'left/right', etc.).[6] However, of greater importance is the way in which the world is constituted by perception in relationship to the body as a mobile object. This is to say that it is exactly insofar as the body is active that the world acquires meaning. The *qualia* of the world are organized by perception in relation to the body as a source of potential and actual action in that world.

In principle all my changes of place figure in a corner of my landscape; they are recorded on the map of the visible. Everything I see is in principle within my reach, at least within reach of my sight, and is marked upon the map of the 'I can.' Each of the two maps is complete. The visible world and the world of my motor projects are each total parts of the same Being.

(1964a: 162)

In this twin map of the visible world and the body's motor projects, objects take on meaning (for example, emerging from, or fading into, the background) in relation to what role they serve as potential objects of human action. The perceptual field thus becomes a field of virtual bodily action, and objects become objects *for* bodily action.

This account of the phenomenal body as the mobile body, and of the phenomenal world as the world constituted for human action, brings out the central role of movement in perception. This account is consonant with work in contemporary psychology and neuroscience, which describes how movement is absolutely crucial for the development of our perceptual faculties. That it is not just by 'perceiving' that we come to grasp the world but rather by seeing how our perception changes through bodily movement, that we begin to get a robust (and meaningful) image of the world.

To demonstrate the importance of movement to perception, we might turn to Andy Clark's account of the Tactile televisual system (TTVS). The TTVS was a prosthesis developed for blind people and consisted of a head mounted camera attached to a backpack unit, in which a 40 x 40 grid of flat-headed 'nails' was placed flush against the user's back. The 'nails' were able to move up and down, and the nail array therefore functioned as very low-resolution 'pixels', providing a tactile representation of the visual imagery delivered by the camera. The important element about the TTVS was that the camera was mobile, shifting with the user's head movements. This meant that, despite the very low resolution of the nail array (not to mention the fact that it provided tactile information, not visual), users were able to start interpreting the tactile information it provided, and use it to navigate the world effectively. What is more, according to users, they very quickly stopped experiencing the array as delivering tactile information to their back and instead began to experience it as a generalized visual experience of the world, to the point where some users were able to 'perform complex perception and 'eye'-hand coordination tasks', including 'face recognition, accurate judgement of speed and direction of a rolling ball with over 95% accuracy in batting the ball as it rolls over a table edge, and complex inspection-assembly tasks' (Clark 2011: 35) (we should remember this case study when we turn to the account of how Merleau-Ponty envisions the incorporation of technological artefacts into the human body and perceptual apparatus).

As Clark describes, the central element in the TTVS is the fact that the tactile information changes in relation to bodily movements, thus allowing perception to accord meaning to the world in relation to the spatiality of bodily action. As he says:

> what determines phenomenology is not neural activity set up by stimulation as such, but the way the neural activity is embedded in a sensorimotor dynamic. . . . For it is arguably the shape of a whole batch of sensorimotor loops that now determines the nature of the visual experience.
>
> *(23)*

Compare this with Merleau-Ponty in *In Praise of Philosophy*, where he states, 'Far from being a simple "displacement," movement is inscribed in the texture of the shapes or qualities and is, so to speak, the revelation of their being' (74–75). In this regard, bodily movement provides a way into the world. It is both a centrifugal force, putting the body out into the world (which is to say investing it with a human meaning, arraying its objects for human action), while at the same time bringing the world into the body (which is to say providing us with a mobile and shifting perspective on the world, filling it out and providing us with a detailed understanding of the world in depth). As Clark says,

> The notion that our perceptual experience is determined by the passive receipt of information, though seductive, is deeply misleading. Our brains are not at all like radio or television receivers, which simply take

incoming signals and turn them into some kind of visual or auditory display. Who would there be to look at the display anyway? The whole business of seeing and perceiving our world is bound up with the business of acting upon, and intervening in, our worlds. And where action and intervention goes, our sense of bodily presence and location swiftly follows.

(2003: 95)

What this means, however, is that the body is not an object like any other. On the one hand the body is an object, given to perception. I can touch it and look at it, smell it and taste it. On the other hand, the body is the sensing body, providing a kind of pre-perceptual grounding for perception. Its movements and actions, both actual and virtual, are not interpreted as separate observable facts. Rather, they constitute the unthought, unperceived foundation on which human perception is constituted. Thus, as Merleau-Ponty says in one of his later works,

> knowledge of my body is not a knowledge, and my movements are not thought as objective factors of knowledge. The awareness that I have of my body is a sliding awareness, the feeling of a power, of a being-able-to. I am aware of my body as an undivided and systematic potency to organize certain unfoldings of perceptual appearance. My body is that which is capable of passing from one such appearance to another, as the organizer of a 'transitional synthesis.' I organize with my body an understanding of the world, and the relation with my body is not that of a pure I, which would successively have two objects, my body and the thing, but rather I live in my body, and by means of it I live in the things. . . . The body appears not only as the exterior accompaniment of things, but also as the field where my sensations are located.
>
> *(1995: 74)*

See here the odd status of the body, in which 'knowledge of the body is not a knowledge' and 'movements are not thought of as objective factors of knowledge'. This is because the body and its movements are prompts to knowledge, and the foundations of perception. When I move my head, I do not keep track of a variety of separate pieces of sense data (that my head moves, that the things that I look at change perspective, that new elements which were previously blocked from view are made clear). When I walk the world does not bob in front of my vision with the rise and fall of my body. Rather, the movements of my body are incorporated and subtracted from my vision (and hearing, and touch, etc.), organizing my perception into a cohesive and unitary field. The body is the organizer of a 'transitional synthesis', bringing together body and world, organizing the world in such a way as to make it accessible to the body.

To fully understand this odd standing of a body which both is and isn't part of the world, which is both 'visible' and 'invisible', we will need to discus in greater detail what Merleau-Ponty calls 'the body schema'.

The Body Schema

The body schema is a concept developed by Merleau-Ponty which speaks to the special knowledge that we have of our body. The body schema is related to the sense of proprioception, the internal, or interoceptive, sense of where the different parts of our body are.[7] The body schema, however, goes beyond proprioception insofar it is not just a collection of individual interoceptive sensations, or isolated possibilities, but is rather a drawing together of the body as a unity. As Merleau-Ponty says in *Phenomenology of Perception*, 'my whole body for me is not an assemblage of organs juxtaposed in space. I am in undivided possession of it and I know where each of my limbs is through a *body schema* in which all are included' (112–113). Elsewhere he states:

> my body is no agglomeration of sensations (visual, tactile, 'tenesthesic', or 'cenesthesic'). It is first and foremost a *system* whose different interoceptive and exteroceptive aspects express each other reciprocally, including even the roughest of relations with surrounding space and its principle directions. The consciousness I have of my body is not the consciousness of an isolated mass; it is a *postural schema*.
>
> *(1964a: 117)*

What is more, the body schema refers not just to the current position of the body but rather constitutes a schematic encompassing all of the possible positions, and thus actions, of the body. 'The body is able to move, to initiate and undertake action, because the body schema is a series, or rather a field, of possible actions, plans for action, maps of possible movements the body "knows" how to perform' (1994: 95).

It is crucial, at this point, to distinguish between the body schema, and another concept in Merleau-Ponty with which it is sometimes confused, the body image. The body image constitutes that image we have of our body as it is given through visual perception, whether directly or via mirrors or other media. The body image is thus the body insofar as it is an object of perception, the sensed body. This has to be distinguished from the body schema as that which grounds perception, the sensing body. As we discussed, perception constitutes the phenomenal world in relation to the field of possible bodily actions, and it is the body schema that provides (or rather is) that field of bodily actions. Discussing this distinction between the body scheme and the body image, Hansen states that the distinction correlates with the task of thinking 'the human body on both sides of the intentional relations'; thus, the body image designates the body as the object or content of intentional (or noetic) consciousness, whereas the body schema characterizes the body as a 'prenoetic' function, a kind of infraempirical or sensible-transcendental basis for intentional operation. 'In contrast to the intentional (and sometimes conscious) nature of the body image, a *body schema* involves an extraintentional operation carried out prior to or outside of intentional awareness'.

(2006: 29)

What this means is that the body schema precedes and conditions the perceptual field, or, as Hansen put it, 'the body as body schema, precedes and informs the constitution of the objective domain (including the body as object, or the body image)' (2006: 40).

In developing his concept of the body schema, Merleau-Ponty frequently draws on empirical case studies of psychological and neurological disorders in which something has disturbed the patient's body schema (such as phantom limb syndrome, in which, despite the obvious visual lack of a missing limb, a patient continues to possess a body schema which includes the missing limb, or in apraxia, in which a limb which is visual present is absent from a body schema [1962: 145]). These case studies show us the important work that body schemas do in organizing perception and aiding us in navigating the world by showing us what happens when they fail to match up with the outside world.

This reference to phantom limbs and cases of apraxia, by showing us that body schemas can change and mutate in relation to physical, psychological, and neurological change, also helps to clarify a crucial fact about body schemas. Although in the quote earlier, Hansen refers to the body schema as 'prenoetic' and a 'sensible-transcendental basis for intentional operation', we should not think of it as a transcendental schema in the style of Kant wherein the schema exists absolutely *a priori*. Rather, while the body schema shapes perception, it is not, therefore, prior to, or untouched by, experience. Rather, the body schema has a history, and is shaped by a diverse set of factors, such as physiology, education, culture, habit, trauma (physical and psychological), environment, and, most importantly for our purposes, technology. For, just as in the case of apraxia in which the body schema can shed things which are biologically part of the body, the body schema can also appropriate things which are not. In his lecture notes, Merleau-Ponty describes how the body schema

can be extended to the things (clothing and the corporeal schema). It can expel a part of the body. It is thus not made of determined parts, but it is a lacunary being (the corporal schema is hollow on the inside) – includes accentuated, precise regions, and other vague regions. (The hollow and vague regions are the point of insertion of imaginary bodies).

(1995: 278–9)

The somewhat cryptic comment about 'clothing and the corporeal schema' refers to a point raised elsewhere, that we frequently incorporate our clothing into our bodily schema since it alternately enables or restricts our bodily field of movement (Young 2005: Ch. 4). As he states,

> If I did not take off my clothes I could never see the inside of them, and it will in fact be seen that my clothes may become appendages of my body. But this fact does not prove that the presence of my body is to be compared to the *de facto* permanence of certain objects, or the organ compared to a tool which is always available. It shows that conversely those action in which I habitually engage incorporate their instruments into themselves and make them play a part in the original structure of my body.
>
> *(1962: 104)*

Nor does Merleau-Ponty stop here, as he identifies several other examples of non-human artefacts which are incorporated into body schemas. These include his famous example of the blind man's cane (discussed in greater detail later), which he states 'cease[s] to be an object for him, and is no longer perceived for itself; its point has become an area of sensitivity, extending the scope and active radius of touch, and providing a parallel to sight' (1962: 165). He also describes how the feather on a hat, and even a car (also discussed later), can be absorbed into the body schema, providing a new 'field of action', and thus reorganizing the field of perception.

This idea, of the incorporation of non-human artefacts into the body schema, obviously holds substantial interest for our discussion of perception and technology. However, we must be careful. If we were to start at this point, we would run the risk of replicating the prostheticizing/parasitizing image of speed discussed in the second chapter, in which non-human artefacts are attached to an already existent and natural human body. Before discussing the issue of Merleau-Ponty and technology fully, we must first turn to another of his central concept, that of the flesh. Only by doing so can we make sure that we do not reconstitute the binary dualities of self and world, human and nonhuman, natural and artificial. Instead, we must understand how the flesh of the body and the flesh of the world are always already intertwined, and thus how, in Hansen's words, the human body is marked by an 'originary technicity' (2006: 100).

The Flesh and the Originary Technicity of the Body

This idea, that we are capable of absorbing elements of the world into our body – developed first in the context of Merleau-Ponty's discussion of the body schema – becomes a major theme of Merleau-Ponty's later work, in his discussion of the flesh. Indeed, according to Mark Hansen this preoccupation with the continuum, or indeed indiscernibility, between self and world, produces a line of continuity linking the early and late Merleau-Ponty.

> Because it is responsible for linking protosensory bodily sense (proprioception) with perception and motility (and indeed for correlating these latter), the body schema is a source of embodied potential. Such a realization is central to Merleau-Ponty's analysis in the *Phenomenology*; it renders that analysis more interesting and far more continuous with the later ontology of the flesh than even the best of Merleau-Ponty commentators have been willing to admit.
>
> *(2006: 42)*

For example, in Merleau-Ponty's writing on the body schema he describes how

> [t]o get used to a hat, a car or a stick is to be transplanted into them, or conversely, to incorporate them into the bulk of our own body. Habit expresses our power of . . . changing our existence by appropriating fresh instruments.
>
> *(1962: 166)*

By way of comparison, in his account of the flesh, Merleau-Ponty describes how 'I adhere to this world which is not me as closely as to myself, in a sense it is only the prolongation of my body – I am justified in saying that I am in the world' (1968: 57).[8] Thus, the central theme of both concepts is that the flesh of the body – as the 'location' for invisible perception – is necessarily intertwined with the visible world, creating a zone of indiscernibility between the two, such that the world is brought into the body, and the body sent out into the world. (Note this relationship between the flesh of the body and the flesh of the world is necessary to ward off the prostheticizing/parasitizing visions of speed and technology described in previous chapters.) The difference between the two is primarily a difference of emphasis. In the earlier writings on the body schema, the emphasis is on the body as the privileged site. The incorporation of the world happens through discrete moments of absorption of technical artefacts: the cane, the hat, the car, the clothes. These are specific elements of the world that are incorporated into the body, that existed outside of, and in opposition to, the self. This is to be compared to his account in *The Visible and the Invisible* in which body and world are fundamentally one via the elemental medium of 'the flesh'.

However, even in the earlier case of the body schema, there are elements which mitigate a reading which affirms a sharp line of separation between self and world. Think here of the long passage in which he describes the habitual incorporation of the artefacts of the hat and the car into the body schema.

> A woman may, without any calculation, keep a safe distance between the feather in her hat and things which might break it off. She feels where the feather is just as we feel where our hand is. If I am in the habit of driving a car, I enter a narrow opening and see that I can 'get through' without comparing the width of the opening with that of the wings, just as I go through a doorway without checking the width of the doorway against that of my body. The hat and the car have ceased to be objects with a size and a volume which is established by comparison with other objects. They have become potentialities of volume, the demand for a certain amount of free space. In the same way the iron gate to the Underground platform, and the road have become restrictive potentialities and immediately appear passable or impassable for my body with its adjuncts.
>
> *(1962: 165)*

While here the emphasis is primarily on the objects of the hat and the car as objects absorbed into the body schema, of their transformation from 'objects with a size and a volume which is established in comparison with other objects' into 'potentialities of volume'. However, insofar as they cease to be objects established in comparison with other objects, that also changes the nature of the objects against which they would otherwise be compared. Although not extensively remarked upon, Merleau-Ponty describes how the 'iron gate to the Underground platform, and the road' have also been transformed into 'restrictive potentialities'. While not explicitly stated, these worldly objects too are absorbed into a corporeal schema (and thus a perceptual field) demarcating a space of bodily action.[9] If, as he says, habitual use results in the fact that 'The blind man's stick has ceased to be an object for him, and is no longer perceived for itself', how would this compare with the way in which my body instinctively moves to the right to avoid the foot of the bed when I am navigating my bedroom in the dark? There are unquestionably differences of degree, of consistency, of 'bandwidth'. But there is a similarity here insofar as both speak to the way in which the perceptual field – and more fundamentally the field of bodily action – incorporate the outside world into themselves, reconstructing the world as a space of continuous potentialities. This is not to suggest that there is no meaningful distinction between self and world, or that all 'things' in the world are incorporated into the body in the same way. Rather it is to say what Merleau-Ponty says, that there is a chiasmal intertwining of the flesh of the body and of the world. Or rather, that there is only the flesh of the world, of which the flesh of the body is a part, a part which has the ability to sense, but is itself also that flesh which is sensed (Grosz 1994: 103).

All of this is an attempt by Merleau-Ponty to remain attentive to the human as a perceiving subject, while at the same time continuing to purge his philosophy of any element of a transcendent, cartesian subject, an unextended mind, seated within the extended matter of the body.[10]

> We have to reject the age-old assumption that put the body in the world and the seer in the body, or conversely, the world and the body in the seer as in a box. Where are we to put the limit between the body and the world, since the world is flesh? Where in the body are we to put the seer, since evidently there in the body only 'shadows stuffed with organs,' that is, more of the visible? The world we see is not 'in' my body, and my body is not 'in' the visible world ultimately: as flesh applied to a flesh, the world neither surrounds it nor is surrounded by it.
>
> *(Merleau-Ponty 1968: 138)*

This is crucial for our understanding of the role of speed and technology in Merleau-Ponty because it fundamentally rejects a distinction between a properly human body and a non-human technology separate from it (as in the first and second encounter between speed and the body discussed in Chapter 2). Here perception is always already mediated via the flesh of the body. Or rather, the flesh of the body provides the chiasmal intertwining between the invisible of perception and the visible of the world. Thus, Hansen describes Merleau-Ponty as having a conception of the 'originary technicity' of the body. The body is always already part of the non-human, always already part of the flesh of the world which conveys the invisible of perception into the heart of the perceptible. The body is always already a 'technics of perception'. Indeed, Hansen pushes this connection further, arguing that it through his analysis of the incorporation of the technological artefact into the body that Merleau-Ponty begins to theorize his anti-humanist account of the flesh, saying,

> the connection between the body schema and technics . . . is precisely what conditions Merleau-Ponty's extension of the body schema to the point of its dissolution, to the point where it no longer serves to specify the boundaries of the body's interiority but rather to mark its ontological interpenetration with the flesh of the world.
>
> *(87)*

What this means is that, in relation to our central question of speed, technology, and perception, we can never fundamentally oppose self and world, or imagine an 'unmediated' perception extended through non-human media, since human perception is always already extended through the flesh of the world.

This excursion through the later Merleau-Ponty's philosophy of the flesh is necessary because it helps us avoid several pitfalls when thinking about the relationship between perception and technology. On the one hand, we avoid the simple distinction between self and world, which can (re)produce a prostheticizing/parasitizing image of technology in which artefacts are super-added to a pure, unitary human body. It also rejects a simple distinction between unextended mind and extended matter, in which perception involves a more or less representative transmission of information from the latter to the former. Both of these points are nicely summed up in a line from Merleau-Ponty's *Primacy of Perception*: 'Our organs are no longer instruments; on the contrary, our instruments are detachable organs' (178). This line (which could well serve as the motto of our investigation of Merleau-Ponty) succinctly describes both the way in which the perceptual field is constituted and unified by the preobjective/presubjective body schema, and the way in which this body schema does not constitute a solid line separating out self from world.[11]

Merleau-Ponty provides multiple examples where the body schema incorporates non-human artefacts as mechanisms for the constitution of the perceptual field. We can here return to his iconic interpretation of the blind person's cane. For Merleau-Ponty, the cane is not to be understood as strictly a medium for information, something separate from the body used to discover information about the world. Rather, as he says 'The pressures on the hand by the stick are no longer given; the stick is no longer an object perceived by a blind man, but an instrument *with* which he perceives' (1962: 175).

> The blind man's stick has ceased to be an object for him, and is no longer perceived for itself; its point has become an area of sensitivity, extending the scope and active radius of touch, and providing a parallel to sight. In the exploration of things, the length of the stick does not enter expressly as a middle term: the blind man is rather aware of it through the position of objects than of the position of objects through it. The position of things is immediately given through the extent of the reach which carries him to it, which comprises besides the arm's own reach the stick's range of action.
> *(1962: 165–6)*

What Merleau-Ponty is describing is the way in which the cane ceases to be one object amongst many, which we might use to measure distance (a ruler, for example) and instead becomes part of the body (or better, incorporated into the body schema).

> If I want to get used to a stick, I try it by touching a few things with it, and eventually I have it 'well in hand', I can see what things are 'within

reach' or out of reach of my stick. There is no question here of any quick estimate or any comparison between the objective length of the stick and the objective distance away of the goal to be reached. The points in space do not stand out as objective positions in relation to the objective position occupied by our body; they mark, in our vicinity, the varying range of our aims and our gestures.

(1962: 166)

The cane in this context constitutes what Andy Clark calls a 'transparent technology': 'Transparent technologies are those tools that become so well fitted to, and integrated with, our own lives and projects that they are . . . pretty much invisible-in-use' (2003: 28). (Here we might think back to the way in which wearers of the TTVS reported that they stopped perceiving it as a separate tactile apparatus, and instead began to respond to it as part of their perceptual field.) As Sara Ahmed puts it,

We must note here that the extension of motility through objects means that the object is no longer perceived as something apart from the body. The object, as with the rest of the body, trails behind the action, even when it is literally 'in front' of the body.

(2006: 131)

Such transparent technologies are not, however, solely restricted to 'passive' technologies which transmit information. Active technologies can also be incorporated into the body schema. There is, of course, Heidegger's famous hammer, and Merleau-Ponty's example of the car. In all of these contexts,

technologies work to expand the body's motile, tactile, and visual interface with the environment; to do so, they call upon – and ultimately, refunctionalize – the body's role as an 'invariant,' a fundamental access onto the world . . . the 'body schema.'

(Hansen 2006: 26)

What is important here is that, even where these technologies are not 'media' *per se*, they still have an effect on human perception. This is because, insofar as these technologies are introduced into a bodily schema, they shape the virtual field of bodily action, which in term shapes the perceptual field. This is important for our discussion of speed and perception because the increasing speed and scope of technologies of both communication and action (think here of the predator drone which both surveilles and kills) serves to reshape the virtual scope of human perception and action, at times on a global scale.

Technology, Perception, and the Encounter With the Other

The last point that we must engage with in this chapter is how Merleau-Ponty's theory of the flesh provides the grounding for the encounter with the other. We began this chapter with a discussion of technologically mediated perception in the case of drone warfare. There the question that emerged was whether the techno-logical mediation of perception alienated and dislocated the drone pilot, making them less likely to view their victims as genuine others rather than as characters 'in a videogame'. As we saw, this was not an anxiety restricted to the specific case of drone warfare. We identified a widespread concern that accelerated perception fundamentally inhibited the possibility of a genuine encounter with the other (and thus implicitly negating the possibility of political solidarity or moral respon-sibility). Having begun to develop a properly Merleau-Pontian account of how technological mediation affects perception, we must now think about how this account relates to his discussion of intersubjectivity. Merleau-Ponty's philosophy is well suited to this task, as, according to Coole, 'his aim is precisely to discover how experience opens us to the other and to what is not ourselves' (103).

For Merleau-Ponty, this 'discovery' is not an easy one, as he struggles with the so-called 'other minds' problem raised by multiple strands of metaphysics. As he says in *The Primacy of Perception*:

> Since I cannot have direct access to the psyche of another. . . . I must grant that I seize the other's psyche only indirectly, mediated by its bodily appearances. I see you in flesh and bone; you are there. I cannot know what you are thinking, but I can suppose it, guess at it from your facial expressions, your gestures, and your words – in short from a series of bodily appearances of which I am only the witness. The question thus becomes this: How does it happen that, in the presence of this manne-quin that resembles a man, in the presence of this body that gesticulates in a characteristic way, I come to believe that it is inhabited by a psyche? How am I led to consider that this body before me encloses a psyche? How can I perceive across this body, so to speak, another psyche?
>
> *(114)*

The answer to this question ultimately lies in Merleau-Ponty's philosophy of the flesh. For Merleau-Ponty, the flesh of the world is inherently intersubjective (or at least marked by a primordial intercorporeity, leading to intersubjectivity). Just as the invisible of our perception is chiasmally intertwined with the vis-ible, so too is the perception of others, linking us all in the flesh of the world. Madison describes Merleau-Ponty's conception of the flesh by saying,

> Perhaps the most appropriate way to construe the meaning of this term . . . would be to say that it is nothing other than *the presence of the other in the*

same. The flesh is the trace of the other, the inscription of the other, in the subject's own selfhood – in its very flesh. What 'flesh' 'means' is that the *subject itself is for another.*

(31)

Merleau-Ponty describes the flesh of the body as not a thing that separates us out from the world, and thus a potential barrier to the encounter with the other, but rather that which submerges us in it: 'The thickness of the body, far from rivalling that of the world, is on the contrary the sole means I have to go unto the heart of the things, by making myself a world and by making them flesh' (1968: 135). Crucially, this 'world', this 'heart of the things' consists of not just objects, but subjects as well, others with whom we enter into a sort of communion. (Thus, just as Merleau-Ponty's theory of the flesh breaks down the distinction between the human and the technological, it also begins to break down the distinction between the self and the other.)

This encounter with the other happens via perception. Not just through our perception of the other, but through our perception of the perception of the other. By perceiving the other perceiving, we recognize our own habits – the bodily practices of perception – and in that we experience the existence of another. We recognize that this other, too, is a chiasmal intertwining of the visible and the invisible, the tangible and intangible. Bredlau describes Merleau-Ponty's account of the intersubjectivity of perception, saying,

> We must recognize, then, that when we perceive other people's bodily interaction with things, we can see them as perceptive. We can perceive others' behavior as their way of having a world, and, in doing so, we can begin to participate in this way of having a world. That is, rather than just observing how others comport themselves toward whatever is around them, we can take up these comportments for ourselves. By joining others in their way of a having a world, however, their way of having a world will be fundamentally changed; it will no longer be their way of having a world but, instead, our way. Our perception will be a collaborative endeavor, and the world we perceive will be a shared world.
>
> *(6)*

This account of the perception of the other then follows from Merleau-Ponty's account that perception is a fundamentally embodied process, and not a passive, disembodied, 'reflective' process.

> We must abandon the fundamental prejudice according to which the psyche is that which is accessible only to myself and cannot be seen from outside. My 'psyche' is not a series of 'states of consciousness' that are rigorously closed in on themselves and inaccessible to anyone but me.

> My consciousness is turned primarily toward the world, turned toward things; it is above all a relation to the world. The other's consciousness as well is chiefly a certain way of comporting himself toward the world. Thus is it in his conduct, in the manner in which the other deals with the world, that I will be able to discover his consciousness.
>
> (Merleau-Ponty 1964a: 116–17)

The fact that perception is embodied shapes not just our own cognition but also our encounter with the other, as perception becomes a material practice in the world, noted by, and intertwined with, the perceptual practices of others.[12]

Note that although Merleau-Ponty specifically emphasizes the dimension of the visible in this discussion (as 'the visible' and 'the invisible' are the central concepts through which he interrogates the two aspects of the flesh), it is not the case that this encounter with the other necessarily, or only happens via vision. While it is definitely the case that vision is one of the mechanisms by which we encounter the other,[13] touch too, for example, can ground our encounter with the other. In a lengthy passage from *The Visible and the Invisible*, we see Merleau-Ponty trace out the way in which the touching of the hand of the other can open up us up to the experience of the other (an example to which we will return in the next chapter).

> If my left hand can touch my right hand while it palpates the tangibles, can touch it touching, can turn its palpation back upon it, why, when touching the hand of another, would I not touch in it the same power to espouse the things that I have touched in my own? It is true that 'the things' in question are my own, that the whole operation takes place (as we say) 'in me,' within my landscape, whereas the problem is to institute another landscape. When one of my hand touches the other, the world of each opens upon that of the other because the operation is reversible at will, because they both belong (as we say) to one sole space of consciousness, because one sole man touches one sole thing through both hands. But for my two hands to open on one sole world, it does not suffice that they be given to one sole consciousness – or if that were the case the difficulty before me would disappear: since other bodies would be known by me in the same way as would be my own, they and I would still be dealing with the same world.
>
> (1968: 140–1)

In addition to vision and touch, Merleau-Ponty also describes the role of language in producing the encounter with the other. Crucially this is not just a matter of the intellectual apprehension of words and ideas, but more the embodied perceptual experience of language, whether through the medium of the written word, or through the visual, tactile, and auditory medium of speech (or signed language).[14] Merleau-Ponty describes how he 'regard[s] language as the reverberation of my relations with myself and with others' (1973: 20) and that 'When I speak or understand, I experience that presence of others in myself or of myself in others which is the stumbling-block of the theory of intersubjectivity' (1964b: 97).

This reference to the 'stumbling-block of the theory of intersubjectivity' drives home a central implication about Merleau-Ponty's theory of the encounter with the other. For Merleau-Ponty, the difficulty that some philosophies have had in explaining the encounter with the other is ultimately rooted in a Cartesian dualism that seeks to split off the body from the mind, leaving no meaningful point of contact through which the encounter might take place. As Levin puts it, 'The disembodied, monadic subject that appears in discourses of metaphysics cannot account for the phenomenological truth: it assumes that an absolute solitude comes first, and then sociability' (39). Merleau-Ponty is very explicit about rejecting such a position, saying,

> we reproach the philosophy of reflection not only for transforming the world into a noema, but also for distorting the being of the reflecting 'subject' by conceiving it as 'thought' – and finally for rendering unthinkable its relations with other 'subjects' in the world that is common to them.
>
> *(1968: 43–4)*

This rejection of conceiving of the 'subject' purely as 'thought' allows for the possibility of the meaningful encounter of the other in the flesh of the world. To return to Levin,

> Rather than being essentially isolated from others, which is how we have understood ourselves in the discourse of consciousness, we are, as bodies, joined inseparably, inseparably bound, to others. What Merleau-Ponty shows us is the fact that *it is by grace of the flesh* that we are gathered with others into a primordial sociality. The body is from the very beginning interactional, not monadic: protosocial, and even protomoral.
>
> *(40)*

This quote notes the moral and political implications of rejecting dualistic accounts of the subject. While the encounter with the other has never guaranteed social or moral behaviour (and hence the 'proto-' in the quote earlier), it does provide the condition of possibility for it. In this regard then, Merleau-Ponty's account of the fundamental intersubjectivity of our embodied material practices of perception also provides the grounding for an understanding of political, social, and moral life. As Coole points out,

> Merleau-Ponty was not content merely to insist on the fact of embodiment in collective life, radical as this insistence is for the dominant

tradition of political thinking that treats political agents as disembodied actors. He wanted to show that (co)existence is simply incomprehensible once mind and body are split.

(2007a: 163)

There is an interesting resonance here with an idea that we engaged with earlier – first in Chapter 4, and then again at the beginning of this chapter. There we noted that the fear that accelerating ICTs might capture human perception and cognition – leading to the alienation and dislocation of the human subject – was fundamentally premised on a Cartesian dualism that presumed that the mind *could* be sheared off from the body. That, in such a framework, the mind was already fundamentally alienated and dislocated exactly because it was held at arms-length from the fleshy corporeality of the world. Here Merleau-Ponty identifies a similar root to the so-called 'other minds' problem. That ultimately, the difficulty that certain strands of metaphysics have in understanding how we encounter the other is based on having sealed the subject off from the world, and thus from the other subjects it might meet there. In both cases, anxieties over our supposed inability to engage with the world (and the others that populate those worlds) are the result of a vision of the subject which is always already constructed in opposition to the world. Instead, if we view the subject (and hence human perception and cognition) as fundamentally embodied, then these problems go away (or at least change their nature).

This turn to embodiment links these two ideas, providing a resolution to the problem that was introduced in our discussion of drone warfare, regarding whether accelerating ICTs fundamentally inhibit the encounter with the other. In Merleau-Ponty's analysis, the encounter with the other is an embodied one, happening in the shared flesh of the world. And as we've seen, perceptual technologies make up part of the flesh of that world, incorporated into the flesh of our own bodies, and shaping our experience of, and encounter with, that world. For Merleau-Ponty, the encounter with the other can happen through the 'mediation' of perceptual technologies exactly because of the originary technicity of our bodies. Perception and cognition never happened 'somewhere else'. They always happened 'here', in the circulating and shifting flesh of the world, whether biological or technological (the cane, the car, the drone, etc.). As Hansen put it,

> Today's digital technologies . . . thus function to actualize the potential of technicity to be a *medium* for being. Through them . . . the transduction of embodiment and technics, of interiority and exteriorization – becomes actualized as a technically specific and technically facilitated intercorporeal commonality.

(84)

Now, this does not mean that a changing technological context has no impact on perception, cognition, or our encounter with the other. Quite the contrary. As Merleau-Ponty has made quite clear, our perception, our body schema, our subjectivity, are not *a priori* givens but instead are shaped by any number of forces, including physiology, psychology, technology, history, culture, politics, economics, etc. Thus, it is necessary to think about *how* changing contexts will shape our perceptions and subjectivities. It is to exactly this question we will turn in the next and final chapter, looking specifically at how the acceleration of perceptual technologies shapes our sense of spatiality, and hence our connection to others (whether social, moral, political, or otherwise). But such an investigation can only properly start from the perspective that perception and cognition are fundamentally embodied things and can therefore never be fundamentally alienated or dislocated from the world. This might not guarantee an ethical or political commitment to the other, but it does provide its condition of possibility. And that is, ultimately, all we can ask.

Notes

1. According to Campanella,

> telepresence is "the experience of presence in an environment by means of a communication medium." Put another way, it is the mediated perception of "a temporally or spatially distant real environment" via telecommunications. In other words, the observer is telepresent in the remote environment, and the observed environment is telepresent in the physical space in which the observer is viewing the scene.
>
> *(Campanella 2001: 27)*

2. See also Eriksen (2001: 2, 52).
3. It's worth noting that Gregoire Chamayou rejects the claim that there was widespread PTSD amongst drone operators but does comment on the extensive stress of drone operators for the reasons discussed later (2015: 8). See also Daggett (2015: 370).
4. Note that arguing that drone pilots aren't necessarily *distanced* from the people they kill (or that some experience stress or trauma in doing so) is not to argue that they are therefore incapable of killing. But, of course, people have always been able to kill people whether they are physically present or not, and much military research goes into figuring out how to make people capable of killing more easily (Grossman 2009). My argument here is simply that we cannot presume that perceiving via a mediated interface makes it impossible to authentically encounter others in a way that might spark a sense of moral responsibility, just as in our unmediated encounters.
5. See also Abram (1996: 45).
6. Note, that this doesn't presume a normative body with a universal physiological make up. Rather, it says that our phenomenological experience will at least partly follow from the particular make up of our particular body.
7. See also Grosz (1994: 91).
8. Tellingly this passage is accompanied by a footnote, in which Merleau-Ponty states, 'As Bergson said in *Les Deux Sources*: my body extends unto the stars'.

9. Merriman does an excellent job of describing this shifting relationship between body, technology, and environment, specifically as it relates to the question of speed.

> As drivers become familiar with their vehicles and find confidence and practical experience, so the various embodied practices and sensations of driving become automatic and habitual, perhaps even functioning in non-cognitive or pre-cognitive ways, as we contemplate, judge, accelerate, move *with* our vehicles. But where do we 'draw the line' or 'make the cut', for these bodies and vehicles also travel *with* countless other things, performing turbulent movements, becoming passage, becoming landscape, moving with landscapes, territorialising and deterritorialising amidst a vibrant turbulent world of movements, affects, sensations, emotions which are engineered by drivers, civil engineers, politicians, safety experts, ergonomists and landscape architects, amongst others. Travellers move with vehicles, tarmac/steel, topography, vegetation, weather.
>
> *(2012: 13)*

10. As Coole puts it, Merleau-Ponty sought to

> contest Descartes' first principle and all that follows from it: the ontological split between mind and body and the accompanying epistemological opposition between subject and object; the primacy of a self-coincident, disembodied, rational consciousness (the *cogito*); the solipsistic ignorance of other subjects that follows from it; the rejection of the senses as valid sources of knowledge; [and] the metaphysical guarantee of truth and the transcendental faith that it is possible or desirable to lay aside one's desires or situation in order to obtain a value-free overview of the world.
>
> *(2007a: 32–33)*

11. We can obviously see a resonance here with Bergson's account of technology as humanity's 'external organs'. What is useful in Merleau-Ponty's account is the way in which he provides a subjective account of what the experience of incorporating these technologies into our bodies looks and feels like. Merleau-Ponty thus provides a phenomenological account of technology use that is lacking (or at least underdeveloped) in Bergson.

12. We might here think back to our analysis of the drone program, and the way we focused on drones as a material form of perception and action which others interact with, in this case in horrifying ways.

13. According to Merleau-Ponty,

> I know unquestionable that that man over there *sees*, that my sensible world is also his, because *I am present at his seeing,* it *is visible* in his eyes' grasp of the scene. And when I say I see *that* he sees, there is no longer here (as there is in "I think that he thinks") the interlocking of two propositions but the mutual unfocusing of a "main" and a "subordinate" viewing. A form that resembles me was there, but busy at secret tasks, possessed by an unknown dream. Suddenly a gleam appeared a little bit below and out in front of its eyes; its glance is raised and comes to fasten on the very things that I am seeing. Everything which for my part is based upon the animal of perceptions and movements, all that I shall ever be able to build upon it – including my "thought," but as a modalization of my presence at the world – falls all at once into the other person. I say that there is a man there and not a mannequin, as I see that the table is there and not a perspective or an appearance of the table.
>
> *(Merleau-Ponty, 1964b: 169–170)*

14. See (Coole 2007b) for a discussion of the embodied character of speech.

Works Cited

Abram, D. (1996) *The Spell of the Sensuous*, New York: Vintage Books.

Ahmed, S. (2006) *Queer Phenomenology: Orientations, Objects, Others*, Durham, NC: Duke University Press.

Bredlau, S. (2019) 'On Perception and Trust: Merleau-Ponty and the Emotional Significance of Our Relations with Others', *Continental Philosophy Review*, 52: 1–14.

Campanella, T. J. (2001) 'Eden by Wire: Webcameras and the Telepresent Landscape', *The Robot in the Garden: Telerobotics and Telepistemology in the Age of the Internet*, ed. K. Goldberg, Cambridge: MIT Press.

Chamayou, G. (2015) *A Theory of the Drone*, Trans. J. Lloyd, New York, NY: The New Press.

Clark, A. (2003) *Natural-Born Cyborgs: Minds, Technologies and the Future of Human Intelligence*, Oxford: Oxford University Press.

Clark, A. (2011) *Supersizing the Mind: Embodiment, Action, and Cognitive Extension*, Oxford: Oxford University Press.

Coole, D. (2007a) *Merleau-Ponty and Modern Politics after Anti-Humanism*, Lanham, MD: Rowman and Littlefield Publishers.

Coole, D. (2007b) 'Experiencing Discourse: Corporeal Communicators and the Embodiment of Power', *British Journal of Politics and International Relations*, 9: 413–33.

Daggett, C. (2015) 'Drone Disorientations', *International Feminist Journal of Politics*, 17(3): 361–79.

Dreyfus, H. L. (2001) 'Telepistemology: Descartes' Last Stand', *The Robot in the Garden: Telerobotics and Telepistemology in the Age of the Internet*, ed. K. Goldberg, Cambridge: MIT Press.

Eriksen, T. H. (2001) *Tyranny of the Moment: Fast and Slow Time in the Information Age*, London, UK: Pluto Press.

Fitzsimmons, S. and Sangha, K. (2013) 'Killing in High Definition: Combat Stress among Operators of Remotely Piloted Aircraft', *Unpublished Paper Presented at CPSA 2013*, Victoria, BC, Canada.

Grossman, D. (2009) *On Killing: The Psychological Cost of Learning to Kill in War and Society*, New York, NY: Back Bay Books.

Grosz, E. (1994) *Volatile Bodies: Toward a Corporeal Feminism*, Bloomington, IN: Indiana University Press.

Hansen, Mark B. N. (2006) *Bodies in Code: Interfaces with Digital Media*, Oxford: Routledge.

Hayles, N. K. (2012) *How We Think: Digital Media and Contemporary Technogenesis*, Chicago: University of Chicago Press.

Heidegger, M. (1971) *Poetry, Language, Thought*, New York: Harper Perennial.

Holmqvist, C. (2013) 'Undoing War: War Ontologies and the Materiality of Drone Warfare', *Millennium: Journal of International Studies*, 41(3): 535–52.

International Human Rights and Conflict Resolution Clinic at Stanford Law School and Global Justice Clinic at NYU School of Law (2012) *Living Under Drones: Death, Injury and Trauma to Civilians from US Drone Practices in Pakistan*. Available at: https://law.stanford.edu/wp-content/uploads/sites/default/files/publication/313671/doc/slspublic/Stanford_NYU_LIVING_UNDER_DRONES.pdf (Accessed August 1, 2019).

Levin, D. M. (1990) 'Justice in the Flesh', *Ontology and Alterity in Merleau-Ponty*, eds. G. A. Johnson and M. B. Smith. Chicago: Northwestern University Press.

Madison, G. B. (1990) 'Flesh as Otherness', *Ontology and Alterity in Merleau-Ponty*, eds. G. A. Johnson and M. B. Smith. Chicago: Northwestern University Press.

Marks, Laura U. (2002) *Touch: Sensuous Theory and Multisensory Media*, Minneapolis: University of Minnesota Press.

Marx, K. (1973) *Grundrisse*, Trans. M. Nicolaus, London: Penguin Classics.

Mayer, J. (2009) 'The Predator War', *The New Yorker*, October 26. Available at: www.newyorker.com/magazine/2009/10/26/the-predator-war (Accessed August 1, 2019).

Merleau-Ponty, M. (1962) *Phenomenology of Perception*, Trans. C. Smith, Abingdon, UK: Routledge.

Merleau-Ponty, M. (1963) *In Praise of Philosophy and Other Essays*, Trans. J. Wild, J. Edie, and J. O'Neill, Chicago: Northwestern University Press.

Merleau-Ponty, M. (1964a) *The Primacy of Perception*, Chicago: Northwestern University Press.

Merleau-Ponty, M. (1964b) *Signs*, Trans. R. C. McCleary, Chicago: Northwestern University Press.

Merleau-Ponty, M. (1968) *The Visible and the Invisible*, Trans. Alphonso Lingis, Chicago: Northwestern University.

Merleau-Ponty, M. (1973) *The Prose of the World*, Trans. John O'Neill, Evanston, IL: Northwestern University Press.

Merleau-Ponty, M. (1995) *Nature: Course Notes from the College de France*, Trans. R. Vallier, Chicago: Northwestern University Press.

Merleau-Ponty, M. (2004) *The World of Perception*, Trans. Oliver Davis, London: Routledge.

Merriman, P. (2012) *Mobility, Space and Culture*, Abingdon, UK: Routledge.

Petranker, J. (2007) 'The Presence of Others: Network Experience as an Antidote to the Subjectivity of Time', *24/7: Time and Temporality in the Network Society*, eds. R. Hassan and R. E. Purser. Stanford, CA: Stanford Business Books.

Watters, E. (2013) 'We Aren't the World', *Pacific Standard*, February 23. Available at https://psmag.com/social-justice/joe-henrich-weird-ultimatum-game-shaking-up-psychology-economics-53135 (Accessed July 28, 2017).

Wilson, C. (2001) 'Vicariousness and Authenticity', *The Robot in the Garden: Telerobotics and Telepistemology in the Age of the Internet*, ed. K. Goldberg, Cambridge: MIT Press.

Young, I. M. (2005) *On Female Body Experience: "Throwing Like a Girl" and Other Essays*, Oxford: Oxford University Press.

7

TOWARDS A PHENOMENOLOGY OF SPEED

Merleau-Ponty and Spatiality in an Accelerating World

Introduction: Hands Across America

In the previous chapter we looked at Merleau-Ponty's phenomenological account of perception, specifically as mediated through his idea of 'the flesh'. In doing so, we looked at Hansen's 'originary technicity' of the body, the idea that perception and cognition were not things that existed in opposition to the world, but are instead seated fundamentally within the flesh of the body and world. This idea has two main consequences: 1) From this perspective, the use of perceptual media is not the superaddition of a prosthetic/parasitic technology onto the already complete human body but rather the continual permutation of the already extended flesh of the body, and 2) This attentiveness to the way in which perception is seated in the flesh of the body also provides a way of thinking about the intercorporeity and intersubjectivity of the world. The flesh of the world, and the reversibility of perception, provides the foundation for the encounter with the other (necessarily rejecting a cartesian monadic vision of the subject as one bound up in unextended spirit rather than always subsumed in extended space). These two points, when brought together, help us to reject modes of analysis which presume that the technological acceleration of perception necessarily results in alienation and dislocation. Rather, from this perspective the encounter with the other can happen just as much via the mediation of technology as it does through the mediation of the body (or perhaps, we might better say that the encounter always happens within the flesh of the world, whether technological or biological).

By way of example, we turn here to the somewhat surprising case: the *Datamitt*. As Canny and Poulos describe:

> One creative experiment in tele-touch took place at SIGGRAPH 93 in Anaheim, California, and simultaneously in New York at the NYU

robotics lab. Ken Goldberg and Richard Wallace connected two simple touch sensors and haptic actuators together to create *Datamitt.* . . . They were placed inside metal tubes on each coast, so that if a participant in Los Angeles placed his or her inside a tube and squeezed, the participant in New York would feel the pressure, and vice versa. What was remarkable about the Datamitt was its low resolution: It was a one-bit sensor/actuator. Either squeeze or no-squeeze with nothing in between.

(Canny and Poulos: 290)

And yet, despite the simplicity of the technology, the user response was surprisingly personal, and visceral. As Andy Clark describes, 'In this simple experiment, people reported a strong sense of personal contact despite the very low bandwidth of the connection' (2003: 112). Canny and Poulos agree, saying the Datamitt

suggests a surprising thesis: Rather than the most difficult of the senses for social telepresence, touch may well be the easiest. At least if the goal is simply to provide a haptic channel with some social value. The meaning of . . . a handsqueeze survives . . . through the Datamitt, even though the pressure data itself is badly distorted.

(290–291)

That a simple handsqueeze – whether mediated through a technical apparatus or not – should provide such a sense of connection, is perhaps not surprising. If we return to Merleau-Ponty's phenomenology of the flesh, we see that the handshake shows up repeatedly as an exemplary site of the encounter with the other. If, as he says, touching our own hand shows us the reversibility of perception, revealing myself as a perceiving subject and a perceived object rooted in the flesh of the world, why should touching the hand of the other not have a similar impact.

The handshake too is reversible; I can feel myself touched as well and at the same time as touching, and surely there does not exist some huge animal whose organs our bodies would be, as, for each of our bodies, our hands, our eyes are the organs. Why would not the synergy exist among different organisms, if it is possible within each? Their landscapes interweave, their actions and their passions fit together exactly: this is possible as soon as we no longer make belongingness to one same 'consciousness' the primordial definite of sensibility, and as soon as we rather understand it as the return of the visible upon itself, a carnal adherence of the sentient to the sensed and of the sensed to the sentient. For, as overlapping and fission, identify and difference, it brings to birth a ray of natural light that illuminates all flesh and not only my own.

(1968: 142)

Elsewhere when discussing the capacity of language to produce an encounter with the other, it is to the handshake that he turns as an example, saying,

> We no more think of the *words* that we are saying or that are being said to us than of the very hand we are shaking. The hand is not a bundle of flesh and bone, it is the palpable presence of the other person.
>
> *(1973: 116)*

Coole describes the importance of this example of the handshake by saying

> Merleau-Ponty is . . . using the handshake to advance an ontological . . . claim and he does so in order to disclose the very possibility of ethical (and political) relations. I know the other as I know the world, he insists, because there is reversibility and because 'he and I are like organs of one single intercorporeity.' If the 'handshake too is reversible,' he reasons, this is because 'synergy' must also exist 'among different organisms' as it does within them. Their landscapes, passions, and actions are interwoven in the overlapping and fission of the flesh.
>
> *(2007: 246)*

What the example of the Datamitt shows us is that the hand we squeeze doesn't necessarily need to be a 'bundle of flesh and bone' to produce this 'palpable presence of the other person'. This also should not be surprising. As Canny and Poulos describe:

> While the fingertips, tongue and lips are extraordinarily sensitive, most of the rest of the body is a rather ordinary touch sensor (compared to what can be built artificially). Shaking hands, kissing, and sexual intimacy stretch the limits of our sense of touch. But other social contacts are dampened through several layers of clothing. Is a hug ineffective because it passes through two layers of woolen sweater? Or for that matter, is a handshake ineffective through a set of gloves?
>
> *(289)*

A handshake through a pair of gloves obviously provides a sense of connection with the other, as it should be said, does a handshake with a prosthesis. What the Datamitt shows is that the other does not even necessarily need to be physically present (or physically present as we usually think of it) for the encounter to produce a feeling of connection. And as Coole points out, such a feeling of connection discloses 'the very possibility of ethical (and political) relations'.

We have already seen, in the previous chapter, that this is not unexpected given the way in which our perception is commonly extended in artefacts and technologies (indeed, through the flesh of the world generally). What is left to be interrogated in greater detail (bringing us back to our discussion of drone warfare) is the particular way in which this extension of perception shapes our sense of spatiality. What is striking about the example of the Datamitt is not just the sense of connection that is produced through the technological apparatus, but the sheer distance that divides the two users. Separated by a continent, the two users still reported a sense of connection, of proximity. What we seek to discuss in this chapter is exactly the way in which various technologies can reshape our sense of spatiality, giving rise to surprising experiences of proximity and connection.

This chapter will therefore proceed in three parts. First, we will begin by providing an overview of Merleau-Ponty's account of space and perception. We will then carry forward our discussion from the previous chapter regarding the incorporation of media into body schemas and cognition – looking specifically at the way in which computers and mobile phones are brought into the body producing an intimate experience of accelerating information flows. With this foundation, we will go on to interrogate the way in which these kinds of incorporations give rise to the trans-location of perception, suturing together diverse places, producing lives lived in multiple spaces simultaneously, or rather, leaving perception to constitute the unique and complex space of an accelerating life. We will draw here on Merleau-Ponty's account of spatiality not as a set or static field, but as a constantly mutating experience of potentiality, always grounded in the unique action space of the body. Attentiveness to this shifting sense of spatiality will help us to trace out the tele-topology of our accelerating world, looking at changes in the relationship between the public and the private, and the near and the far. It will also allow us to better understand changing opportunities for political solidarity and identity, as we discuss new protest tactics and forms of social movement building.

Merleau-Ponty and Spatiality

For Merleau-Ponty, space cannot be understood as abstract, objective, Euclidean space. Rather, space is a malleable medium which organizes itself around the gravitational pull of embodied perception.

> In psychology, as in geometry, the notion of a single unified space entirely open to a disembodied intellect has been replaced by the idea of a space which consists of different regions and has certain privileged directions; these are closely related to our distinctive bodily features and our situation as beings thrown into the world.
>
> (Merleau-Ponty 2004: 43)

What this means is that the world borrows from, and is organized according to, the privileged spatial dynamics and orientations of the human body. Though in an abstract Euclidian spatiality, objects are organized according to simple relative positions, none of which has primacy, our bodies have a specific relationship to space which grounds certain spatial orientations. The perceptual field is organized and oriented in relation to the body schema, and its privileged spatial orientations of the body.

> Thus, since every conceivable being is related either directly or indirectly to the perceived world, and since the perceived world is grasped only in terms of direction, we cannot dissociate being from orientated being, and there is no occasion to 'find a basis for space or to ask what is the level of all levels'.
>
> *(1962: 295)*

By a 'level of all levels', he is referring to some sort of abstract space which could organize all objects in absolute terms. This kind of objective account of space can only ever be secondary to a primary embodied perception, overlaid on top of perception via the act of reflection. Perception always presumes a 'level' which relates to the specific orientation of the human body, which therefore necessarily shifts according to location and nature.

> The primordial level is on the horizon of all our perceptions, but it is a horizon which cannot in principle ever be reached and thematized in our express perception. Each of the levels in which we successively live makes its appearance when we cast anchor in some 'setting' which is offered to us. This setting itself is spatially particularized only for a previously given level. Thus each of the whole succession of our experiences, including the first passes on an already acquired spatiality.
>
> *(1962: 295)*

This process of 'casting anchor' in a 'setting' is to posit, corporeally, a 'ground' according to which space will be organized, investing that space with meaningful spatial orientations, such as up and down, left and right, in front of and behind. This level will, of course, be temporary, situational, and we are capable of 'anchoring' in diverse ways, such as when I invert my bodily schema to make sense of an upside down picture or when I place myself 'within' a map to navigate it, converting its abstract cardinal coordinates into meaningful directions of left and right I can act on.

As discussed, however, this spatial orientation does not just rely on the body schema in terms of its brute physical location. The body schema isn't just a collection of proprioceptive data of the body's current condition but is also a virtual space of corporeal action. This serves to present to perception potential objects of human action, helping us to organize space into figure and background. All of this is to say that perception works to invest space with a *human* meaning.

What is more, this constitution of space via human perception doesn't just affect those things which we can directly perceive. Merleau-Ponty describes how perception serves to 'fill in' those areas of space blocked to human perception. He gives the example of how, when faced with only one side of a lamp (as, of course, all things present only one side to us) we do not therefore assume that the back is absent. Indeed, what is more, it is not so much that we presume the presence of an absent side through a reflective intellectual action. Rather, even in 'immediate' perception, we grasp the object as whole, though we are presented with 'incomplete' sense data.

> I grasp the unseen sides as present, and I do not affirm that the back of the lamp exists in the same sense that I say the solution of a problem exists. The hidden side is present in its own way. It is in my vicinity. Thus I should not say that the unseen sides of objects are simply possible perceptions, nor that they are the necessary conclusion of a kind of analysis or geometrical reasoning. It is not through an intellectual synthesis which would freely posit the total object that I am led from what is given to what is not actually given; that I am given, together with the visible sides of the object, the nonvisible sides as well. It is, rather, a kind of practical synthesis: I can touch the lamp, and not only the side turned toward me but also the other side; I have only to extend my hand to hold it.
>
> *(1964a: 14)*

It is this fact, that 'I have only to extend my hand to hold it' that is at the heart of this constitution of the 'incomplete' object as whole. It attests to the fact that the lamp is not a collection of sense data, of impressions and perspectives, but is rather a thing in the world, present to my body for possible action. My body schema has learned through a lifetime of grasping things how three-dimensional objects – how lamps – *work*, and thus this knowledge is applied in the constitution of a perceptual field. This is not, of course, to say that this might not turn out to be wrong. The lamp might turn out to be a cardboard cut-out, a *trompe l'oueil* painting, or some other such thing. This merely speaks to the extent to which this body schema is not an *a priori* or transcendental schema but is rather constructed out of physiological fact, individual history, and cultural context, and thus can be wrong in its grasp of the world. Indeed, it is exactly the fact that it can be mistaken which supports the idea that perception is not simply the passive reception of sense data, but an active orientation that can be 'wrong' (for certain values of wrong). This is why, no matter what facts we know about astronomy, it doesn't change the fact that we perceive the sun changing size depending on how close it is to the horizon (because, of course, the analysis of relative size and distance in terms of bodily perspective usually works in the constitution of a spatial and perceptual field, when applied to non-astronomical bodies). The entire existence of optical illusions attests to the active, bodily constitution of perception.[1]

Thus, the perceptual field serves not just to organize and orient present sense data but also to fill in absent sense data in order to 'complete' the perceptual field. What is more, this process is not just limited to 'completing' partial objects 'within' the visual field. Rather, it extends beyond the visual field by presuming, and presenting to perception, the continuity of the perceptual field.

> When we reach the limits of the visual field, we do not pass from vision to non-vision: the gramophone playing in the next room, and not expressly seen by me, still counts in my visual field. Conversely what we see is always in certain respects not seen: there must be hidden sides of things, and things 'behind us', if there is to be a 'front' of things, and things 'in front of us', in short, perception.
>
> *(1962: 323)*

This introduces a crucial point, that the perceptual field expands beyond the perceptual field, or rather that the perceptual field immediately apparent to us presumes, and is situated within, a wider horizon of space which is also shaped by our bodily schema, and expectations about how space and objects within it work. This factor is especially important to our discussion of space and speed, as it begins to describe how we relate to spaces which are not immediately present to us.

Thinking Distance

The non-objective nature of space means that even when we relate to much longer distances, they too are organized as part of our perceptual field, if not in such a straight forward manner. Rather, as we've seen, even what is absent is included in the perceptual field, and what is distant is continuous with what is near (even if, and this is crucial, it is continuous exactly insofar as it is viewed as separate). Consider this passage in which Merleau-Ponty provides an account of how our relationship even to the furthest reaches of the world take on a human meaning.

> Whatever be the validity of our universal concepts, the antipodes will never exist for us like the things we perceive around us. They will never be simultaneous with the world that I perceive; I cannot believe in it in the same way that I believe in the things that surround me. Between the antipodes and us there is only a linkage of motivations; I know that others have been there, that I in principle can go there, but that I would take time to go there and that when I will be there I will not be at the antipodes. This ubiquity of thought that makes me believe that the antipodes

exist rests on a transmutation of here to there. . . . In this sense the world of idealization encloses a certain relativity. It is only true as limited and reincorporated into a more concrete given.

(1995: 78)

Two crucial points are made here. 1) Despite the existence of universal concepts of space and time, the question of space is always a question of how things 'exist for us'. We can happily look at a map and understand the objective relations of all space, but in relationship to my embodied perception, the antipodes take on an orientation of 'farness' which is relatively to my bodily situation. 2) This is what I mean when I said that in the perceptual field what is distant is continuous with what is near, even if this is insofar as it is viewed as separate from what is near. As this passage makes clear, the antipodes are defined exactly insofar as they are distant from me. And they are distant exactly insofar as they are beyond my ability to act on them (as Clark says 'Distance . . . is what there is not action at' [2003: 89]). They take on an orientation, a *meaning* in relation to my bodily location, a meaning which would necessarily be lacking when we treat the antipode merely as a point on a map. When we look at a map, we take in space (and therefore time) as simultaneous, as co-present with itself. In terms of embodied perception, however, this is impossible. The antipodes 'will never be simultaneous with the world that I perceive' exactly because it is given meaning in terms of its distance from my ability to act on it.

At the same time as our embodied perception can create a separation between near and far, parcelling out space according to its relation to our bodily schema's space of virtual action, it can also suture together spaces which are widely disparate, even on a planetary scale.

We have forgotten the notion of *Boden* ('ground'), because we have generalized it, situating the Earth among the planets. But, Husserl says, imaging a bird capable of flying to another planet: it would not have a double ground. From the sole fact that it is the same bird, it unites the two planets into one single ground. Where I go, I make a ground there and attach the new ground to the old where I lived. To think two Earths is to think one same Earth. . . . Our soil or ground expands, but it is not doubled, and we cannot think without reference to one soil of experience of this type.

(Merleau-Ponty 1995: 77)

We, of course, do not need to imagine a bird but rather can bring to mind the history of space flight, and how it has changed humanity's relationships to space, and to the earth. This is not to say that most people think that they will go into space (any more than we might expect to visit the antipodes). It is rather that space, and the moon, have now been incorporate into the virtual space of human bodily action in a way that was previously impossible. Here is where the question of speed becomes central to the phenomenology of space. The speed of the rocket provides a potential conduit of action between the earth and the moon, changing its phenomenological relationship to the previous world of human action.

Now, there is a seeming contradiction here between the embodied perception which separates off the antipodes as 'distant' yet can incorporate the moon into the 'ground'. Partly this is a function of the fact that our phenomenological experience of space is not purely a binary opposition between 'near' and 'far'. Rather space is experienced on a continuum of increasing difficulties of expressing action, increasing abilities, costs, and likelihoods of travelling a given distance. However, it also speaks to the relative mutability of the perceptual field in terms of the ways in which it orients us to the flesh of the world. We can, for example, Merleau-Ponty says, anchor our perception in different ways in the world to reorganize the perceptual field. Merleau-Ponty points out that the relativity of motion is resolved in perception by anchoring on one specific object (and only ever one specific object at a time).

> What makes part of the field count as an object in motion, and another as the background, is the way in which we establish our relations with them by the act of looking. The stone flies through the air. What do these words mean, other than that our gaze, lodged and anchored in the garden, is attracted by the stone and, so to speak, drags at its anchors. The relation between the moving object and its background passes through our body. How is this bodily mediation to be conceived? How does it come about that the relations of objects to it can differentiate them as in motion or at rest? Is not our body an object, and does it not itself need to be determinate in relation to rest and movement?
>
> *(1962: 326)*

For our purposes, what is especially important is that this ability to anchor perception in diverse locations is not just confined to immediate space. Rather, just as we said that distant spaces are linked to nearer ones via the perceptual field, so too can we anchor our perception to distant spaces, splitting ourselves in two.

> Even in waking life things are no different. I arrive in a village for my holidays, happy to leave my work and my everyday surroundings. I settle in in the village, and it becomes the centre of my life. The low level of the river, gather in the maize crop or nutting are events for me. But if a friend comes to see me bringing news from Paris, or if the press and radio tell me that war threatens, I feel an exile in the village, shut off from real life, pushed far away from everything. Our body and our perception

always summon us to take as the centre of the world that environment with which they present us. But this environment is not necessarily that of our own life. I can 'be somewhere else' while staying here, and if I am kept far away from what I love, I feel out of touch with real life.

(1962: 333)

In this case, anchoring on a distant space reinforces this sense of distance as 'non-simultaneity' discussed earlier. This account is important for understanding the way in which the speed and scope of contemporary information technologies can make us feel alienated from where we are, keeping us 'far away from what we love', and trapping us where our body physically is. Note here that exactly what is important is the fact that though one has information about Paris, one is unable to act there. The anchor of one's perceptual field, and the location of one's space of bodily action are opposed to one another, resulting in a situation where one feels 'out of touch with real life'.

This is not, however, the only possible relation of the near and far. Via various technological innovations, there are increasingly ways in which information flows do not just anchor our perception in distant locations but allow us to have effects there as well. In this regard, much like the bird which is able to fly between the earth and the moon, technology can suture together diverse grounds, creating new spaces. Thus Merleau-Ponty describes how

> A friend's speech over the telephone brings us the friend himself, as if he were wholly present in that manner of calling and saying goodbye to us, of beginning and ending his sentences, and of carrying on the conversation through things left unsaid.
>
> *(1964b: 43)*

Here the speed of communication first inaugurated by the telegraph wire becomes robust enough to carry a human voice, and with it, a phenomenological experience of being able to interact with what was once distant (reach out and touch someone) (Petranker 2007: 175–6). What is more, we see here a return to Merleau-Ponty's account of how language can be a conduit for the encounter with another, via the technological medium of the telephone.

By acknowledging the way in which the telephone can 'bring the friend himself', Merleau-Ponty is noting the way in which reciprocal embodied action can suture space together. The distance of space is annihilated not just in the instantaneity of the data transfer across phone lines, but in my perceptual field which parcels out spaces of 'nearness' and 'distance'. Nearness and distance become not matters of objective space (as, of course, they never were), but instead questions of bodily capability, of a virtual space of action, and thus of a technical apparatus which can transmit flows of information and action fast enough, and densely enough, to shape our perceptual field in ways that suture distant spaces together. We can, of course, shift from this relatively pleasant image of a phone call with a friend to the horrific image of a drone operator murdering a civilian on the other side of the world. The point here is not that such shifting spatialities are inherently good, or liberatory, or unifying. The encounter with the other provides the conditions of possibility for political solidarity and moral responsibility, but it has never guaranteed it. Rather, what we are trying to identify here is the way in which technological change grounds shifting phenomenological topology of an accelerating world. It is to this shifting topology that we turn next.

Incorporating Media

In terms of tracing out the phenomenological topology of an accelerating world, our goal is, in some ways, to develop a more nuanced understanding of that most cliched statement about life in a world of accelerating ICTs: 'the feeling one has that the world is at one's fingertips' as Hayles puts it. She goes on to describe this feeling in better detail saying,

> The ability to access and retrieve information on a global scale has a significant impact on how one thinks about one's place in the world. I live in a small town in North Carolina, but thanks to the web, I do not feel in the least isolated. I can access national news, compare it to international coverage, find arcane sources, look up information to fact-check a claim, and a host of other activities that would have taken days in the pre-internet era instead of minutes, if indeed they could be done at all. Conversely, when my computer goes down or my Internet connection fails, I feel lost, disoriented, unable to work – in fact, I feel as if my hands have been amputated. . . . Such feelings, which are widespread, constitute nothing less than a change in worldview.
>
> *(2012: 2)*

In this passage, Hayles invokes multiple themes from our investigation of Merleau-Ponty – the way that technologies can be incorporated so fully into our body schema that their removal can feel like the loss of a limb; the way that technologically mediated changes in the space of information, communication, and action can serve to change my perception of spatial characteristics such as nearness, distance, and isolation; and finally, that together these tendencies 'constitute nothing less than a change in worldview'. In this section, then, we will turn to the question how accelerating ICTs can be incorporated into our body schemas (and perceptual networks more broadly), and discuss how this shift in our body schemas produces a shift in our perception of space. At stake here is a rejection of accounts which view contemporary ICTs as having a dislocating effect on human existence. In its place, I wish to argue for a better understanding of the way in which these technologies produce an experience of translocalization, suturing together diverse spaces and producing a unique and shifting topology in which values of near and far, present and absent still exist, but in ways which don't directly map onto 'objective' space. The political and ethical implications of such shifts are diverse, and I will try to gesture towards some of the ways in which this framework could shape our political analysis (as I did in the previous chapters discussion of drone warfare). Again, my point is not that such changes are necessarily 'good' or 'bad' but rather that assuming a kind of flat 'distancelessness' as the consequence of accelerating ICTs will leave us ill-equipped for understanding the spatial and perceptual character of the present political and technological moment.

As we saw in our discussions of Spinoza and Bergson, the idea that the human body is marked by an originary technicity – a primal relationship to speed and acceleration – is in no way restricted to Merleau-Ponty. There are many authors who have viewed the history of the human body and mind as the ongoing process of supplementation by technological artefacts, what Bernard Stiegler calls our 'technogenesis'. What we are specifically interested in is how a technology can be so thoroughly integrated into the body as to radically affect the shape and scope of the subject's perceptual field. Just as the blind person's cane can extend the radius of human touch, so too can digital technologies extend the space of other aspects of the human sensorium over a much wider distance. At its absolute limit, this translates into what is terms 'telepresence', the ability to fully transport the human sensorium to a different locale. Cognitive scientist Andrew Clark describes what this would look like in its most extreme forms, saying,

> True telepresence, insofar as it is achievable, would seem to require a high bandwidth multisensory bath of information with local sensory stimulation: in effect, the full virtual reality body suit, with feedout and feedback connections for sight, sound, hearing, touch, and smell, as well as heat and resistance sensing. Also – perhaps crucially – the user needs the ability not just to passively perceive but to *act upon* the distance environment and to command the distant sensors to scan intelligently around the scene.
>
> *(2003: 93)*

Though work continues on immersive media and 'virtual reality' platforms which might someday develop these technical capabilities, thus far this kind of experience is still science-fictional. However, we should not imagine that this is the only way to produce the experience of telepresence. As our discussion of the TTVS in Chapter 6 indicated, we do not necessarily need access to high bandwidth sensory information to give the experience of embodied perception. Rather, as Clark points out in an overtly Merleau-Pontian moment 'Our sense of personal location has more to do with this sense of an *action-space* than with anything else' (2003: 94). This is to say that it is our ability to take action in the world which grounds perception, shaping our sense of spatiality and location. This is why even when they have high-definition screens and high bandwidth connections, teleconferencing suites rarely give us the feeling of tele-presence. It is not just that we cannot physically affect the space on the other side of the screen. This could easily be surmounted. It is that the camera angle is essentially unmoving. Since the perspective is disconnected from our bodily movements, the camera cannot be effectively integrated into our body schema. Thus, ironically, the TTVS system, despite its incredibly low bandwidth (and arbitrary interface) gives an embodied experience of perception and location in a way that a high-definition visual experience frequently does not. As Clark puts it, 'What seems to matter in these cases is the presence of some kind of local, circular process in which neural commands, motor actions, and sensory feedback are *closely and continuously correlated*' (2003: 104). In other words, the vector of perception incorporates itself into the body schema in a continuous enough way to produce the transparency of the sensing medium (whether it be cane or video camera), and its constitution as embodied perception. In a world in which telepresence, telemanipulation, and telerobotic technologies prolifer-ate, even where they do not reach the gold standard Clark provides earlier, the simple fact is that we will have more experiences of being tele-present. This will serve to radically shape our sense of spatiality.

Indeed, this point raised earlier – that the most effective telepresence media are not necessarily those with the highest bandwidth, or that most faithfully recreate the experience of immediate vision (think here once again of the *Datamitt*) – brings us to another point. Incorporating technologies into the body schema is not necessarily just a matter of extending perception in a linear fashion. Extensions of the body do not just perfectly replicate perception in its 'natural' form. The cane does not just reproduce vision (or touch for that mat-ter) in a non-biological form. To think of it this way is to adhere to what Clark calls the 'crutch' image of technology, viewing technological artefacts as simply recreating the 'natural' capabilities and functions of the human body. Instead, many technologies introduce a new sense into the body, one which can become part of the body schema, but which therefore *changes* the body schema and in doing so *changes* the perceptual field, and therefore *changes* cognition. (Here we see an echo of Bergson's account of the relationship between technology and the body wherein new technological organs induce 'new needs' and 'new organizations' of the body).

In many ways, this should not be surprising. Merleau-Ponty regularly describes how history, biology, culture, and personal experience, shape bodily perception. Again, we need to remember that, though Merleau-Ponty's account of how the perceptual field is shaped by a pre-perceptual schema, we should not think of this as an *a priori* schema in a Kantian sense. Rather, the schema is developed *a posteriori* in a feedback loop with the world in which it exists. This is why Hansen invokes Deleuze's language of 'transcendental sensibility' to describe it (2006: 8). And this is also why, when attempting to investigate technologies which translocate embodied perception, we should not just be searching for the technologies that most faithfully replicate the experience of 'immediate' or 'natural' bodily experience and presence, the 'gold standard' telepresence platform discussed earlier. What is more, this should also factor into how we think about translocation. Frequently we see a distinction made between a complete, 'natural', immediate location, and an uncanny, unnatural 'dislocation'. Such a dichotomy ignores the way in which technologies might produce, indeed, might *seek* to produce, a *different kind of location*, a different kind of spatiality, which carries only some of the characteristics of what we think of as 'immediate' location. Clark quotes technologists Jim Hollan and Scott Stormetta who state:

> [much] telecommunications research seems to work under the implic- itly assumption that there is a natural and perfect state – *being there* – and that our state is in some sense broken when we are not physically proximate . . . in our view, there are a number of problems with this approach. Not only does it orient us towards the construction of crutch- like telecommunications tools but is also implicitly commits us to a general research direction of attempting to imitate one medium of com- munication with another.
>
> *(2003: 109)*

The counter-example Clark provides is e-mail, saying that contrary to a 'crutch' view of e-mail in which it is just a degraded way of having a face to face conversation,

> e-mail is *nothing like* face-to-face interaction, and therein lies its virtue. It provides *complementary functionality*, allowing people informally and rap- idly to interact, while preserving an inspectable and revisitable trace. It does this without requiring us both to be free at the same time . . . The tools that really take off, Hollan and Stormetta thus argue, are those that 'people prefer to use [for certain purposes] even when they have the option of interacting in physical proximity . . . tools that go *beyond being there*.
>
> *(110)*

To interrogate this idea of novel technological embodiments giving rise to novel phenomenological experiences, we might want to think about the ways in which embodied perception and our sense of spatiality are shaped by an increasingly ubiquitous ICT: texting.

Texting, Smartphones, and Spatiality

Although in principle a much slower, intermittent, and less information dense form of communication than talking on the phone, texting has become immensely popular. A survey of US adults shows that between March 2006 and May 2011, the number of individuals who send or receive text messages climbed from 31% to 61%. What is more, this statistic skews heavily according to age, with only 48% of those age 50–64 using text messages, compared to 89% of those aged 18–29 (Rainie and Wellman 2012: 90). Indeed, the numbers go up even more when we look at teenagers, for whom texting is a far more common form of communication than actually talking on the phone. According to Rainie and Wellman, this is for a variety of reasons.

> Teens prefer mobile texting . . . because they can do it privately from their personal phones, and because texting is unobtrusive – it can be done silently while in a class, out with friends, or even at home with parents. Unlike phone chats, texting can be asynchronous: Busy teens can leave messages for each other.
>
> *(90–91)*

Here we see exactly what Clark was discussing earlier; the reasons that texting has taken off are exactly the reasons that make it different than 'immediate' 'face-to-face' communication and perception. It's asynchronous, it's low-bandwidth (and therefore silent), it can be done parallel with other activities. This has resulted in its integration as one of the central mediums of communication in our accelerating world. Texting allows for a constant, low-level contact with absent others regardless of their distance from you (the experience of texting is the same whether the recipient is in the next room or in another country). The result is that the use of texting in one's daily life can shape one's sense of spatiality in several key ways.

First, is the constant virtual presence of absent others (and your virtual presence to those absent others). As Rainie and Wellman put it, 'The small size of mobile phones also gives users a sense that their social networks are easily accessible where they are: the diminutive device potently symbolizes a network in their pocket' (95). No longer do we assume that people are only accessible when at certain discrete locations we have a phone number for, and only at specific times when they are not otherwise occupied. Now the presumption is that the inaccessibility of individuals will be a rare and temporary phenomenon.

> This easy and constant accessibility changes how people relate. For networked individuals, this switch to perpetual access that is untethered from places gives them more control of their outreach to others and their available to others. This also affects people's sense of time, place presence

and social connectedness. This, in turn, leads to new notions about when it is possible – and permissible – to be in touch with others. People's expectations about the availability and findability of others have sharply expanded since the Mobile Revolutions.

(95)

Of course, debates over the desirability of this kind of ubiquitous connectivity are ongoing. On the one hand, the expectation of constant availability which many workers feel in relation to their jobs is a profoundly stressful experience. On the other hand, those in, for example, long-distance relationships, describe the important role that this kind of ubiquitous, low-level communication plays in maintaining a sense of intimacy and connection. My goal here is not to decisively evaluate the benefits or dangers of this kind of technology, but to seek to understand the way in which this shift in expectations of findability constitutes a mutation in our sense of spatiality.

While the individuals which are part of our social and electronic network are clearly not present in an 'immediate' way, they *are* present in a virtual, but still effective and affective, way (otherwise the virtual presence of our bosses would not provoke stress, nor the virtual presence of our lover, affection). We might not be able to go so far as to mimic Merleau-Ponty's statement that 'A friend's speech over the telephone brings us the friend himself' when it comes to texting, but it definitely produces a sense of what Rainie and Wellman call the 'present absent' (103). The present absent necessarily occupies a space which is neither near or far, which sutures together distant space, but in a less robust way than a 'gold-standard' telepresent suite might, resulting in a virtually present space of connection which fades in and out of focus, depending on our current activity (Petranker 2007: 181).

This experience, it should be noted, is not just informational or imaginary (I receive a text from an individual and imagine them as virtually present as I read the note) but is embodied as well. Phones are very much integrated into our body schema and our interactions with them shape our perception in very concrete ways. As Hassan puts it, 'so intimate have we already become with mobile phones, personal computers, PDAs, and so forth, that it is already possible to view these as our cyborg extensions into the network, technologies that unite us with it and it with us' (47). (Clark reports 'Finnish youngsters have dubbed the cell phone "kanny," which means extension of the hand' [2003: 9].) This meshes well with Merleau-Ponty's insight that the habit of typing serves to integrate the perception and knowledge of the keyboard into our bodies. Indeed, the keyboard exists alongside the cane, the feather, and the car, as a key example of our body's ability to 'appropriate fresh instruments' for ourselves.

> Habit expresses our power of dilating our being-in-the-world, or changing our existence by appropriating fresh instruments. It is possible to

know how to type without being able to say where the letters which make the words are to be found on the banks of the keys. To know how to type is not, then, to know the place of each letter among the keys, nor even to have acquired a conditioned reflex for each one, which is set in motion by the letter as it comes before our eye. If habit is neither a form of knowledge nor an involuntary action, what then is it? It is knowledge in the hands, which is forthcoming only when bodily effort is made, and cannot be formulated in detachment from that effort.

(1962: 166)

This points out the way in which, when texting with someone, we are not focusing on the keyboard or the act of typing, so much as we are *communicating*, enacting language's ability to produce a sense of connection with the other.[2] This serves to materialize the connection with the other, shaping your perception of spatiality (again, similar to Merleau-Ponty's account of the phone call). This incorporation of the materiality of the cell phone extends beyond the keyboard interface to the whole of the object itself. Anyone who has extensively communicated via cell-phone can tell you about how the vibration which accompanies a text notification can have profound physiological and psychological effects – excitement for the individual expecting a text back from a lover, dread for the individual expecting a work text. Indeed, even the weaknesses of the mobile phone can direct our attention to the ways in which it shapes our sense of spatiality (as a broken hammer makes us more attentive to its nature). When, for example, poor reception interrupts a text conversation, we suddenly find that someone who was near has suddenly become distant, and we feel like a power we once had is now gone (think of Hayles' confession that when her internet link is broken, 'I feel as if my hands have been amputated').

This ability for our cellular connection to be severed – and thus for our virtualized conception of spatiality to be disrupted – brings our attention to another way in which texting and mobile phones shape our relationship to space – the way that they change even our experience of 'immediate' space. The ubiquitous presence of mobile phones (frequently with Wi-Fi capabilities) makes us attentive to the materiality of our surroundings. Being around thick concrete, underground, in a space with lots of other network data, or behind rebar- all of these begin to take on additional meaning for us. Our acquisition of a wireless mobile phone develops what Gilbert Simondon called a 'technogeographic milieu' (Mackenzie 2010: 126). Once again, we see a Merleau-Pontian echo in the way in which changes in the field of action serve to change the way in which perception is constituted, and the way in which space, and objects, are accorded meaning. In the same way that the subsumption of the car into our body schema gives a new meaning to the space of the entry gate ('too small'/'just big enough'), so too does the incorporation of the mobile phone give new meaning to architecture and location ('Proximity to Wi-Fi routers and cellular antennae', 'Opaqueness to electromagnetic radiation'). In a tenuous but also very real, way, we can say that the space of wireless frequencies becomes tangible too us. We watch people navigate this space as they get up and move about the room, hunching over or standing on tip toes in an attempt to get a connection.

This point brings us to the final way in which texting and mobile phones shape our sense of spatiality. As discussed, the increasing ubiquity of mobile phones has resulted in increased expectations of findability. Thus, you do not assume that you are only able to contact individuals at specific locations at specific times. What this means is that the values of 'specific times' and 'specific locations' begins to wane. As Rainie and Wellman point out, the constant low-level contact which texting and mobile phones provide has resulted in changes in the way in which some people relate to planning meetings in physical space.

> Rather than people stating precisely where they will be and when, people use their mobile phones as they draw near a gathering, repeatedly reporting their whereabouts and approximate arrival time, and often point out landmarks so that those meeting them will be able to place them and even see them as they approach. They understand from the beginning that the initial time and place for the meeting are approximate and changeable. They are more careless about arriving at the proper time and they fuss less about knowing the proper place ahead of time. Sociologist Bernie Hogan calls this 'soft time' and 'soft location'. It is part of networked individuals' shift from place-based connections to person-based connections, with 'a flexible lifestyle of instant exchange and constant updates'.
>
> *(2012: 99)*[3]

In this changing practice of planning meetings, we see a changing sense of spatiality. Rather than a map marked by specific important and stable locations, space becomes marked by vectors, velocities, and tendencies, as individuals spiral into, and out of physical proximity. This softening of location and time isn't just a matter of convenience, or busyness, but rather marks a genuine change in perception of spatiality. The access that some people have to mobile internet, and to services such as google maps, softens space even further, as we can travel without worrying about finding ourselves 'lost', or unable to connect 'here' to 'there'.

This changing relationship to space has formal political implications, for example, in terms of tactics and strategies for public demonstrations and protests. Analyses since the mid-2000s have increasingly commented on the role that smartphones have played in organizing mass demonstrations and occupations (here in addition to the specific role of texting I include other applications available on smart phones, including access to maps, social media platforms, the ability to take and upload videos and pictures, etc.). Rainie and Wellman discuss the central role that cell phones played during the occupation of Tahrir square during the Arab spring.

> Mobile phones played an important role because many more people owned them than personal computers. Those in Tahrir Square at the center of the revolt relied on mobile phones to learn about fast-paced events that were unfolding around them and then share those stories via the internet. They – and others – sent bulletins by Twitter and text, and uploaded protest (and repression) videos to Youtube, thereby spreading the flow of information worldwide. . . . Mobile phones were so essential to the group that they ingeniously kept them charged by tapping into street lamp wires to obtain electricity.
>
> *(209–210)*

Manuel Castells in turn provides an account of the role that texting and Twitter played in organizing actions as part of the Occupy Wall Street protests.

> An unpublished study by Kevin Driscoll and Francois Bar at the University of Southern California Annenberg Innovation Lab collected Occupy tweets continuously beginning on October 12, 2011, by comparing them against an evolving set of approximately 289 related keywords and phrases. During the month of November, they observed approximately 120,000 Occupy-related tweets on a typical day with a peak of over 500,000 during the raid of Zuccotti Park on November 15th. The analysis by Gilad Lotan on Twitter traffic related to the movement shows that the peaks are associated with crucial moments in the movement, such as the first attempt to evict the occupation of Zuccotti Park on October 13. In most instances of threatened police action against occupations, Twitter networks alerted thousands, and their instant mobilization in solidarity played a role in protecting the occupiers. Using Twitter from their cell phones, the protesters were able to constantly distribute information, photos, videos and comments to build a real-time network of communication overlaid on the occupied space.
>
> *(2012: 171–2)*

The integrated use of these technologies allowed for much quicker responses to police actions on behalf of protesters, allowing for a more dynamic use of spatial tactics. What is more, as discussed earlier the fact that texting (or using other communication technologies embedded in smartphones) connect spaces both locally and globally, these technologies allowed for connections with global activist networks who provided support and Information. Thus, during the Egyptian revolution,

> [w]hile protesting, organizers leveraged their networks and resources. They continued to communicate with the experienced activists from Tunisia and Serbia who provided practical advice, such as sniffing lemons, onions, and vinegar for relief from tear gas, using spray paint to cover windshields of police cars, and shielding their bodies with plastic bottles or cardboard.
>
> *(Rainie and Wellman 2012: 209)*

This is not to suggest that there aren't dangers or drawbacks to the use of texting and smartphones, or the changing spatialities that they inculcate, or that their political impact is uniformly positive. It is merely to provide one set of examples of the way in which they make robust, concrete changes in our sense of space, in ways that shape how we organize politically. This cuts against accounts which see, in accelerating ICTs, only an alienating or dislocating effect.

What we find in this brief engagement are multiple ways in which the embodied practices of perception and communication afforded by the mobile phone as technical apparatus serves to shape our perception of space, both in terms of 'physical' 'immediate' space, as well as a virtual space of 'absent presences'. Not all of these hew exactly to the image Merleau-Ponty provides of an incorporated technology shaping our sense of spatiality. But again, we should be careful that we do not assume that our embodied perception of spatiality will be unchanging or will change only in regular ways. The entire point of Merleau-Ponty's analysis is to understand the way in which changing conditions of biology, culture, history and personal experience shape the schema, which in turn shapes perception. We must therefore be attentive to the ways in which new technologies might shape our sense of perception and spatiality in unexpected ways. This is the point that is lost when people treat information and communication technologies as necessarily disembodying and virtualizing. As N. Katherine Hayles points out:

> our interactions with digital media are embodied, and they have bodily effects at the physical level. Similarly, the actions of computers are also embodied, although in a very different manner than with humans. The more one works with digital technologies, the more one comes to appreciate the capacity of networked and programmable machines to carry out sophisticated cognitive tasks, and the more the keyboard comes to seem an extension of one's thoughts rather than an external device on which one types. Embodiment then takes the form of extended cognition, in which human agency and thought are enmeshed within larger networks that extend beyond the desktop computer into the environment.
>
> *(2012: 3)*

Reshaping Space

Our engagement with the case study of texting and smartphones earlier provided an example of both the ways in which technologies can be incorporated into our body/schema, and the way in which this can shape our sense of spatiality. What is important to note, in the context of a discussion of speed and perception, is the way in which technologies that accelerate flows of information and action do not serve to despatialize experience, transporting us to the no-place of cyberspace. While these technologies certainly *change* our sense of spatiality, producing a novel phenomenological topology of space, they never succeed in genuinely taking us out of space (whatever that might mean). This is contrary to a vision of the despatializing effects of accelerating ICTs developed by, for example, Albert Borgmann, based off of his reading of Heidegger.

> As Heidegger pointed out in 1905- already, we have been annihilating space and time in earnest through planes, radio, film, and television. Information technology in particular does not so much bring near which is far as it cancels the metric of time and space. Heidegger . . . consider[ed] the role technology has had in providing for 'communication over vast distances,' and concluded, correctly, I believe, that technology does not make present what is distant. 'Everything,' he says, 'gets lumped together into uniform distancelessness'.
>
> *(2001: 98–9)*

As we have been arguing, our experience of space in an accelerating world is not one of 'uniform distancelessness', though it might not be the spatiality of previous historical moments. What we have been attempting here, is rather to engage in a Merleau-Pontian phenomenological topology which looks at how new technologies shape new embodied perceptions, and thus new spatialities. This is what we did in the previous section in our discussion of texting and mobile phones. Now, I cannot do the same for all of the other technologies that invest our accelerating world – not just due to space constraints but also because they change so rapidly. Instead, what I would like to do is engage with the more general question of how accelerating perceptual technologies are shaping our sense of spatiality. I will do this by looking at two key spatial oppositions which are shaped by an accelerating perception – public and private, and near and far.

Public and Private

Many people have remarked on the way in which ubiquitous telecommunications devices have begun to break down the line between public and private. This is, perhaps, most obvious in the case of the so-called 'work-life' divide.

E-mail, mobile phones, teleconferencing, and virtual desktops mean that in many ways work is capable of expanding to all hours of the day. Usually this story is told in terms of the steady erosion of the private by the public, the domestic by the economic. Rainie and Wellman, however, point out that this breaking down of the line between public and private is less a homogenization under the sign of a ubiquitous public, than an increasing interpenetration of the two, decoupled from immediate location.

> The interpenetration of home and work goes in both directions. In one direction, workers bring work home from the office to finish off jobs or they may stay home full or part time. . . . For others, the new media tethers them to their jobs – they cannot leave work behind when they head out the office door. On the one hand, many feel so burdened by time pressures and the constant threat of demands that they respond and complete tasks even when they are away from their place of work. On the other hand, many feel liberated by being able to avoid long, tedious, and tense commuting. They enjoy the prospect of being able to do 'home' activities such as personal browsing of the web, sharing Facebook updates, shopping, and emailing family and friends while they are at work. In short, 'home' activities have invaded work while 'work' activities have invaded homes.
>
> *(16)*

Now, these effects of accelerative technologies can't be read in isolation from the broader social and economic contexts in which they exist. The invasion of 'home life' by work is an extension of the usual capitalist processes of real subsumption – enhanced, certainly, by communication technologies, but not reducible to them. Thus, Wacjman 'argue[s] against the view that ICTs extend and colonize all time outside the workplace' (138) and instead suggests that '[r]ather than conceiving of technology as an autonomous force determining the organization of work' we should look at how 'that technology is itself crucially affected by the antagonistic class relations of production' (89). Furthermore, as Rainie and Wellman point out, these same technologies provide opportunities for workers to fight back, clawing back some of their own time during work hours, setting up temporary private spaces, while in the archetypal public space of work. Wajcman agrees, saying,

> Multiple mediated forms of connection and distance, and the different negotiations that take place around access and availability do disrupt what we once thought of as boundaries between public and private, work and family, labor and leisure. However, rather than worrying about technology intruding on, and poaching, time from intimate moments that we used to think of as somehow 'private', we would be better off

reformulating the question in terms of the control that individuals can and do exercise over when and where they make themselves available.

(2016: 138)

She goes on to argue for a nuanced account of the impact of ICTs on our sense of spatiality and relationships.

Many critics stress that, by allowing employers to contact their employees at all hours, mobile technologies encourage work problems to colonize the times and spaces once reserved for family life. Others, however, argue that by making place irrelevant, these devices afford novel opportunities for intense connectedness, deepening strong ties. Rather than fragmenting relationships, time spent using communication tools might make relationships more durable.

(139–140)

This is not to suggest that these efforts are symmetrical, or that we should not be concerned about this appropriation of private life by work. Indeed, an attentiveness to these effects can mean attending to ways to limit them, such as laws limiting contact after working hours (such as France and several Scandinavian countries have done), or developing stronger cultural morays which value slow, private time. However, this kind of approach does encourage us to recognize that accelerating ICTs do not simply produce one homogenous public space. They can also provide new opportunities for privacy, even creating private spaces in formerly public spaces. As Rainie and Wellman say,

Mobile phones have made conversations more private than they were in the era when the household phone sat in the middle of the house so that everyone at home could hear at least one end of a phone conversation. Texting has brought another dimension to person-to-person contact by helping it become more private, even in close quarters.

(17)

This is especially important for those individuals who might not have access to private space over which they have control. Think here of a queer teenager, attempting to maintain a relationship in the context of a disapproving parent, or a victim of domestic abuse seeking help or information under the surveillance of their abuser. As Wajcman puts it:

The same technologies can mean very different things to different groups of people, collectively producing new patterns of social interaction, new relationships, new identities. Rather than simply reading them as adding to time pressure and accelerating the pace of life, mobile modalities may be creating novel time practices and transforming the quality of communication.

(2008: 68)

Again, the claim here is not that such effects are symmetrical, or universally good. Moreover, such effects are crucially dependent on various decisions made by technology makers, on whether to prioritize privacy, or to make surveillance easier in the devices and networks they create. The point, however, is to understand that changing the line between public and private does not inherently mean the subsumption of the latter by the former. Rather, this interpenetration of public and private space greatly changes our experience and sense of spatiality, making us feel more exposed and 'findable' in our previous alone, private time but also allowing us to carve out bubbles of private time in seemingly public space (as anyone who has ever 'sexted' in a crowded restaurant knows). The point – as it always is in our Merleau-Pontian frame of analysis – is how and where we are able to take action, and thus how that shapes our perceptual field and sense of spatiality. As Andy Clark describes:

> Next time you are on a crowded train or in a subway station, look at all the people around you talking on their cell phones. Where are they? Well, clearly, they are with you in the station or on the train, but often, they are not much engaged with these local surroundings. They are, temporarily at least, jacked into a web of personal and business communications, which deliberately disrespects current physical location. Draw the lines of proximity and distance according to the criterion of effective action, and a virtual neighborhood emerges; one in which the speakers are more proximal to their colleagues or loved ones than to the strangers on the platform.
>
> *(2003: 89)*

Note how Clark is very careful not to describe this phenomenon as one of dislocation, or virtualization, or subsumption into some distanceless non-space (or homogenous public). Though these technologies certainly allow us to 'disrespect current physical location', this is to draw new lines of proximity and distance 'according to the criterion of effective action'. Sometimes this will serve to transform a private space into a public space. Sometimes it will carve a private space out of a public space. Sometimes it will even serve to shift expectations about what public and private space (and public and private behaviour) are. As Rainie and Wellman go on to describe changing privacy practices in a networked age,

> Blogs often become quasi-public diaries, and social media such as Facebook, Twitter, and foursquare-enable people to inform others of their

whereabouts and to announce their momentary thoughts and doings. . . .
At the same time, heretofore private activities invade public spaces as
people speak openly of intimate affairs on their mobiles in public spaces
and work on their laptop in coffee shops (hoping that others won't peek
too much).

(17)

We might find some, or all of these development undesirable (although I would
emphasize that understandings and practices of privacy have shifted greatly
over time, and thus to be chastened before judging any particular development). But the crucial point to understand is that all of them involve an evolv-
ing, but always embodied, sense of spatiality.

Near and Far

In the quote earlier, when Clark asks the question 'Where are they?' of train
passengers using their cell phones, he notes that the question of space is not
just one of quality (public or private) but also one of location (near or far).
Our sense of spatiality is shaped by the speed and difficulty with which we are
able to project actions. Says Clarke, 'Our sense of personal location has more
to do with this sense of an *action-space* than with anything else' (2003: 94).
This perception of action space serves to parcel out space and mark it with the
qualities of 'near' and 'far'. 'Distance . . . is what there is not action at' (Clark
2003: 89). This follows from our account of Merleau-Ponty, insofar as a sense
of spatiality emerges from the virtual space of action contained within our
body schema. Telecommunication and telemanipulation technologies therefore
serve to change the action space, altering our perception of spatiality (and note
this holds not just for technologies that allow physical manipulation of objects
but also communication technologies, as in Merleau-Ponty's discussion of the
phone call which 'brings us the friend himself'). What is crucial here is that,
once again, the extension of perception does not result in the collapse of space
into homogeneous 'distancelessness' nor does it allow us to transcend into a
virtual non-place of cyberspace. This is important to reiterate because failing
to acknowledge this means missing out on two other central aspects of our
understanding of how the spatiality of 'nearness' and 'farness' are experienced
in an accelerating world. The first is that not all subjects have the same experience of this new teletopology, and the second is that, to the extent that distant
spaces can be brought near and sutured into our action space, there will be a
wide variety of ways in which we will be able to act at a distance.

In regard to the first point, while we've critiqued the Heideggerian-inspired
reading that accelerating ICTs collapse the world into a homogenizing distancelessness on the grounds that it ignores the complex and embodied phenomenological engagements with, and incorporations of, technologies that

Merleau-Ponty describes, it is also worth pointing out that this homogenizing narrative ignores the profound variety of different subjects' experiences of, and access to, accelerating ICTs and the complex teletopologies they produce. This means that the phenomenological topology of an accelerating world is not, itself, a static, uniform, or objective space, but will differ quite widely depending on the subject and their particular location and status. As a fundamental starting point, in Chapter 4 we discussed the digital divide, and the way access to accelerating ICTs is shaped by a variety of questions of wealth, infrastructure, governmental regulation, monopoly capitalism amongst a host of other variables. From this perspective, what technologies you have access to, at what bandwidth, at what cost, with what kind of restrictions or surveillances, will vary widely from person to person on a global level, with real consequences for each person's phenomenological experience of the spatiality of the world.[4]

More than this however, other non-technological aspects of an individual's situation can have effects on their experience of spatiality. A rich vein of work has been produced since at least the 1980s, developing Merleau-Ponty's idea that one's phenomenological experience is shaped not just by biological (or technological) factors but also by 'the cultural apparatus with which my education, my previous efforts, my personal history, have provided me' (1962: 71). Work has been done to interrogate the way in which phenomenological experience is shaped by social categories of race, gender, sexuality, etc. Thus, for example, Iris Marion Young's work in feminist phenomenology describes the way in which gendered social relations decrease the effective space of action available to bodies gendered as female, which produces consequent effects on these bodies' phenomenological experience of the world, saying,

> The space, that is, that is *physically* available to the feminine body is frequently of greater radius than the space that she uses and inhabits. Feminine existence appears to posit an existential enclosure between herself and the space surrounding her, in such a way that the space that belongs to her and is available to her grasp and manipulation is constricted and the space beyond is not available to her movement.
>
> *(40)*

Sarah Ahmed explores similar themes in her *Queer Phenomenology*, looking at the way in which categories of race and sexuality shape the phenomenological experiences of certain bodies to feel as if they are effectively integrated into the 'flesh of the world', discussing the

> 'white world' and how it feels to inhabit a white world with a black body. We might say, then, that the world extends the form of some bodies more than others, and such bodies in turn feel at home in this world.
>
> *(129)*

These social categories shape phenomenological experiences mediated via accelerating ICTs as much as anything else. Thus, by way of example, we might think of our earlier discussion of the way in which mobile phones and social media play a role in shaping our experience of space. We might look to Twitter as a one medium by which our sense of spatiality is shaped and extended, suturing together different global spaces, warping our perception and experience of local ones, and potentially giving rise to moments of connection with others. Such an analysis would need to take into consideration the way in which Twitter, like many other social media platforms, is actively hostile to women, people of colour, and LGBTQ individuals. Death threats, harassment, marginalization, are all par for the course for many users of this platform. In this regard, these extended, technologically mediated spaces are just as marked by an experience in which 'the space that belongs to her and is available to her grasp and manipulation is constricted and the space beyond is not available to her movement'.

Returning to the second limitation of a vision of spatiality under accelerating ICTs as homogenizing and distanceless, such an approach ignores the fact that, to the extent that distant spaces can be brought near and sutured into our action space, there will be a wide variety of ways in which we will be able to act at a distance. The telephone, or the text, might, as Merleau-Ponty states, 'brings us the friend himself' but certainly not in a way that would allow me to hug them (although it may certainly allow me to console them). The point being different technologies will produce the opportunity for different types of actions and will therefore produce a different sense of presence – thinner, more diffuse, more focused, more intense. For some commentators, this means that these forms of presence will always be, as we discussed in the introduction, 'less than' – less authentic, less human, less real. As Hubert Dreyfus says in his discussion of telepresence and telerobotic technology:

> Nor is it just a question of giving robots surface sensors so that, through them as prostheses, we can touch other people without knocking them over. Even the most gentle person/robot interaction would never be a caress, nor could one successfully use a delicately controlled and touch-sensitive robot arm to give one's kid a hug. Whatever hugs do for people, I'm quite sure tele-hugs won't do it. And any act of intimacy mediated by any sort of prosthesis would surely be equally grotesque if not obscene. By why am I so sure tele-intimacy is an oxymoron? I suspect it is because any sense of intimacy must draw on the sense of security and well-being each of us presumably experienced as babies in our caretaker's arms. If so, even the most sophisticated forms of telepresence may well seem remote and abstract if they are not in some way connected with our sense of the warm, embodied nearness of a flesh-and-blood human being.
>
> *(52)*

There is, of course, a deep tautology in this analysis, as Dreyfus argues that telerobotics cannot produce real intimacy because intimacy isn't the kind of thing that can be produced by telerobotics. But more than being logical incoherent, this also ignores the empirical evidence. Dreyfus' certainty aside, there are numerous examples of how even very narrow bandwidth telerobotic interfaces can produce experiences of connection and intimacy. We saw this in our discussion of the Datatmitt earlier. Another example Clark describes is

> the LumiTouch, a prototype picture frame. When one user touches the frame, the frame of a connected-but-distant picture lights up. If the distant partner see this, and picks up her frame and squeezes, a feedback disply area lights up on the originating frame, its color and intensity varying according to the force, location, and duration of the distal squeeze. Over time, two distant participants can learn to exchange a kind of private emotional language of touch using the device.[5]

The fact that Dreyfus' certainty that 'tele-hugs won't do' what real hugs do can be disproven even by these relatively simplistic examples is the result of starting from the assumption that only perceptions and actions which mimic those of the 'naturally occurring human body' can be authentic, and insofar as perceptual technologies will always fall short of this standard, they will always be 'degraded', 'inauthentic' forms of human experience.[6] Implicit in this is the assumption of some kind of authentic (if not quite *a priori*) human perceptual schema. For Merleau-Ponty, however, the human body schema and perceptual field are profoundly mutable. Our perception field, and our body schema, can incorporate all sorts of things that bear no resemblance to the human body and allow for action quite wildly different from what a 'natural' human body can do (whatever that might mean). Our human body can, according to Merleau-Ponty, incorporate clothes, and feathers, and canes, and cars, and keyboards, and language, and telephone wires. Why would Datamitts or mobile phones or VR suits be any different? Or rather, because they are all different in their own unique ways, they will all shape human perception and action in their own unique ways. Indeed, one of the points that was raised in our earlier discussion was that frequently what makes a technology useful/desirable is that they function in ways not identical to our immediate biological senses, creating new bodies with new capacities. And given our discussion in the previous chapter of the social implications of technologically mediated perception, we might wish to think about what forms of political solidarity and moral responsibility become possible with such new bodies and spaces.

Thus, we might return to our earlier discussion of the role of social media and ICTs in organizing and grounding social movements and protests. In their discussions of the various protest movements, commentators have remarked on the way that social media allows not just information but also affects, to be shared and circulated, creating both local and global communities. Thus, in relation to the Arab spring Hussein and Howard discuss how

> younger generations of mobilizers felt disenfranchised by their political systems, saw vast losses in the poor management of national economies and development, and most importantly, a consistent and widely shared narrative of common grievances – a narrative which they learned about from each other and co-wrote on the digital spaces of political writing and venting on blogs, videos shared on Facebook and Twitter, and comment board discussions on international news sites like Al Jazeera and the BBC.
>
> *(13)*

Carmen Leccardi provides an optimistic account of how this shifting spatiality of near and far can have effects on the formation of political communities and subjectivities, saying,

> In the context of discovered political subjectivity, the new communication and information technologies present themselves as perfect 'global' tools to stimulate the growth and consolidation of this democratic space-time. Individuals and groups, even those spatially distant, can share perspectives, mobilize civic resources, promote opinion formation, and elaborate a direct response to social and political institutions whose credibility is declining.
>
> *(32)*

Robert Hassan provides a similarly account, arguing,

> The exercise of a democratic choice is currently building a grassroots politics that is developing across cyberspace and across the physical world. The consequences of neoliberal speed and commodification . . . being consciously rejected by millions of people across the world today. The most important development here is that it is being done from within the network society itself, using the tools of speed and instrumentalism that run counter to the ways they were intended. Using the panoply of connectivity that ICTs provide, activists, theorists, and the many who are simply fascinated by what computers can do are creating alternative times and spaces where alternative visions can be projected and alternative politics developed. Global networks have developed and continue to develop, where ideas are formed and discussed and political action is translated into agency in the physical realm.
>
> *(2007: 56)*[7]

Now, again, this is not to suggest that the effects of these new spatialities are inherently or inevitably good, or liberatory. These same spatialities allow for the emergence and organization of white supremacist communities (Bob 2012) or the intervention of malign foreign actors into national democratic conversation (as we have seen from Russian operatives in national election cycles in multiple different countries). To say that political solidarity is possible via technologically accelerated perception does not promise us that this will be solidarity around issues or identities that we approve of. But again, 'unmediated' perception cannot promise this either. All we are saying is that these new modes of perception, embodiment, and spatiality do not automatically negate the possibility of these kinds of connections.

Now, we might wish to debate whether we like the kinds of spatiality they give birth too. We might wish to forego certain technologies or shape our encounters with technology (or our technologies themselves) in certain key ways out of political and ethical concern. (Indeed, the entire point of our discussion in Chapter 2 of typologizing different types of encounters between speed and the body was to have a framework of political analysis and judgement on the effects of accelerative technologies.) What we cannot do is reject such as spatiality as unnatural, inhuman, or inauthentic *a priori*. To do so is, at the very least, to limit our ability to understand this new accelerating world, and at most to miss out on some potentially useful possibilities. More than anything, it is to invoke a mistaken understanding of the human, and its place in an always shifting spatiality, and an always mutating technogenesis.

Conclusion: Inhuman Speeds

This chapter ends on one of the reoccurring themes of the book as a whole: that debates around speed are frequently debates around the nature of the human. Throughout the text we have seen the way in which anxieties around speed, social acceleration, and technology frequently turn on essentialist accounts of human nature. What is more, these accounts of the human are frequently rooted in the terrain of the body. Thus, in Part I we saw the way in which the Gibsonian and Rousseauian narratives take speed to be a fundamentally inhuman phenomena, either destroying, or capturing the body. In our discussion of accelerating perceptions in Part II we saw thinkers like Virilio, Andrejevic, Heidegger, Dreyfus, Abram, and Borgman, for whom acceleration is a danger to the natural tempos, rhythms, and spatialities of human bodies. At root here is a strong normative conception of the human body, which is threatened by technological acceleration. This is why I have more than once pointed to the creeping ableism of these positions, as thinkers, in their defence of an essentialist humanity, posit a normal and norma*tive* human body. Such positions are unable to accept the idea of a spectrum of bodily difference or imagine bodies in complex interrelation with human artefacts and societies, as to do so would be to lose the bulwark of the natural, 'healthy', hermetically sealed human body which could be opposed to a degenerative, parasitic technological speed.

Curiously, this dramatic investment in a normal/normative body might seem at odds with another claim I made about many 'anti-speed' thinkers and movements in Chapter 4, namely that they are examples of what Nietzsche calls 'despisers of the body'. At first it might seem like there is a tension between these two points – between Rousseau or Virilio's valorization of the 'natural', 'healthy' human body, and a despiser who seeks to transcend the limits of the earthly body. But, of course, there is a connection because the human body that these thinkers attach so strongly to is never the actually existing human body in all of its differences and 'imperfections'. Rather it is an idealized – in many ways mythological – body which contains and secures an essentialized account of human nature. Indeed, it is not surprising that these 'natural', 'healthy' human bodies are so often rooted in the past. Rousseau imagines his perfect healthy human body in the mists of the 'state of nature' (think here of Stiegler's account of Rousseau's position as, 'The man of nature, without prostheses, is robust, as robust as a man can be – and it is civilization that will weaken him' [1998: 115]), Virilio in a time before the coming of dromocracy. For these thinkers, the human body is not the empirical body, with its variations and complexities, its entanglements, and dependencies. These thinkers are despisers of the body not in spite of their attachment to the normative body but because of it. The actual body can never live up to their normative ideal, and thus always must be found wanting, seen as corrupt, decaying, and weak. We might think here of the horror of Virilio who laments the coming of the 'para- or quadriplegic' body captured by the 'vision machine', as if such bodies do not already exist, human bodies living valuable lives. Here we see a bodily echo of the account of *ressentiment* against speed we documented in the first chapter. The positing of a normative world and body which the real world and body can never live up to, and thus must be punished, rejected, and escaped from.

What we come back to is a desire for stable and secure borders, boundaries, and trajectories, and a vision of speed as disruptive, as something which breaks down barriers and disturbs settled lines of time. Political movements, orientations, and subjectivities which are invested too resolutely in certitude and stability, whether that be the borders of a country, the boundaries of a 'healthy' body, or the trajectory of a teleological narrative of time, will find experiences of speed which challenge those lines as inherently threatening, provoking a reactionary *ressentiment*-laden response which can, in specific contexts, lapse into violent or authoritarian attempts to forcibly reinstill the world with the stability they crave. While *ressentiment* against speed is clearly not the only source of reactionary, authoritarian, xenophobic, or violent political behaviour, in a world of accelerating flows of people, goods, and information it is necessary for us to interrogate how anxieties over these accelerating flows can contribute to such movements, and what kinds of practices, institutions, and narratives might be useful in pushing back against them. As I argue throughout the text, combating *ressentiment* against speed, at a variety of levels and sites, is a crucial component in seeking a more just, equitable, and diverse world.

Now, once again, saying this is not to say that all anxieties around speed are necessarily reactionary, or that any and all attempts at deceleration are necessarily authoritarian. Desires for stability and security are natural and ground many calls for justice, equality, and democracy. Throughout this text I have tried to reject modes of analysis which are unilaterally 'pro-speed', and to acknowledge the various violence, inequities, and injustices that can result from social acceleration. We need not accept all forms of social acceleration and can and should reject some accelerative technologies and modes of organization at both the individual and social level. Crucially, decisions around both social acceleration and accelerative technologies should be subject to democratic decision making rather than the whims of the market, monopolistic capitalist formations, or the militarist state.

However, as we seek greater democratic control over questions of social acceleration, we should recognize that affects of fear, anxiety, and resentment around speed, and its potentially disruptive effects, can produce reactionary, violent, and authoritarian decisions. That is why, ultimately, this book has focused on two intertwined projects.

First, to understand the affects and perceptions that give rise to these *ressentiment*-laden investments, and potentially develop practices, policies, and narratives which can loosen their hold on individuals and societies. Thus, our accounts of *ressentiment* in Nietzsche, affects in Spinoza, or 'closedness' in Bergson, help us to understand the roots of reactionary political orientations in different responses to social acceleration. And topics as diverse as our discussion of mindfulness in Chapter 5, smartphone use in transnational protest movements in Chapter 6, and the 'Transborder Immigrant Tool' in Chapter 3 articulate practices, narratives, or policies which can reject these reactionary responses and produce ethically valuable and political useful responses to, and appropriations of, technological acceleration.

This attempt to develop helpful practices, policies, narratives, and organization is aided by the book's second project, to develop frameworks of analysis which help us to understand and evaluate speed, without being premised on normalizing and *ressentiment*-laden accounts of the human, the body, or time. In these frameworks we have rejected accounts which seek to find speed as *fundamentally* and *essentially* opposed to either politics or humanity, even as we have sought to develop critical mechanisms which might seek to reject or challenge specific instances of social acceleration Thus, Spinoza's *conatus*-based interpretation of speed which provides us with a rubric for determining which forms of social acceleration might be helpful for human bodies and societies, and which are harmful. We can also think of Bergson's account of open morality, and the way in which it helps us judge how we might like technological and scientific advancements to develop and become integrated into society. None of these frameworks require an unthinking acceptance of all forms of social and technological acceleration. However, they do require that we reject an essentializing account of the human, and recognize the multiple tempos that have constituted human bodies, lives, and societies throughout history (and therefore the dangers that can lurk in a unilateral reactionary rejection of speed and acceleration).

Indeed, this point, of the multiple tempos of human bodies and societies, is perhaps the most important one. It returns us to a claim that was raised in the introduction. That although we are undoubtedly going through a noteworthy period of social acceleration, speed is by no means a new phenomenon or political problem. The question of speed and acceleration has been reoccurring theme throughout the history of Western political theory. Indeed, if we take the story of the acheulean axe seriously, the question of speed has been a central one for as long as there have been humans. In this regard, although in Chapter 2 I raised the Spinozist point that 'no one has yet learned how fast the body can go', we might also say that no one has yet acknowledge how fast the body goes, that we consistently fail to grasp the multiple tempos – some fast, some slow – that constitute human bodies and societies. It is my contention that acknowledging this co-constitution of speed and the body is a crucial step in developing politics, and political theory, for an accelerating world.

Notes

1. What is more, optical illusions speak to the *a posteriori* nature of this perceptual schema, as intercultural testing has shown diverse responses as to whether or not individuals are 'fooled' by them. See Watters (2013).
2. As Merleau-Ponty puts it, 'When someone – an author or a friend – succeeds in expressing himself, the signs are immediately forgotten; all that remains is the meaning. The perfection of language lies in its capacity to pass unnoticed' (1973: 10).
3. See also Crang (2007: 75–6).
4. As Coole puts it in her account of Merleau-Ponty, 'the practical, perceiving body – is situated in socioeconomic and historicocultural contexts to which it responds and which transfigure it. This enables him to combine corporeal and historical materialism' (108).
5. Petranker makes the inverse argument, noting the physical proximity is no guarantee of connection, saying of various telepresence experiences such as the Datamitt:

    > Compare these examples to the pseudopresence typical of a commercial interaction between a customer and a salesperson, and the difference is clear. Presence grounded in intimacy depends not at all on physically inhabiting the same "here" and "now," nor is such co-inhabiting a guarantor of presence.
    > *(182)*

6. And once again, we should be attentive to the implicit ableism of this vision of the normal and normative human body.
7. See also Hassan (2009: 210).

Works Cited

Ahmed, S. (2006) *Queer Phenomenology: Orientations, Objects, Others*, Durham, NC: Duke University Press.

Bob, C. (2012) *The Global Right Wing and the Clash of World Politics*, Cambridge: Cambridge University Press.

Borgmann, A. (2001) 'Information, Nearness, and Farness', *The Robot in the Garden: Telerobotics and Telepistemology in the Age of the Internet*, ed. K. Goldberg. Cambridge: MIT Press.

Canny, J. and Paulos, E. (2001) 'Tele-Embodiment and Shattered Presence: Reconstructing the Body for Online Interaction', *The Robot in the Garden: Telerobotics and Telepistemology in the Age of the Internet*, ed. K. Goldberg. Cambridge: MIT Press.

Castells, M. (2012) *Networks of Outrage and Hope: Social Movements in the Internet Age*, Cambridge, UK: Polity.

Clark, A. (2003) *Natural-Born Cyborgs: Minds, Technologies and the Future of Human Intelligence*. Oxford: Oxford University Press.

Clark, A. (2011) *Supersizing the Mind: Embodiment, Action, and Cognitive Extension*, Oxford: Oxford University Press.

Coole, D. (2007) *Merleau-Ponty and Modern Politics After Anti-Humanism*, Lanham, MD: Rowman and Littlefield Publishers.

Crang, M. (2007) 'Speed=Distance/Time: Chronotopographies of Action', *24/7: Time and Temporality in the Network Society*, ed. R. Hassan and R. E. Purser. Stanford, CA: Stanford Business Books.

Dreyfus, H. L. (2001) 'Telepistemology: Descartes' Last Stand', *The Robot in the Garden: Telerobotics and Telepistemology in the Age of the Internet*, ed. K. Goldberg. Cambridge: MIT Press.

Hansen, Mark B. N. (2006) *Bodies in Code: Interfaces with Digital Media*, Oxford: Routledge.

Hassan, R. (2007) 'Network Time', *24/7: Time and Temporality in the Network Society*, ed. R. Hassan and R. E. Purser. Stanford, CA: Stanford Business Books.

Hassan, R. (2009) *Empires of Speed: Time and the Acceleration of Politics and Society*, Boston, MA: Brill.

Hayles, N. K. (2012) *How We Think: Digital Media and Contemporary Technogenesis*, Chicago: University of Chicago Press.

Hussein, M. M. and Howard, P. N. (2012) 'Democracy's Fourth Wave? Information Technologies and the Fuzzy Causes of the Arab Spring', Unpublished Paper, presented at *International Studies Association*, April 1–4, 2012, San Diego, CA, USA.

Leccardi, C. (2007) 'New Temporal Perspectives in the "High-Speed Society"', *24/7: Time and Temporality in the Network Society*, eds. R. Hassan and R. E. Purser. Stanford, CA: Stanford Business Books.

Mackenzie, A. (2010) *Wirelessness: Radical Empiricism in Network Culture*, Cambridge, MA: MIT Press.

Marx, K. (1973) *Grundrisse*, Trans. M. Nicolaus, London: Penguin Classics.

Merleau-Ponty, M. (1962) *Phenomenology of Perception*, Trans. C. Smith, Abingdon, UK: Routledge.

Merleau-Ponty, M. (1963) *In Praise of Philosophy and Other Essays*, Trans. J. Wild, J. Edie, and J. O'Neill, Chicago: Northwestern University Press.

Merleau-Ponty, M. (1964a) *The Primacy of Perception*, Chicago: Northwestern University Press.

Merleau-Ponty, M. (1964b) *Signs*, Trans. R. C. McCleary, Chicago: Northwestern University Press.

Merleau-Ponty, M. (1968) *The Visible and the Invisible*, Trans. A. Lingis, Chicago: Northwestern University.

Merleau-Ponty, M. (1995) *Nature: Course Notes from the College de France*, Trans. R. Vallier, Chicago: Northwestern University Press.

Merleau-Ponty, M. (2004) *The World of Perception*, Trans. O. Davis, London: Routledge.

Petranker, J. (2007) 'The Presence of Others: Network Experience as an Antidote to the Subjectivity of Time', *24/7: Time and Temporality in the Network Society*, eds. R. Hassan and R. E. Purser. Stanford, CA: Stanford Business Books.

Plato (1994) *Gorgias*, Trans. R. Waterfield, Oxford, UK: Oxford World Classics.

Rainie, L. and Wellman, B. (2012) *Networked: The New Social Operating System*, Cambridge, MA: MIT Press.

Stiegler, B. (1998) *Technics and Time, 1*, Trans. R. Beardsworth and G. Collins, Stanford, CA: Stanford University Press.

Wajcman, J. (2008) 'Life in the Fast Lane? Towards a Sociology of Technology and Time', *The British Journal of Sociology*, 59(1).

Wajcman, J. (2016) *Pressed for Time: The Acceleration of Life in Digital Capitalism*, Chicago: University of Chicago Press.

Watters, E. (2013) 'We Aren't the World', *Pacific Standard*, February 23. Available at: https://psmag.com/social-justice/joe-henrich-weird-ultimatum-game-shaking-up-psychology-economics-53135 (Accessed July 28, 2017).

Young, I. M. (2005) *On Female Body Experience: "Throwing Like a Girl" and Other Essays*, Oxford: Oxford University Press.

INDEX